AN INTRODUCTION TO Islam FOR JEWS

In loving memory of Miles Lerman,
who spent a lifetime dedicated to creating a world of
understanding, tolerance, and mutual respect
among all people.

David Lerman, Shelley Wallock,
Brooke Lerman, Julia Lerman, and Ted Lerman

AN INTRODUCTION TO Islam FOR JEWS

Reuven Firestone

120
JPS
Nourishing Mind and Spirit
2008 • 5768
Philadelphia

JPS is a nonprofit educational association and the oldest and foremost publisher of Judaica in English in North America. The mission of JPS is to enhance Jewish culture by promoting the dissemination of religious and secular works, in the United States and abroad, to all individuals and institutions interested in past and contemporary Jewish life.

The Jewish Publication Society
2100 Arch Street, 2nd floor
Philadelphia, PA 19103
www.jewishpub.org

Design and composition by Desperate Hours Productions

Manufactured in the United States of America

08 09 10 11 12 10 9 8 7 6 5 4 3 2 1

Library of Congress Cataloging-in-Publication Data:

Firestone, Reuven, 1952-
An introduction to Islam for Jews / Reuven Firestone.
p. cm.
Includes bibliographical references and index.
ISBN-13: 978–0–8276–0864–1 (alk. paper) 1. Islam. 2. Islam—Essence, genius, nature. 3. Islam—Relations—Judaism. 4. Judaism—Relations—Islam. I. Title.
BP161.3.F57 2008
297.02'4296—dc22
2007047352

To Sa`di and Isma`il
Abu Sneineh

Contents

Preface

Islam is a complex religious civilization that remains largely unknown to Jews, despite the fact that the future of the Jewish people has become profoundly affected by developments in the Muslim world. For our own personal edification and understanding, therefore, for responsible decision-making within the Jewish community and for a world of greater understanding and compassion, writing a book on Islam with the particular interests of Jews in mind is an important undertaking. This book will treat issues and items that are of particular interest to Jews, as well as some that would be of benefit for Jews to understand even if they may not be of obvious interest. It will therefore concentrate on some topics that do not appear in most introductions to Islam. It will likewise omit some subjects found in other introductions that are not of particular importance to Jews. I naturally concentrate on issues of personal interest that I assume are of interest to other Jews as well. I love the languages of Hebrew and Arabic, for example, and I naturally tend to note their similarities in relation to religious issues. I am fascinated by the ways that Islam and Judaism have so many parallels, yet are separate religious systems. Please note: this book is written by an individual and not a scholarly community, and it is only one single volume. It cannot hope to represent all the various internal perspectives of Muslim groups and all the analyses of scholars of religion. It need not and should not be your only source for information on Islam.

As any sensitive reader knows, an author can never dissociate himself or herself from what he or she has written. Because of this truth, it is appropriate to reveal something about myself for the sake of full disclosure.

I am a liberally observant Jew, trained as both a rabbi and an academic. I have lived for some six or seven years in Israel and have raised my children in Jewish day schools in the United States and Israel. We all speak Hebrew in my family, and I am writing this introduction while in Jerusalem. In addition to scholarly works on Islam and its relationship with Judaism and Christianity and pre-Islamic indigenous Arabian culture, I have written an introduction to Judaism for Muslims.[1]

I grew up in a household that was deeply Jewish but that respected the wisdom and arts of those who lived outside our own particular religious and cultural framework. Despite sensitivity to the universal value of humanity that I learned from my family, growing up in America naturally instilled within me a number of vague prejudices that were simply imbedded in Jewish or American culture. As a result, when I first traveled to Israel as a naïve American Jewish teenager in 1970, I had a vague, unarticulated expectation that the Jewish Israelis would be heroic and upright while the Arabs would be dishonest and deceitful. This evaluation was hazy and indistinct, and I had not thought about it in any kind of conscious way. In fact, it was only some years later that I understood how these prejudices affected my general outlook. I would certainly not define myself as a racist, but like virtually everyone in my generation, I had absorbed vague judgments about self and other that infused my general thinking about the world around me.

But soon after arriving in Israel, I was surprised to find some quite unheroic Israelis and some quite upright Arabs. I found myself living in the Muslim Quarter within the aged Ottoman walls of the "Old City" of Jerusalem, where I remained for a few months exploring its alleys and warrens. I also ventured out into the newer sections of the city both in the east and west as well as the villages in its vicinity. I became particularly close to two young Muslim Arab cousins who had each recently married, and I was privileged to spend quality time with them and their extended families.

This was during a very special period in Israel. The Palestinians that had come under Israeli control were relieved to find that the Israelis did not engage in a campaign of rape and pillage as they had feared during the 1967 War. They were happy when many of their villages were hooked into the electric grid for the first time, and they enjoyed the fruit of that early period when Israelis swarmed into the territories and spent money freely, thus buoying the economic status of many Palestinian families. There was a general feeling at this time among both Israelis and Palestinians that the situation was temporary, so the two sides encouraged engagement at a variety of levels. I felt welcomed as a Jew in the homes of many Arabs, and I took full advantage of that welcome in order to learn something of the culture, the language, the music, and the religious worldview of my new friends. That golden age soon passed. The political situation became increasingly tense and violent over the years, and misunderstandings and cultural misreadings sometimes caused hurt between my friends and me. But our relationship remained strong and we remain close to this day.

That first visit in 1970 was not spent entirely among Arabs. I also lived on a border kibbutz for a few months and found a deep personal affinity with the struggles and dreams of Zionism. My experience among Jews deepened my sense of connection with my collective past and aspirations for a common future when Jews would live in peace in the state of Israel. I subsequently returned to Israel many times to study and work and visit, as many American Jews do. But I always spent time with my Arab friends, and I always kept very closely in touch with their developments. It was that profound experience in 1970 that forever changed my life. I found myself continually being drawn back to the relationship between Jews and Arabs and between Judaism and Islam. I found that the most rewarding area of study for me in college and beyond was Judaism, then Islam, and then the study of religion in general. And I found that the most meaningful area of activism for me would be in improving relations between Jews and Muslims. I returned not only to Israel to study and live, but also to other parts of the Middle East. Most recently I took a sabbatical in Cairo with my family, where my children attended an Egyptian school. Having lived in Israel and having attended American Jewish day schools and Israeli schools, it was a moving and most positive experience for them to live among and attend school with Arabs, most of them Muslim.

Because of my experiences, my general approach to Islam is sympathetic, but also, I hope, realistic. I feel no need to be polemical, because I do not feel threatened or fearful of Islam. I have learned that Islam, like Judaism and Christianity (and I would suppose all religions), allows for certain expressions and behaviors that I would consider terribly problematic, and others that I consider transcendent and even sublime. I do not believe that religion is the cause of the world's problems, but I do believe that it can be part of the solution. Religion has proven to be a very effective means of rallying large numbers of people to engage in extraordinary behaviors, sometimes tremendously inspiring and sometimes terribly malevolent. While religion is not the cause or the sole solution to the world's problems, it can make them worse, and it can alleviate them.

I just mentioned that my general approach to Islam is sympathetic. That may strike the reader as odd, since one would generally expect a writer to claim an objective approach that is neither sympathetic nor condemning. In the study of religion, however, I question whether a purely objective approach is possible. Religion is so powerful, its images and ideas so potent, and its engagement so energetic, that it is probably impossible to remain neutral. One finds oneself attracted or even deeply moved by certain aspects and indifferent or perhaps even repulsed by others. The result is that the observer cannot help but form an opinion at various times, despite the intent to withhold judgment.

I consider it my responsibility, therefore, to convey my general attitude toward Islam, and that general attitude is indeed sympathetic. This is only partly based on my studies. It is true that the more I understand it, the more appreciative I become. But my approach is also based on my understanding of Jewish values. I take the famous dictum of Rabbi Hillel and apply it not only to human individuals but also to human collectives: "Do not judge your fellow until you have been in his place."[2] As I come to understand the complexity of issues that drives my fellow to act the way he does, I can appreciate his behavior even if I do not always agree with it. In fact, I may be sympathetic even when I disapprove of his behavior. This is my approach also to larger collectives, in this case to Muslims and to the religious system of Islam.

One of the reasons that religionists tend to think negatively of other religions is that they employ different methods for judging their own religion than they use to judge the religion of the other. Jews and Judaism have often been victimized by this problem over the ages as the ignorant or enemies try to prove that Judaism is a primitive or even evil religion. The simplest way this false comparison is made is to compare the "best" of one religion with the "worst" of another. One can do this with a variety of topics, but one particularly relevant topic today is war and peace. If one compares the peaceful verses of the Torah with the militant verses of the Qur'an, one will evaluate the two quite differently than if one compares the militant verses of the Torah with the peaceful verses of the Qur'an (we will treat these issues more fully below).

The Jewish reader will certainly compare Islam with Judaism. This is natural, even inevitable, and I do not consider it inherently problematic. In fact, comparing the two has contributed greatly to my enjoyment in writing this book. But it is important to compare fairly and not to compare in order to score points. This requires, among other things, comparing apples with apples. For liberal, Westernized Jews, for example, it is neither accurate nor fair to compare traditional Islam with nontraditional forms of Judaism. There is a range of positions in Islam on most issues, just as there is a range of positions in Judaism. Keep in mind that Islam did not experience the European Enlightenment and Christian Reformation in the same way as did the peoples living in Europe, including the Jews (this will also be explored in some detail in the pages to follow). In order to engage in an honest assessment, one must be willing to apply the same methodology to judge the religion of the other as one applies to one's own religious tradition.

To conclude these remarks, here are some thoughts on a how a non-Muslim can write a book about Islam. I do not believe that anyone can fully and intimately make sense of the spirituality and meaning of another's religion.

There is a certain discomfort, therefore, that I feel as a non-Muslim taking on the responsibility to teach Islam to Jews. I have tried as best I can to be conscious of this limitation, and I have often tried to imagine how I would feel if, say, a Muslim were writing this book to teach Judaism to Muslims. With that sense of awesome responsibility and limitation, I have agreed to take on this project. The Jewish sages have taught that one is not responsible to solve all the problems of the world, but neither is one free to disengage from working diligently to this end (Mishnah, *Pirkei Avot* 2:16). I hope and pray that I have represented Islam accurately and fairly, and that my work will bring a little more understanding in a very confusing world.

A Note on Islamic Sources

Last, a note is required on referencing Islamic sources. There is an ongoing debate in the Muslim world over the use of authoritative texts to support norms of behavior and expectations of belief, but there is no argument over the absolute authority of the Qur'an. To Muslims, the Qur'an is Scripture, the perfectly accurate record of the divine will as revealed to God's prophet, Muhammad. There are of course differences of opinion over how verses should be understood, just as there are in Judaism and Christianity, but there is almost no disagreement over the actual text of the Qur'an. Because of the core position of the Qur'an, I will often provide the qur'anic source around which certain conclusions or arguments are constructed. The translations that are provided are my own, though they are influenced by the work of Muhammad Pickthal, Muhammad Asad, and Thomas Cleary.[3] I provide the chapter and verse of every citation so the reader can check it against his own text.

There is more controversy over the use of the next authoritative layer of religious literature, the *Ḥadīth*, which will be discussed in detail below. I will occasionally cite the *Hadith* when it is particularly relevant, and I also provide my own translations, but I will try to limit my citations to bilingual sources that are most readily available in college libraries. The most widely available translation of an authoritative *Hadith* work is the bilingual edition of *Ṣaḥīḥ Bukhārī*, published in Pakistan by Kazi Press,[4] so I try to limit my reference to this work.

The use of terms in religious discourse is sometimes controversial and even polemical, and this applies also to the word for the deity. The most common term for God in the Qur'an is Allah, which means, simply, "the God." Some Muslims prefer that non-Muslims use the term "Allah" when referencing God in the Qur'an, because it conveys respect to the particularity of Islamic discourse. I prefer to use the word "God" for the simple reason that it is the English term and this is an English-language book on Islam. I would similarly use "God" rather than the current popular Hebrew term "Hashem" when referencing God in the Torah. A second reason I prefer this term is that in the recent past, some non-Muslim religious polemicists have referred to Allah as if it is the "false god" of a "false" religion known as Islam, whereas God is the "true God" of another, "true" religion. In order to avoid any such insinuation I stick with the term "God" for all references to the One Great God that is worshiped by all monotheists.

References to God, Muhammad, and the prophets in Islamic religious discourse are usually followed by short references of praise. God (Allah in Islamic texts) is often followed by the word *"ta`allā,"* meaning "most high." Muhammad or "the Prophet" is usually followed with the phrase *"ṣallā allāhu `alayhi wasallam,"* meaning "God's prayer and peace be upon him" (this is often shortened in English to PBUH: "peace be upon him"). Islamic prophets such as Abraham, Moses, and Jesus are usually followed by the words *"`alayhi al-salām,"* which finds a direct Hebrew parallel, *`alav ha-shalom* meaning "peace be upon him." I use the typical English mode of reference without these additional tributes. This is simply a matter of English prose style and does not imply disrespect.

Finally, a few words on the use of the terms "Islam" and "Muslim." In Jewish parlance, there is a religion called "Judaism," a religionist called a "Jew," and an adjective that defines both: "Jewish." Jewish can refer to a book or a person, something referencing the religion of Judaism or the person of a Jew. In Islamic discourse it is a bit more complicated. "Islam" references the religion, and "Islamic" is an adjective that references all things relating to the religion and its civilization. "Muslim" refers to a person, a religionist who follows the religion of Islam. But "Muslim" is also an adjective, and while the difference in adjectival meaning between "Islamic" and "Muslim" is somewhat fluid in English usage, I use the two terms for two different categories in this book. "Islamic" references only issues and things that have to do with the religion of Islam. "Muslim" references issues and things that have to do with Muslims. Therefore, the world in which Muslims make up the majority population is referenced here as "the Muslim world." Similarly, a "Muslim state" is a nation-state in which the majority population is Muslim, but it could be organized politically as a secular monarchy, a democracy, or a dictatorship. Conversely, an "Islamic state" is a nation-state in which the organizing principle is Islam. At the time of this writing, therefore, Iran would be an "Islamic state," and Egypt a "Muslim state." Similarly, "Muslim community" references a community that is defined by being composed of Muslims. In contrast, "Islamic community" would reference a community in which the organizing principle is Islam.

The book is divided into three parts and is designed to be read consecutively. The first is a survey of Islamic history that concentrates on the emergence of Islam, though it offers a larger framework for understanding the development of Islam through the modern period. The second part is an examination of Islam as a religious system and treats theology, scripture, its interpretive literatures, the tradition, and religious law. The largest part is the third, which treats how Islam is practiced. A fair amount of religious terminology is used in the book. Words are defined early on and a glossary and index will help the reader to understand the terminology and seek out specific information.

It is my hope that the reader will come away from this book with a deeper appreciation of Islam—and of Judaism—and a greater understanding for some of the behaviors of both Muslims and Jews. Understanding allows for better leadership and improved decision-making, and when one has grounding in a subject, positive engagement is more likely and more apt to be successful. The ultimate goal is no less and no more than a little bit of *tikkun*, to use an important Jewish term—making our world a better place for us all and our children.

Acknowledgments

I am indebted to my students and colleagues at Hebrew Union College and the University of Southern California for their stimulating and challenging engagement with me in courses, seminars, and conferences. I have had the privilege of being energized and forced to think carefully and creatively by their insightful comments and difficult questions. The Fulbright Bi-national Committee in Egypt and the Center for Arabic Study Abroad at the American University in Cairo graciously supported my 2006 sabbatical in Egypt, where I began writing this book. Special thanks are due to Dafer Dakhil, Don Miller, Khaled Abou Al-Fadl, Brie Loskota, Mustafa Abu Sway, Mahmoud Ayoub, Mehnaz Afridi, Muhammad al-Hawari, Fred Denny, Marc Sable, Aziza Hasan, F. E. Peters, Ismail Bardhi, Cathryn Goddard, Khaleel Mohammed, Yusuf Murigu, Steffi Meyer, Muhammad Ali Salama, Jennifer Mapes, Fred Donner, Steve Fogel, and my dear brothers Sa`di and Ismail Abu Sneineh. Although I am indebted to all for their insights, I take responsibility for any and all errors that may be found in the book. Special thanks also to the library and support staff at HUC and for an administration that has always been supportive of my academic, religious, and community interests.

PART ONE

A SURVEY OF ISLAMIC HISTORY

CHAPTER 1

Why an Introduction to Islam Specifically for Jews?

Certainly, Jews can, and should, read general introductions to Islam. But there are questions and issues that are unique to the history and practice of Jews and Judaism that these general books on Islam do not address. If we look closely at Judaism and Islam, we see many parallels in practice, theology, and religious outlook. We may also note commonalities in the language, history, and culture of the two religions. In these, Judaism and Islam may be more similar to each other, interestingly enough, than either is to Christianity. But there are very important differences as well, some quite clear and some more subtle, that distinguish between these two distinct religious civilizations. It is fascinating to learn the complex ways in which we are both so similar to and so different from each other.

Today, as the 21st century unfolds before us, there is a wide gap between impressions and understanding of Islam, between media representation and informed knowledge. Jews, as never before, have a pressing need to understand the history, theology, and practice of Muslims and Islam. This book—designed specifically for the Jewish reader hungry for that understanding—is one of the first to fill that gap.

Although written by a Jew, this is not a "Jewish" introduction to Islam. It is not intended to be a Jewish analysis. In other words, Islam is not subject in this book to appraisal based on Jewish values or Jewish political interests or needs other than the fact that it treats issues that are of interest to Jews. There is no attempt here at moral evaluation. This is a nonjudgmental approach to the study of an extremely complex phenomenon.

For the past few centuries, most Jews have lived among and under the rule of Christians (although earlier, during most of the Middle Ages, most Jews lived under the rule of Muslims). Jews entered modernity through the Christian world, and all of the great Jewish achievements and calamities of modernity were influenced one way or another by the profound underlying relationship between Jews and Christians that had been developing for centuries. Although the ambivalences that have marked this foundational relationship continue to a greater or lesser extent today and will undoubtedly influence the future, it has become clear that the religious civilization that is having the greatest impact on Jews in the 21st century is Islam, both in the Middle East and in the West.

The conflict between Israel and its neighbors is at its core one of competing nationalisms, but religion has become increasingly identified with it. Islam has taken a much greater role in Palestinian political and social movements. The Middle East in general as well as the entire Muslim world has experienced a similar growth in the influence of Islamic perspectives in government, social movements, and even science. As the Muslim population and the impact of Islam have increased in the West, they have had a growing influence on Jews' sense of identity and security. Yet Jews know precious little about Islam. Responsible decision-making is impossible without understanding. For the sake of the future of the Jewish people and the future of the world as a whole, it is important to develop a firm, sober, realistic understanding of Islam and how Islam affects the outlooks and behaviors of Muslims as they act in the world.

Having said that, it is critically important to understand that Islam, like Judaism and Christianity, is an extraordinarily complex and multifaceted religion. It cannot be reduced to simple slogans, despite the attempts by some of its enemies and some of its self-appointed spokespeople to do so. So much of what we think we know about Islam is only a very small part of the whole picture (and it is not even necessarily accurate). What comes to mind is the famous story of the blind men and the elephant, a parable that came to the West through the great Muslim thinker Jalāl al-Dīn Al-Rūmī. Unable to see the elephant, they can only feel a part of it, and depending upon where they touch, they believe the elephant to be like a water spout (from the trunk), a fan (from the ear), a pillar (from the leg), and a throne (from feeling the back). No single part alone provides enough to form an accurate understanding of the elephant, yet each is a critical component without which one could not make sense of the animal. Even with the whole picture of the elephant, we cannot predict its behavior, but we can have a better sense of understanding its form, and also a greater sensitivity and compassion for its needs and desires.

CHAPTER 2

Arabs and Israelites

The terms "Arab" and "Muslim" describe different aspects of identity. "Arab" refers to a geography, a language, and a culture. "Muslim" refers to a religious identity. And while this book is an introduction to the religion of Islam rather than the ethnicity of Arab culture, the two are closely associated because Islam emerged out of an Arabian geographical, cultural, and linguistic context. Arabs existed long before Muslims, but Islam emerged as an Arabian—as opposed to Israelite or Greco-Roman—monotheism.

Arabia and the Bible

The Bible is one of the earliest sources referring to Arabia and Arab peoples, and it does so repeatedly, particularly in its early genealogies in the book of Genesis. These genealogies show how the Israelites viewed their relationship with neighboring peoples; they also set the stage for the great biblical saga of the Israelites and their relationship with God.

In the ancient world, where there were no mass media and people tended to stay in their towns and villages from birth to death, travelers who journeyed beyond their districts would notice that the farther they traveled, the more difficult it was to understand the language of the people they met. If they traveled far enough, they would encounter people who spoke a truly foreign language that was completely incomprehensible to them.

The farther away one moved from one's home, the less protected one was. In this world, people appeared to exist on a spectrum of relationship in which kinship, language, physical characteristics, and geographical proximity were all related. The many genealogies in the Bible were a means for making sense of these complex interrelations from the perspective of ancient Israel. The nearby Moabites, for example, who spoke a language that is so similar to Hebrew that the Israelites and Moabites could easily understand one another, were considered to be close relatives through Abraham's nephew, Lot (Genesis 19). Other peoples, who lived farther away and who spoke dialects or languages that were more difficult to understand, were placed farther away from Israel in the genealogical tables of Genesis.

The Arabs are an interesting group, because they exist in a number of biblical genealogies, some placing them distant from Israel through the genealogical lines of Kush and Yoktan in Genesis 10, or very close to Israel through Ishmael and Keturah in Genesis 25. This placement probably reflects the fact that, while Arabic-speaking peoples originated and were concentrated in the Arabian Peninsula, which was relatively far away from the Land of Israel, some lived in nomadic Arabian tribes based in desert or arid areas right on the border. Some of the names that are closely associated with Arab peoples are listed in both sets of genealogies. Sheba and Dedan, for example, are both descendants of the faraway Kush in Genesis 10, but also of Abraham and Keturah in Genesis 25. This probably reflects the reality that different traditions had arisen to explain the relationship of these two groups with Israel. Since it wasn't clear which was more correct, both were included in the genealogies.

None of these families, nor any of the individuals listed in these biblical genealogies, are called Arabs. It seems that the term did not become common in the Bible until later. But we know that they refer to Arabs because the names seem to reflect Arabic linguistic forms or roots, are associated with places that are known to be in Arabia, or reflect economic or cultural aspects of nomadic groups such as Arabs. Hagar, for example, whose son Ishmael would become closely associated with Arab peoples, was told by an angel in Genesis 16:12 that he would live outside of settled areas and engage in the common nomadic activity of raiding settled peoples. In 21:20, Ishmael is again described as living outside of settled areas and engaging in hunting rather than farming. These references reflect the different economies of pastoral nomadism, which was closely associated with Arabian culture, and village agriculture, which was associated with Israelite culture. Some of Ishmael's sons have strong Arabic names, such as Hadad, which means "smith" and is a common name among Jewish, Christian, and Muslim Arabs today.

In the genealogy reflecting Abraham's relationship with Keturah after the death of Sarah, Midian is their son and \`Efa their grandson. Midian is known in ancient Arabian inscriptions and texts to be a region of northwest

Arabia just south of today's Aqaba on the caravan route from Sheba and Dedan. The Midianites, as we learn from the story of Joseph in Genesis 37:25–28, were long-distance traders who brought Joseph from the Land of Israel to Egypt. And they are associated with Ishmaelites, whom we also know represent Arab peoples in the Bible through Ishmael's genealogy. Midianite Arabs transported incense grown in Arabia that was so important in the sacrificial system of the Jerusalem Temple and interacted repeatedly with the Israelites. In fact, Moses married one! Her name is Tziporah, the daughter of the Midianite priest and tribal leader Jethro. "Tziporah" is a Hebrew word for incense, as is "Keturah." These are all associated in the Bible with ancient Arab peoples and with their most important economic contribution to the Mediterranean world: the cultivation and export of incense.

Most foreign peoples are regarded with suspicion by the Bible, and Arabs are no exception. The wariness results from a particular nature of ancient Near Eastern geopolitics. Before the establishment of empires, small communities competed with one another over scarce resources and were not averse to raiding their neighbors. The Israelites themselves had great difficulty moving beyond the bickering and backbiting tribal system into a unified kingdom, as the books of Judges and Samuel so eloquently narrate. The united kingdom under David and Solomon hardly lasted two generations, collapsing under Solomon's son, Rehoboam, and animosity between the divided kingdoms of Israel and Judah was even great enough for them to engage in wars against one another (1 Kings 15:16). The Israelites always seemed to be on the verge of being attacked by or attacking their non-Israelite neighbors, and that anxiety is expressed throughout the historical narratives. It is in this context that we must understand the biblical view of Arabs, since the Arabs, like the Canaanites, Arameans, Moabites, Edomites, Egyptians, Babylonians, and virtually every other ethnic or national people, were potential enemies of Israel.

The term "Arab" (Heb. *'aravi*) only occurs in post-Exilic texts, meaning texts that were written down after the Babylonian destruction of the Jerusalem Temple in 586 BCE. When Isaiah prophesies the destruction of the hated Babylonian Empire, he likens the future of the capital city of Babylon to the total destruction of Sodom and Gemorrah. The city will be so desolate that even Arabs who travel the barren wastes of the desert would not choose to set up their tents there: "Nevermore shall it be settled nor dwelt in through all the ages. No Arab shall pitch his tent there, no shepherds make flocks lie down there. But beasts shall lie down there, and the houses be filled with owls . . ." (Isa. 13:20–21).

When some of the exiles from Babylon returned to Judah to rebuild the Temple, they were opposed by a coalition of peoples, including Samaritans and Arabs (Neh. 6:1–16). One of the tribal groups that the Israelites fought later was called the Hagarites, and they appear to be Arabs, not only because they are associated with Ishmael's mother, Hagar, but also because of their location in an Arabian ethnic region and the description of their homes in 1 Chron. 5:10: "And in the days of Saul, they made war on the Hagarites, who fell by their hand; and they occupied their tents throughout the region east of Gilead." In 5:19–20, those enemy Hagarites are associated with other names of Hagar's descendants, namely, Yetur and Nafish, both sons of Ishmael in Genesis 25:12. We must keep in mind that in the ancient world, tribal groups were in a constant state of alert because of the threats of neighboring peoples. Read in the context of other non-Israelite communities and peoples, the biblical view of Arabs is not particularly negative.

Arabs in Rabbinic Literature

Jews continue to interact with Arabs after the destruction of the Temple by the Romans in 70 CE. By that time, large Jewish communities already had been established in Mesopotamia and Egypt, both of which bordered great deserts and contained substantial numbers of Arab peoples. Small Jewish communities had sprung up in Arabia itself by this time, and the Talmud and Rabbinic literature refer to Arabs as Ishmaelites, Arabs, or *Tayaye*. The latter term, "*tayaye*," is found in the Babylonian Talmud and refers to seminomadic traders living in the vicinity of the Babylonian Jewish community of Pumbedita,[1] or desert-dwelling warriors and guides who roamed northern Arabia and Sinai. Interestingly, Talmudic references to Tayaye are always neutral or positive. The Tayaye respect Jews and Judaism and even know biblical traditions and some proper Jewish religious ritual. One served Rabbah bar bar Hana as guide in the Sinai Desert, led him to Mount Sinai, showed him where the earth swallowed Korah (Numbers 16), and revealed the spot where "heaven and earth kiss."[2] "Ishmaelites," on the other hand, are not positively portrayed, and Arabs are referenced as sinful and hopeless idolaters who "worship the dust at their feet" (BM 86b), and engage in repugnant sexual practices. The different references certainly refer to different subgroups, but they may also reflect attitudes of various Jewish communities, since the term "Tayaye," for example, may be found in Jewish texts only in the Babylonian Talmud (the term is also found in Persian and Syriac Christian sources from the same period).

By the time of the emergence of Islam, Jews and Christians had established communities in many parts of Arabia, from the northern deserts to the most southern regions along the Arabian Gulf and the Red Sea. They brought their scriptures, their stories, and their religious lore and practices with them. Monotheism and monotheistic practices were thus not unfamiliar to Arabs living deep within the peninsula even generations before the birth of the Prophet Muhammad. The important city of Najran, some 400 miles southeast of Mecca on the southern border of today's Saudi Arabia and Yemen, was a thriving center for Christianity in Arabia. On the other side of Mecca, some 300 miles due north, was the oasis community of Yathrib, the home of a thriving Jewish community.

CHAPTER 3

Pre-Islamic Origins

Judaism and Christianity in Pre-Islamic Arabia

By the generation of Muhammad's birth in about 570 CE, most of the Middle East had abandoned its local polytheistic religious systems and had taken on Judaism, Christianity, or Zoroastrianism, the state religion of the Persian Empire. Despite the penetration of these three religions into Arabia, the peninsula was never controlled by any foreign power. Arabia lay in a strategic location between Mesopotamia and Egypt, and between India and Africa. It produced valuable incense and was known for its gold; yet, the harsh climate, the lack of a significant water supply, and the fierce independence of its inhabitants made it impossible to conquer.

As a region that lay outside the political control of contemporary empires, Arabia was a natural refuge for dissidents. Since the Roman Empire had become Orthodox Christian by the 4th century and the state religion of the Persian Empire was Zoroastrianism, religious as well as political dissidents sought refuge outside their reach. We know, for example, that dissident (or sectarian) Christians were persecuted by the Orthodox religious establishment of the Byzantine Empire and fled to Persia and Arabia. As Rabbinic Judaism became the established form of Judaism in the Land of Israel and Babylonia, sectarian Jews may have fled their own religious establishments as well, and Arabia was a logical refuge, since it lay beyond the reach of any powerful players in other parts of the Middle East.

There are many signs of Jews living in Arabia before the advent of Islam.

References to Jews are found in inscriptions and graffiti and texts written many years later that tell the history of the period. One particularly interesting find is an inscription showing the Jewish expression of conclusion, "peace."[1]

Although Jews populated Arabia for centuries before the emergence of Islam, we do not know precisely what kinds of Jews they were and what kinds of Judaism they practiced. The Qur'an, which is the earliest Islamic text, seems to describe some Jewish ideas or practices that are quite strange to any kind of known Judaism. In a curious verse criticizing Judaism and Christianity for not upholding pure monotheism, for example, the Qur'an says, "The Jews say that `Uzayr is the son of God, and the Christians say that the messiah is the son of God" (Q.9:30). Most Western scholars have understood from this that the Qur'an was simply wrong in its assessment of Judaism. More recently, however, some scholars have noted that the originally Jewish books known as 4 Ezra (14:9, 50, also known as 2 Esdras) and 2 Enoch (22:11) associate a near-divine or angelic status to the biblical personages of Ezra and Enoch. It is possible that Jews who held such views had to settle far away from mainstream Jewish communities that would have found such thinking unacceptable. Their very special regard for Ezra could easily have been misconstrued by early Muslims (as it apparently was by the established Jewish communities in the Land of Israel and Babylonia) as compromising true monotheism.

In south Arabian inscriptions, references to pagan deities of the ancient tradition virtually disappear in the 4th century and are replaced with references to the one God referred to as "the Merciful" (RHMNN), or simply, "God," and usually qualified as "Lord of heaven" or "Lord of heaven and earth." These are not only Jewish epithets. In later centuries they become names for God in Islam, who is referred to in the Qur'an on occasion as *al-Raḥmān*.

According to legend, an Arab tribal leader named Abū Karib As`ad (c. 383–433 CE) of the tribe of Himyar in South Arabia, went to the town of Yathrib with the intention of conquering it. A large Jewish community was living in Yathrib at the time, and two Jewish leaders convinced Abū Karib not only to refrain from the conquest but to convert to Judaism. The two are referred to in the story as *aḥbār*, the Arabic form of the Hebrew *ḥaverim*, which the Babylonian Talmud refers to as religious leaders of slightly lower status than rabbis. According to this story, when Abū Karib returned to Yemen with the two rabbis,

> . . . the Himyarites blocked his path, saying: "You will not enter Yemen because you left our religion." Then he invited them to his religion . . . so they said: "Let's test it by the fire." He agreed. There was a custom in the Yemen that a fire would judge between them when they had their differences. It would consume the guilty and let the innocent go unharmed. So the Himyarites went forth with their idols and their

> religious objects, and the two rabbis came out with their sacred texts hanging like necklaces from their necks.[2] They stopped where the fire would blaze out. When it blazed forth [the Himyarites] were terrified and withdrew, but their comrades held them back and commanded them to be patient. So they held their ground until the fire consumed their idols, their offerings, and those who carried them. The two rabbis then came out with their scripts hanging from their necks, their foreheads sweating but otherwise unharmed. So the Himyarites took on his religion from then on. This is the origin of Judaism in the Yemen.[3]

Abū Karib's son Yusuf (Joseph) became a great warrior and ruled southern Yemen for some 38 years during the middle of the 6th century, but he became entangled in the power politics of his generation. While the great empires never actually conquered Arabia, they had proxies in the peninsula and especially in the wealthy and well-watered south. The Christians living in the region were naturally allied with Christian Ethiopia (Abyssinia), just across the narrow Red Sea. The Jews naturally allied with the Persian Empire, under which the great Babylonian Jewish academies were able to practice and develop Rabbinic Judaism. Persia and Byzantium fought each other through proxies, much like the United States and the Soviet Union did in the 20th century, and relations between Jewish and Christian communities played themselves out in Arabian battles that represented extensions of the competing powers. As the fighting intensified, the synagogue in the town of Najran was burned. Shortly thereafter, Yusuf put Najran to siege and massacred many of its Christian inhabitants. This is memorialized in Christian martyrologies and is also reported in early Muslim histories. Eventually, an invasion force of Christian Ethiopians managed to defeat the Jewish Himyarite army and kill Yusuf, thus ending this short period of Jewish political and religious dominance in southern Arabia.

Indigenous Arabian Monotheism

In addition to indigenous Arabian polytheism and some forms of Judaism and Christianity practiced in the peninsula, there is evidence that other forms of monotheism were practiced there. These seem to have been expressions of indigenous Arabian monotheisms, no doubt influenced by the success of Judaism and Christianity in the Middle East in general. The Qur'an refers to a believer who is neither polytheist, Jew, nor Christian as *ḥanīf*. It refers to those who had abandoned prevailing polytheistic religions. Abraham, for example, is a *ḥanīf*. Because the Torah of Judaism had not yet been revealed when Abraham followed the divine command, the Qur'an does not consider him to have been a Jew. It refers to him, rather, as both a *ḥanīf* and one who submits to the divine will (*muslim*). The use of the word *"muslim"* in this context does not suggest Abraham was a member of an established Muslim community, because the religion had not yet been founded. It means, simply, that he *submitted* himself to the one God: "Abraham . . . was a *ḥanīf muslim*, not one of the polytheists" (Q.3:67). The Qur'an also commands Muhammad to be a *ḥanīf* like Abraham: "Lift up your face to the *ḥanīf* religion, and be not among the polytheists" (Q.10:105).

Of course, Islam itself was an indigenous form of Arabian monotheism, and the believers in that monotheism were led by the Arabian prophet, Muhammad. But Islam was not the only form of Arabian monotheism guided by a living prophet. Even during the lifetime of Muhammad, a rival prophet named Musaylima led a community in the region called Yamāma to the east of Mecca. Like Muhammad, Musaylima claimed to have received revelation from God the Merciful (*al-Raḥmān*), and he established a *ḥaram* (sacred area) that paralleled the function of the *ḥaram* in Mecca. At one point in their competitive careers, Musaylima approached Muhammad to share their prophetic mission together, but Muhammad refused to join with Musaylima and accused him of being a false prophet. Musaylima outlived Muhammad, but was killed in a battle waged under the authority of the first caliph of the young Muslim community, Abū Bakr.

Pre-Islamic Arabia was thus a complex geographical entity socially, economically, and religiously. Arabia held a mix of religions, and it was virtually the only significant part of the Middle East in which the dominant religious form was still polytheism.

Pre-Islamic Arabia

The term *"jāhiliyya"* is an Islamic reference for Arabia (and sometimes the entire world) prior to the revelation of the Qur'an. Its literal meaning is "ignorance," the assumption having been that Arabia was a helplessly ignorant place, stuck in the terrible error of idolatry prior to the coming of Islam. The historical worldview conveyed by the use of *jāhiliyya* is quite clear. Pre-Islamic Arabia represented the Dark Ages of Arabian civilization that, while holding potential, was unable to blossom until the coming of God's word in the Qur'an as articulated through the mouth of God's last and greatest prophet, Muhammad. The stark contrast between the dark ignorance of the *jāhiliyya* and the enlightenment of Islam is a foundation of all Islamic worldviews.

The Qur'an itself associates polytheism with immorality and evil behavior, and monotheism with ethics and righteousness. The equation moves in two directions. Idolatry breeds immorality, and immorality encourages the depraved act of idolatry. The one and only God of the heavens and the earth is righteous and therefore demands ethical behavior. Conversely, anyone who is truly ethical must arrive at the realization of the one just God.

Islam thus represents itself as a powerful model of ethical monotheism long before such an idea became fashionable in the West among Jewish Reformers. A section of the Qur'an in Sura 17 directly equates ethical behavior with monotheistic commitment.

> 22Do not make up another deity aside from God, or you will sit condemned and deserted. 23Your Lord decreed that you worship only God and show kindness to parents. Whether one or both reaches old age with you, do not rebuff them, but speak kindly to them. . . . 26Give relatives their due, along with the poor and the wayfarer, but do not squander carelessly . . . 33And do not take a life, which God has made sacred, except for just cause. . . . 34And do not approach the property of the orphan . . . 39This is some of the wisdom your Lord revealed to you. Do not make up another deity beside God, or you will be thrown into hell, condemned and banished.

The geographical context for these words is the west-central area of Arabia known as the Hijaz, which was populated by Bedouin nomads moving through the arid steppe in small extended family groups, or Arab villagers living in small oases where dates could be cultivated. All residents of this region were Arabs, whether Jews, Christians, or indigenous polytheists or

THE ONENESS OF GOD

One of the most famous and beloved early suras (chapters) of the Qur'an exhorts the polytheistic inhabitants of Mecca in a beautiful rhymed prose style that is unfortunately lost in translation (Sura 107):

> 1Do you see the one who rejects the religion?
> 2That is the one who repels the orphan,
> 3who will not encourage feeding the needy.
> 4So, woe to those who pray
> 5yet are not attentive to their prayer;
> 6those who want to be seen
> 7but who refuse small acts of kindness.

monotheists. All spoke some version of Arabic, and all shared common aspects of Arabian culture in this unique peninsula called *shibh jazīra* in Arabic, meaning "resembling an island."

Although the residents of Arabia shared a common general culture, they were hardly a unified community. The peninsula had never been governed by any overarching political organization. As a result, there was no concept of law as we know it. The kinship group therefore became the basic organizational body for social, cultural, religious, and political purposes, providing protection and support, and creating a powerful sense of tribal solidarity. The tribal system was the organizing principle for all of Arabia, whether nomadic or settled. Individuals identified themselves and their loyalties in terms of their kinship groups, beginning with the nuclear family and broadening out to larger extended family and clan groupings, eventually to the tribe. Nomads, seminomads, agriculturalists, and urban dwellers all identified themselves according to this system.

THE BEDOUIN

Though smaller in numbers than the population of Arab agriculturalists during this period, the nomadic Bedouin represented the dominant culture and worldview. The name "Bedouin" is derived from the Arabic word for desert, *al-bādiya,* and they were tremendously successful at living in adverse desert conditions and in achieving political and cultural dominance in the region. Ironically, although more powerful than their Arab agriculturalist brethren, the Bedouin could never accrue real material wealth. They simply could not carry many things along with them, so they would distribute the goods and flocks that they acquired among the families and clans within the tribes. Although nomadic, the Bedouin could not live entirely alone in the desert, because they needed the date products that supplied them and their camels with food for long treks and trading journeys. The great mobility afforded to camel nomads made them formidable raiders of settled areas, for they could attack settled peoples by stealth and then retreat into the desert where they could not be followed. The Bedouin therefore established a kind of symbiotic relationship with Arab villagers, who supplied them with dates and other goods. The Bedouin, in turn, provided "protection" from other raiders and also served as traders and suppliers, traveling long distances in their overland caravans to transport goods between Arabia, the Mediterranean, and Mesopotamia.

Kinship rules and expectations were determined by "custom." Custom in this sense refers to an unwritten but powerful set of norms that legislated a wide range of behaviors within and between kinship groups (one of the pillars of tribal unity, for example, required all members to act together in war). The tribal leader was "first among equals," usually a tribal elder or *sheikh* (which simply means "elder" in Arabic). It was customary for the younger people of the tribe to emulate the most prestigious elder, whose behavior and sayings were known as his tribal *sunna*, the tribal custom.

The socioeconomic system, borne of a harsh desert environment, dictated that the fit survive, at times by seizing resources (livestock, food, or control of land) from weaker kinship groups. The larger the kinship group, the more secure and powerful its protection. The meager environment, however, could not support groups beyond a relatively small critical mass except during certain rainy times of the year. Large groups therefore broke into smaller units that could be raided and absorbed by others. Sometimes smaller groups would grow naturally through their own success and become competitive with the larger tribe. And large tribes sometimes broke into groups that became semi-independent or even eventually unrecognized by the tribe.

Although a complex web of obligations and expectations lay within the kinship group, each extended tribal unit considered itself independent of every other and, therefore, felt no inherent obligation to those outside the tribe. Raiding the resources of unrelated or distantly related tribes was not only acceptable, but also commendable, and raiding has even been termed the "national sport" of the ancient Arabs.

Islam emerged in this environment of competitive and suspicious tribalism. The system was certainly not anarchic, because all the players knew the rules of engagement between kinship groups. But it was a disorderly system that bred distrust and a constant threat of conflict and battle between kinship groups. As we will see, Islam became a means for transcending the divisiveness and violence of the pre-Islamic era by building a kind of *religious* tribalism meant to unify the bickering disunity of the *jāhiliyya*.

CHAPTER 4

The Emergence of Islam

Tradition, History, and the Meaning of Narrative

The first century of Islam was a busy time of expansion, conquest, and consolidation, when an obscure people burst forth from the Arabian desert and managed to subdue and control empires. It was a revolutionary time that would change human history forever, yet there are almost no contemporary sources that inform us of that critical period. Virtually all sources we have that treat the life of Muhammad, his prophetic mission, the revelation of the Qur'an, and the success of the Muslim movement were written at least 100 years later, and they were all written by Muslim religious scholars who were hardly objective historians. This fact has raised a good deal of controversy among some Western scholars, who have suggested many theories to account for the emergence of Islam. These range from considering Islam to have been a break-off from a Babylonian Jewish sectarian movement to suggesting that Muhammad was an imaginative creation of a religious community that actually emerged generations later. We have no intent to pursue these ideas here, though they call into question the reliability of our sources for early Islam.

The problem of sources is not unique to Islam. It is equally problematic in Judaism and Christianity. For example, there are no contemporary literary sources that describe the biblical Patriarchs and Matriarchs, the Exodus from Egypt, the giving of the Torah at Mount Sinai, the emergence of the religion of the Bible, or the conquest of Canaan. And there are no contemporary sources that treat any aspect of the life of Jesus or his mission. In fact, for all three great monotheistic scriptural religions, we rely largely on the religious writings of the followers of the religions themselves. These sources were often written by people who had particular interests that might distort their perceptions and depictions of events, so scholars try to develop techniques that will help them sift through the data for information that they believe is historically accurate and sound. The result is always a variety of perspectives about the history of these emerging religions. No historian is certain exactly what happened and how it occurred.

This is certainly the case with Islam, which emerged at a time before the Arabic language even had a functional writing system. However, the oral nature of pre-Islamic Arabian culture greatly admired storytelling, and epic stories and poems were remembered and recited regularly by experts. The first historical works written by Muslims retained much of this storytelling style, with literate individuals collecting and recording the memories of ancient days told by those who heard their narratives orally from their elders, who in turn heard them from their own. There remains a great deal of controversy over the accuracy of oral histories, even in our own day, when we take oral histories of Holocaust survivors or witnesses to events who are cross-examined in a court of law. Because this book is an introduction to Islam, we are less concerned with what actually happened than we are with what Muslims believe happened. We want to understand how Muslims view their own history and how that history impacts their lives as religious people. In what follows, therefore, we follow the basic outlines of early Islamic history as told by traditional Muslim sources.

From Creation to Abraham

Unlike either the Hebrew Bible or the New Testament, the Qur'an is not organized chronologically in any way. In fact, it seems that it is purposefully anti-chronological and contains very few references to occasions in the mission of its own prophet, Muhammad. On the other hand, it references Creation and many of the stories and personalities that are found in the Hebrew Bible and New Testament, from Adam to Jesus. It also contains references to ancient tribes and prophets that are not found in the Bible, and these too appear without any kind of chronological order.

Although the Qur'an is not interested in chronology, the earliest Muslim historians were. They reorganized the qur'anic references to individuals and events in their great universal histories, beginning with Creation and ending with the major events in their own generation. They also took the huge and constantly growing compendium of oral traditions among the Arabs and organized them chronologically and in relation to the traditions and histories of neighboring empires and peoples. We thus read in such historians as Muhammad b. Jarīr al-Ṭabarī (9th–10th century) about the kings of Persia and even India, along with the history of Greece and Rome, Israel, Arabia, and the goings-on in the great Muslim empires.

Many of the hundreds and thousands of short vignettes that make up these multivolume universal histories find parallels in the Bible, in the Jewish interpretive literature called midrash, and in the New Testament. In many cases it seems that the Muslim historians mined Jewish sources for details to fill out the short qur'anic references to biblical characters. In others, it appears that later Jewish sources took some of their information from Muslim sources. One well-known example of the latter is in the midrash called *Pirkei de-Rabbi Eliezer* (chapter 30), in which Ishmael's wives have the names of Muhammad's wife, `Ā'isha, and his daughter, Fāṭima.

The history of the world in the great Muslim compendia contains many of the stories found in the Bible, including Creation, the stories of Adam and Eve, the expulsion from the Garden, Cain and Abel, many of the biblical genealogies, the story of Noah and the Flood, and other narratives that take place in ancient Persia and Arabia. Many of the stories are recognizable from parallels in other literatures, but they are unique in their Islamic narrations, and the core of many are found in the Qur'an.

Abraham's Monotheism in the Qur'an

Abraham is the first monotheist, and he comes to know God through rational thinking, suggesting that any rational person can (and should) believe in the unity of God. Abraham's deductive discovery of God is found in the Qur'an in two suras:

> Remember when Abraham said to his father *Āzar*: Do you take idols as gods? You and your people are clearly in error! Thus We show Abraham the kingdom of the heavens and the earth, in order that he will be certain. When night came down upon him he saw a star. He said: This is my Lord. But when it disappeared he said: I do not like things that disappear. And when he saw the moon shining, he said: This is my Lord. But when it disappeared he said: If my Lord will not truly guide me, I will be led astray. And when he saw the sun shining he said: This is my Lord. This is greater. But when it vanished he said: O my people, I am free from what you associate [with God]. I have turned my face as a monotheist (*ḥanīf*) toward Him who created the heavens and the earth. I am not an idolater. (Sura 6: 74–79)

The second qur'anic passage is also found in a slightly different form in the Jewish midrash:

> And among these was Abraham, when he came to his Lord with a whole heart. He said to his father and his people: What is it that you worship? A fake? Do you desire gods other than God? What then is your opinion of the Lord of the worlds? He glanced at the stars and said, I feel sick! When they turned their backs and left him, he turned to their gods and said: Will you not eat? What is the matter with you that you do not speak? So he attacked them, giving them a blow with his right

MECCA, THE KA`BA, AND THE ZAM-ZAM

Mecca, Muhammad's birthplace, was the religious center for polytheism in the region, and many religious rituals and festivals were held there. In the center of the town was a large black, basalt stone structure called the Ka`ba, meaning the "cube," for its shape. Inside the Ka`ba were many figurines, images, and idols representing the gods of the various indigenous Arabian pantheons. Other sacred sites with pillars and images were scattered within the protected limits of the town called the *ḥaram*. People throughout the region would come to the *ḥaram* of Mecca, especially during special periods of the year, to pay obeisance to the images of their gods and to trade. A large industry grew up around the pilgrimages and trading fairs in Mecca, which supplied its population with a good deal of wealth.

Next to the Ka`ba was a spring called *Zam-zam* for the gurgling sound it produced along with its water. According to the Islamic interpretive literature called "Prophetic Tales," which functions similarly to the Jewish Midrash, the spring that God brought forth for Ishmael after Hagar's expulsion from Abraham and Sarah's family was the Zam-zam in Mecca (compare Gen. 21:14–21).

Ishmael would grow up in Mecca and, with the help of his father Abraham, raise up the foundations of the Ka`ba as the House of God and serve as its caretaker. Ishmael, whose descendants eventuate in Muhammad, is known in Islamic tradition as a Hebrew immigrant to Arabia who assimilated with locals to become Arab himself. The very center of Islam's sacred history thus extends from the sacred history of the Bible, just as the divine revelation that is the Qur'an is considered an extension and correction of the Bible.

> hand. Then they [the people] came back to him quickly. He said: Do you worship what you carve, though God has created you and whatever you make? They said: Build a pile [of fuel] for him and caste him in the blaze. They designed a snare for him, but We made them inferior. He said: I am going to my Lord. He will guide me! (Sura 37: 83–99)

Abraham is mentioned in the Qur'an more than 100 times in some 25 chapters. Only Moses appears more often than Abraham. The Qur'an seems to extend the biblical story of the expulsion of Hagar and Ishmael in Genesis 21 to Arabia, where Abraham and Ishmael raise up the foundations of the sacred Ka`ba in Mecca (Q.2:125–132). Abraham establishes Ishmael there and charges his sons to be forever submitters (*muslims*) to God, after which the family of Ishmael becomes the keeper of the Meccan House of God and the sacred shrines that made it a center of pilgrimage.

Abraham to Muhammad

According to Islamic tradition (this is not explicit in the Qur'an itself), the descendants of Abraham begin to backslide in Arabia over the generations and descendants to polytheism. The corruption is so great that they end up converting the monotheistic Ka`ba into a pagan shrine. According to this scenario, the sacred sites in Mecca that Muhammad would later claim for Islam were thus monotheistic in origin. The Qur'an is quite explicit that Muhammad's role as God's prophet was to reform the corrupted Arabian religion and bring the people back to the original monotheism of father Abraham.

The other side of Abraham's family remained in Canaan and the history of the family follows the basic storyline known from the Bible: the biblical Patriarchs and Matriarchs; Joseph and the decent into Egypt; Moses and Pharaoh; the redemption from Egypt and the receipt of the Torah at Mount Sinai; the desert experience; the kingships of Saul, David, and Solomon. These and many other biblical tales and personalities are also referenced in the Qur'an, including references to Korah, Elijah, Jonah, Haman, Ezra, John the Baptist, Mary mother of Jesus, Zakariah, and Jesus among others unknown from the Bible.

This long and wonderful history is both entertaining and thick with meaning at many levels. Throughout is the underlying theme that, despite the true divine revelation of earlier scriptures given to righteous prophets of old, the peoples to whom those books were given soon engaged in backsliding. They failed to live up to the divine will. The qur'anic narrative thus opens up not only the possibility but the necessity for another revelation that will bring idolaters and errant monotheists alike back to the right path. In great mercy and compassion, God would send his final messenger with the divine word in a book called "the Recitation"—the Qur'an. This would be the last call to humanity to wake up and come to its senses by following the word of God as spoken by the last and greatest prophet, Muhammad.

Muhammad in Mecca

According to Islamic tradition, Muhammad was born in 570 CE into the clan of Hāshim within the tribe of Quraysh in Mecca. Muhammad's father, Abdallah, died shortly before his birth, and his mother, Āmina, died some six years later. The Banū Hāshim was a respectable clan but not the most powerful within the larger tribe. The Quraysh (which, like the Hebrew *karish*, means "shark") was the most powerful tribe in Mecca and had considerable influence in the surrounding area. Most of its members were worshipers of the traditional Arabian pantheons.

Muhammad spent some of his younger years as a shepherd among the Bedouin of the region, as was custom among some urban folk, in order to learn the noble life of the desert nomad, but he soon returned to Mecca and grew up there as an orphan under the care of his uncle, Abū Ṭālib. He thus experienced both the material equality of the Bedouin lifestyle and the urban tendency to accrue wealth among those who were able, all through the eyes of an underprivileged orphan. He was not among the well-off in Mecca, and he suffered the experience of an orphan in an environment lacking the kind of safety net that was a part of traditional Bedouin life. Poor but not destitute, his lack of means kept him a bachelor until the age of 25, when he was noticed by a widow of 40 named Khadīja.

Khadīja's family was engaged in the caravan business. Mecca was in a perfect location for this business, as it is situated halfway between the spice-growing area of southern Arabia and the Mediterranean world that required that product. In such an ideal location, the Meccans could easily transport goods and provide the armed security necessary to move it through the ungoverned expanses of Arabia. The economy of Mecca was thus supported by its two great pillars: transportation and the religious tourism industry associated with pilgrimage to the Ka`ba.

Muhammad had a reputation for honesty and trustworthiness. When he married Khadīja, he became the manager of her transport business, and it is possible that he accompanied a caravan or two northward to the Mediterranean. Some traditions insist that he did so, even as a child under the care of his uncle, Abū Ṭālib. In one of them, his prophetic status was discovered by a Christian monk who, after taking one look at Muhammad, pulled off his shirt to reveal the "mark of prophecy" between Muhammad's shoulders that the monk recognized from ancient manuscripts. More important for our purposes, if he had traveled northward, he certainly would have met some of the Jews and Christians who lived in northern Arabia and Gaza, the usual endpoint on the northern caravan journey.

Muhammad may have married into wealth, but the tradition depicts him as being uneasy with some aspects of his new life. He was troubled by the inequities of Mecca, with the existence of the poor and those without adequate care. He would regularly remove himself from the commotion of the town to a cave in nearby Mount Ḥirā', where he would meditate. Things changed radically after he reached the age of 40, in the year 610 CE.

On one nighttime retreat during the month of Ramadan, on a day later named the Night of Power, he was confronted by a heavenly being or voice who commanded, "Recite!" He responded either that he was not a reciter, or he asked what he should recite, when he was again commanded, "Recite!" Again he hesitated, after which the first revelation of the Qur'an was brought down from on high. The first five verses of chapter 96 are considered Muhammad's first revelation:

> 1Recite! In the name of your Lord, who creates:
> 2Creates humanity from a clot.
> 3Recite! For your Lord is most generous,
> 4Who teaches by the pen,
> 5teaches humanity what it knows not.

These lines appear in a rhymed prose style known as *saj`*, a form not unlike some pre-Islamic oral poetry recited by individuals who were thought to have been possessed by demons. The demons endowed them with hidden knowledge and enabled them to recite complex Arabic forms. The context for this revelation is not found in the Qur'an itself, but is provided by interpretations. According to one, Muhammad thought that he had become possessed by such a demon and said, "None of God's creatures was more hateful to me than an [ecstatic] poet or man possessed . . . Woe is me, poet or possessed!" In a fearful frenzy he ran up the mountain to throw himself off and end what seemed to have become a life of demonic possession, but halfway up the mountain he heard a voice from heaven saying: "O Muhammad! You are the messenger of God and I am Gabriel!" When he looked up, he saw Gabriel standing on the horizon, and Gabriel repeated his words, "O Muhammad! You are the messenger of God and I am Gabriel!" Whichever direction Muhammad turned, he saw Gabriel.

Muhammad returned home and greatly doubted his experience, but Khadīja and her cousin, Waraqa (who had converted to Christianity and was familiar with holy books and traditions), believed that he had been contacted by an angel of God. According to some accounts, the second revelation he received was the beginning of the qur'anic sura called "The Pen" (Sura 68):

> 1By the pen, and what they write,
> 2You are not, by God's favor, possessed.
> 3In fact, you have an endless reward
> 4and a powerful inner strength.

After these revelations there was silence for a while, and Muhammad began to doubt himself and his worthiness to receive divine revelation. Finally, a third revelation came that not only reassured him but gave him his first instructions:

> 1By the early morning light
> 2And by the night when it is still
> 3Your Lord has not left you nor does He hate you.
> 4What follows will be better for you than what has already been.
> 5Your Lord will surely give to you and you will be content.
> 6Did He not find you an orphan and shelter you?
> 7And find you drifting and guide you?
> 8And find you needy and enrich you?
> 9So do not oppress the orphan!
> 10And do not drive away the beggar! (or, the seeker)
> 11And declare the kindness of your Lord! (Sura 93)

While these are considered the earliest revelations, they occur toward the very end of the Qur'an. As mentioned previously, the Qur'an seems to be consciously anti-chronological, and the earlier revelations tend to be organized toward the back of the book. They are powerful messages fully consonant with this expression of ethical monotheism. Interestingly, it is rarely clear to what events they are responding. Numerous methodologies have been devised to try to put them in chronological order, and an entire genre of literature called "Occasions of Revelation" emerged in Islam in an attempt to do so. The various attempts tend to contradict one another, however, depending on the ordering method employed. Still, there is a generally accepted sequence of revelation for much of the Qur'an among Muslims and, as will become clearer below, that presumed sequence has a powerful impact on the meaning of the verses themselves.

Muhammad would receive revelations periodically until the end of his life some 22 years later. Sometimes they arrived in response to pressing issues of the hour. Sometimes despite pressing issues, revelations would not come. And sometimes words would be revealed in what might appear to be a random manner incomprehensible to the human mind. It took some time and more revelations before Muhammad felt ready to preach in Mecca, and his preaching was first met with tolerance and curiosity. He seems to have been a powerful orator, and his messages turned some of the most basic assumptions of *jāhiliyya* culture on their head. He preached an ethic of divine commands in place of the old tribal traditions. He warned of a Final Judgment and reward and punishment in a world to come, and he preached that a universal ethic of religion must be the basis for human solidarity rather than the divisive interests of tribe and faction.

As his message of ethical monotheism became stronger, its implications became increasingly clear to the powerful people who ran the polytheistic religious tourism industry and who hoarded their wealth at the expense of the unfortunate. As Muhammad's following grew, he was increasingly considered a threat to the religious establishment of Mecca. In turn, the Meccan establishment became an increasing threat to his safety and that of his followers.

He was protected by tribal rules that would not allow the killing of a fellow tribesman, and he had personal protection through his influential uncle Abū Ṭālib and his Hāshimite clan, but he and his followers were still subject to scorn and even physical abuse. Some fled to neighboring Abyssinia (part of today's Ethiopia), governed by a Christian king who afforded them asylum. The pressure continued to mount. In 619 CE his enemies declared a ban against his clan, hoping that the pain of boycott would encourage his kinsmen to force Muhammad to end his preaching. Though the boycott was unsuccessful, Muhammad suffered a personal blow that same year, when both his beloved Khadīja and his protector, Abū Ṭālib, died. He was becoming persona non grata in his own native town, and rumors had it that a plot was brewing to kill him. If a member of each clan within the Quraysh tribe would be involved in the murder, it would be impossible for Muhammad's clan of Banū Hāshim to avenge the death. Just as things were looking extremely bleak for the Prophet and his growing band of believers, an unlikely development was occurring in the oasis settlement of Yathrib, some 300 miles to the north.

Yathrib

Yathrib was an agricultural center made up of a number of small clan settlements. The area was blessed by a high water table that allowed palm trees to reach the abundant water in aquifers lying under the desert sands, and was populated by several clans and tribes. Many Jews were counted among them. Two of the major clans of Yathrib, the Aws and the Khazraj (sometimes they are referred to as tribes), were engaged in a blood feud that was making life in the settlement virtually impossible. The tribal system of blood vengeance had emerged in the expansive Arabian steppe, where tribes in conflict lived far enough apart from one another to avoid most contact when engaged in a blood feud. In the open desert wilderness, innocent non-players could thus usually avoid the violence. In the close quarters of a settled environment, however, where varied kinship groups shared the same water sources, markets, and thoroughfares, one was constantly bumping into members of enemy clans. Removing innocent bystanders from the conflict in such an environment was impossible—so the toll tended to mount as one excessive act of revenge invited another.

During the pilgrimage season following the deaths of Khadīja and Abū Ṭālib, six men from one of the warring clans came to Mecca and met with Muhammad. They had heard of his honesty and trustworthiness, and after talking with him, they joined his followers with the hope that he would help them resolve the tribal violence in their home. They then returned to Yathrib. The following year, they came back to Mecca for the pilgrimage and brought with them more members of their clan, along with a few representatives of the enemy clan. They all pledged allegiance to the Prophet, and Muhammad sent a representative to accompany them, recite the Qur'an (as much as had yet been revealed), and give them religious instruction. The seed for a community of believers was thus planted in Yathrib.

Meanwhile, conditions were not improving between the warring factions. On the third pilgrimage, 73 men and two women sought out Muhammad and pledged loyalty to him. He was invited to begin the process of resolving the disputes that had so divided that town. Muhammad demanded certain conditions in return. His family and followers must be allowed to join him, they must be supported until they could find a means of livelihood for themselves, and they must be afforded protection and treated as full citizens. Yathrib would soon be called Medina, short for *medīnat al-nabī*, the City of the Prophet.

Muhammad in Medina

The transition from Mecca to Medina in 622 is referred to in Islam as the Hijra, or emigration (sometimes spelled "Hegira" in English). It indicates a major transition in Islam, not unlike the Exodus in biblical history. The Hijra marks the beginning of Islam as a societal religion. In Mecca before the Hijra, Muhammad was a fiery prophet who foretold the doom of hell for unethical nonbelievers, and the good tidings of heaven for those who repented of their evil ways and accepted the unity of God. In Medina, without the daily harassment of the Meccan opposition, Muhammad had the overall support of the larger community. He was thus able to move in a new direction to develop a complex religious and social system with a set of rules and laws. In Mecca, Muhammad was a prophet. In Medina, he was still a prophet, but he was also a religious and political leader, and eventually also a military leader and strategist. But success was not immediate, and it did not come easily.

Resolving the Blood Feud

The first order of business was to resolve the blood feud that was raging in Medina, and this was accomplished by reforming the notion of social responsibility. Muhammad managed to begin the process of transcending tribal bickering by creating a larger unit of Medinans who would retain their traditional kinship ties while developing a sense of trans-tribal responsibility. This change is symbolized in a document called the Pact (sometimes called the "Constitution") of Medina. This formal document placed all the various kinship and religious groups into one community called the *umma* (the modern Hebrew word for nation, *ummah*, is linguistically related). The *umma* became a kind of supertribe, and each subgroup within the *umma* would retain its own basic group ties and internal responsibilities, but each was also required to have a greater allegiance to the overall community as a whole. According to the Pact of Medina, the various factions of Medina. . .

> are one community [*umma*] to the exclusion of all men. The Quraysh emigrants according to their present custom shall pay the blood-payment within their number and shall redeem their prisoners with the kindness and justice common among Believers.[1] The Banū `Awf according to their present custom shall pay the blood-payment they paid in the *jāhiliyya*; every section shall redeem its prisoners with the kindness and justice common among Believers. The Banū Sa`ada, the Banūl-Ḥārith, and the Banū Jusham, and the Banūl-Najjār likewise. . . . The God-fearing Believers shall be against the rebellious or him who seeks to spread injustice, or sin or enmity, or corruption between Believers; the hand of every man shall be against him even if he be a son of one of them. . . . God's protection is one; the least of them may give protection to a stranger on their behalf. . . . To the Jew who follows us belong help and equality. He shall not be wronged nor shall his enemies be aided. The peace of the Believers is indivisible. No separate peace shall be made when Believers are fighting in the way of God.

> Conditions must be fair and equitable to all. . . . The Jews of the Banū `Awf are one community with the Believers—the Jews have their religion and the Muslims theirs—their freedmen and their persons, except those who behave unjustly and sinfully, for they hurt but themselves and their families. The same applies to the Jews of the Banūl-Najjār, Banūl-Ḥārith, Banū Sa`ida, Banū Jusham. . . . Loyalty is protection against treachery. The freedmen of the Tha`laba are as themselves. The close friends of the Jews are as themselves. None of them shall go out to war save with the permission of Muhammad, but he shall not be prevented from taking revenge for a wound. He who slays a man without warning slays himself and his household, unless it be one who has wronged him, for God will accept that. The Jews must bear their expenses and the Muslims their expenses. Each must help the other against anyone who attacks the people of this document. . . . [2]

The raging feud was thus ended, but all was not rosy in Medina with the coming of Muhammad. To begin with, most Medinans did not accept him as a prophet. He had the status of clan leader in his capacity as chief of those who accompanied him from Mecca. Yet in his capacity of arbitrator for the entire joined community, he had a certain authority that trumped that of traditional clan leaders. This caused resentment in some quarters. His collective authority was based on his role of messenger of God, from whom he received revelations from time to time in the form of commands that were supposed to apply to the whole community. As more and more people accepted Muhammad's leadership, his community grew. He held authority over members of clans unrelated to him, since they had become interested in his religious and social ideas. The new social and religious innovations, imposed on the traditional social system, threatened those who were loyal to the old tribal system and caused anxiety. If such tensions hampered a process of unification throughout the lifetime of the Prophet, they were controlled well enough for a community of Believers to grow and succeed.

The Economic Problem

Economics was also problematic for the Believers. They were not self-supporting, hardly a respectful position for an ascendant religious and socio-political leader to be in. The Medinan economy was based on agriculture, and since all the arable land was already cultivated, new sources of sustenance had to be found. Muhammad and the Believers therefore turned to a traditional solution: the raid. But whom should they raid? In the traditional system, one could only raid outside the tribe. Of course, the Medina Pact prevented any kinds of raiding among the many communities and villages within the precinct of the Medina oasis. The most natural target would be the Meccan caravans carrying goods between southern Arabia and the Mediterranean, but they were manned and protected by Quraysh, who were kinsmen of Muhammad and his core followers from Mecca. Yet, the Quraysh had threatened their own kinsmen in Muhammad and his followers, and they had expelled them from their homes. The Meccan Quraysh had broken the sacred ties of kinship. They could therefore be considered fair game for attack.

After a number of feeble attempts and one minor success, Muhammad managed to capture a major caravan in 624 at a raid memorialized as the "Battle of Badr." Although the Muslims hoped to surprise the caravan, the tables were turned because the Meccans learned of the impending attack from allies in Medina. As a result, when Muhammad arrived on the scene of battle, he found himself outnumbered three to one, but by the time they discovered the surprise, they were committed. To the astonishment of both the raiders and the Meccans, however, they were overwhelmingly victorious, which success was considered—by the Medinans, at least—to be the result of divine intervention that brought Muhammad tremendous prestige.

To Muhammad, the Meccan Quraysh had forfeited any ties of privilege through kinship by virtue of their persecution of him and his followers. The Meccans may have been in agreement about the severance of kinship responsibility, but they capitalized on the incident by claiming to tribes throughout the region that Muhammad was breaking the sacred Arabian rules of relationship. That there would be a counterattack was clear to everyone. It

THE BATTLE OF BADR

The Battle of Badr is one of the few historical occasions in the life of Muhammad referenced directly in the Qur'an:

> 123God made you victorious at Badr when you were lowly, so be conscious of God, and be grateful. 124When you said to the Believers, Is it not enough that your Lord help you with 3,000 angels sent down? 125No! If you would only be patient and conscientious, when they immediately came upon you like that, your Lord would help you with five thousand illustrious angels. 126God did this to make good news for you so your hearts will be at ease. Victory comes only from God, the mighty, the wise.

occurred the following year, in 625, when the Meccans sent some 3,000 infantry and 200 cavalry against Medina at the Battle of Uḥud, a hill within the Medinan oasis.

The result of this battle was not another miraculous Muslim victory. In fact, Muhammad himself was wounded in the heat of the fighting. Rumor spread that he had been killed, and the Medinans lost three times the number of warriors as the Meccans. Surprisingly, however, when the Quraysh could have pressed their advantage to overrun the Medinan forces entirely and kill Muhammad, they chose to return to Mecca. The reason for this retreat remains unclear to this day and is debated by historians. The Muslim histories suggest that the Meccans saved face in the battle, which may have been enough for them. It is often the case that when a confederation of clans joins together in battle, continued unity may be threatened if a leader fights too long and loses too many warriors. The wife of the Meccan warrior who wounded Muhammad is cited in the sources as saying, "We have paid you back for Badr!" And Abū Sufyān, the leader of the Meccan forces, was said to have shouted to his troops from the top of the hill, "You have done a fine work. Victory in war goes by turns: today is in exchange for the day of Badr."

Whatever the reasons, the Meccans retreated without pressing their advantage. With the end of this battle, the Muslims concentrated on internal issues, and they were assisted with the continuing revelation inspired in Muhammad. The lull in fighting was not complete, of course, for the nature of life in Arabia was such that tribes and clans were constantly maneuvering for influence and for scarce resources. Muhammad's growing community sent out expeditions to gain influence and followers or to raid in nearby areas. The Meccans engaged, as always, in making and reforming alliances with neighboring tribes and communities, and the growing strength of the Medinans became increasingly problematic. The tension between Muhammad's Medinan community and Mecca continued to grow.

Finally, the Meccans put Medina to siege with overwhelming force for some two or three weeks in 627. This engagement was called the Battle of the Trench. The Meccans had assembled far more fighters than previously by rallying neighboring tribes, and the sources cite numbers between 7,500 and 10,000 warriors. Muhammad knew of the impending attack and dug a trench—the *khandaq*—around the obvious openings to the oasis settlements in order to slow the attack. It was constantly manned by the outnumbered Medinans and succeeded in preventing the expected cavalry charge. A number of forays were attempted, but they were held off, and the overwhelming Meccan infantry never made a serious attempt to crush the defense. After a few weeks of virtual stalemate, the Meccan alliance began to crumble. Shortly thereafter, the siege was ended and the attackers returned to their homes.

Neither side was victorious, but as was common in these kinds of encounters, each side made the claim of victory. It was clear, in any case, that the combined forces of the Quraysh and its allies could not overwhelm the Muslims and their supporters in Medina. The net result was a rise in the prestige of Muhammad and his followers. Within three years, Mecca would come under the control of the Believers.

The Problem of Authority

Throughout his prophetic mission, from the moment of receiving his first revelation to his last, Muhammad was plagued by the problem of authority. People were simply unsure whether Muhammad was truly a prophet. Sources tell us that while he was still in Mecca, some of the Quraysh sent a representative "to the Jewish rabbis in Medina and said to them: 'Ask them about Muhammad; describe him to them and tell them what he says, for they are the first people of the scriptures and have knowledge which we do not possess about the prophets.'"[3] People were naturally suspicious of someone claiming prophethood, and the Qur'an itself unabashedly reports accusations against Muhammad: "Or they say, 'Hasn't he invented it?' Say [to the accusers], 'Then bring a chapter like it or call on anyone you can aside from God if you are truthful!'" (Q.10:38). The Qur'an also contains many verses defending itself against attacks on its authenticity: "This Qur'an could not have been invented without God. It is, rather, a confirmation of what preceded it, an exposition [or, 'filling out the details'] of scripture, in which there is no doubt" (Q.10:37). One repeated response to the suspicion against the Qur'an is that its message is no different from the authentic revelations known to Jews and Christians. "He has sent down to you the scripture in truth, confirming that which was before it as He revealed the Torah and the Gospel" (Q.3:3).

The problem that Muhammad faced, as any prophet or leader of a new religion, was how to demonstrate that he was telling the truth when he claimed to be God's prophet. Because new religious movements tend to attract the youth and often exhibit an energy and vibrancy that has faded from established religions, they are always opposed by those establishment religions, which find them threatening. It then becomes the burden of those representing the new religious movement to prove the validity not only of the message, but also the medium for the message. No matter the nature of the revelation, if it is not accepted as authoritative, it will not attract the necessary following to sustain the movement. In the case of Islam, it was both the prophethood of Muhammad and the divine revelation of the Qur'an that was suspect and had to be proven to the community.

When a new religion succeeds, it naturally retains a feeling of hostility toward the establishment religions that tried to defeat it. We observe this anger and resentment in early Christianity, in early Islam, and in the religion of ancient Israel.[4] The natural animus expressed in the Qur'an toward the religious opposition is most vehement in reference to the traditional religious establishment of Arabian polytheism, which posed the strongest threat to emerging Islam.

The pagan Meccan establishment abused Muhammad and his community both socially and physically, most especially Muhammad's own tribe of Quraysh, which controlled the sacred shrines and religious tourism industry in Mecca. The Qur'an also contains much invective against Judaism and Christianity. And more qur'anic anger is directed against Jews than Christians. This fact has puzzled some students of Islam, particularly because in the 7th century when Islam emerged as a religious system, Christianity was the religion of the Roman Empire, while Judaism was the religion of a dispersed and largely powerless minority. It would follow, therefore, that Christianity was a much more powerful and threatening establishment religion to Islam than Judaism. But the reason for the greater hostility directed against Jews is the result of a certain accident of history.

When Muhammad fled his hometown of Mecca to save his life from the threat of the polytheistic Qurayshi Arabs, the town to which he escaped had a large and established Jewish community but few Christians. It was therefore an Arabian Jewish community that opposed his prophethood in his new home, rather than an Arabian Christian community. Had he fled southward to Najran, where a large number of Christians lived, rather than northward to Medina, he would have encountered an organized Christian community and few Jews, and the situation would have been reversed.

CHAPTER 5

Muhammad and the Jews of Medina

When Muhammad arrived in Medina, it appears that he expected the Jews to welcome him and to accept his prophetic status. After all, the Jews were a monotheistic people who had their own prophets. They would know a prophet when they saw one. Muhammad was disappointed. The Jewish community of Medina refused to accept his prophethood and religious leadership, although a few individuals did join his followers.

This rejection became a very serious issue for the Muslims, because the Jews were known and respected by the Arabs as a wise and ancient community of monotheists with a long prophetic tradition. Their rejection of Muhammad thus represented a major blow to his authority in Medina, not only as a prophet, but as a leader in general. As the relations between Muhammad and the Medinan Jews deteriorated, it became apparent that there was only enough room in Medina for one expression of monotheism. With this realization, the stakes grew higher and the tactics on both sides became radicalized. In the end, the clash concluded violently. The conflict between Muhammad and the Jews of Medina has become a controversial issue in Jewish-Muslim relations to this day. There is a tendency on both sides to see the situation in simplistic terms, which not only fails to do justice to the complexity of the situation, but also reinforces negative stereotypes that are not accurate reflections of reality.

It is difficult to reconstruct exactly what occurred during the fateful year or two after Muhammad's arrival in Medina when the conflict between Muhammad and the Medinan Jews played itself out. Jews were clearly included in the Pact of Medina at the very outset of Muhammad's residence there and were thus afforded the same rights as other groups. Ironically, some early Muslim sources state that the Jews inadvertently brought converts into the new community of Believers because of the nature of their ancient monotheistic status.

According to ibn Ishāq, the author of the most authoritative and ancient biography of Muhammad:

> `Āsim b. `Umar b. Qatāda related on the authority of some of the elders of his tribe that when the apostle [Muhammad] met [members of this tribe of Medinan Arabs] he learned by inquiry that they were of the Khazraj tribe and allies of the Jews. Muhammad invited them to sit with him, expounded Islam to them and recited the Qur'an. Now God had prepared the way for Islam in that [this tribe of Arabs] lived side by side with the Jews who were people of the Scriptures and knowledge, while they themselves were polytheists and idolaters. The Arabs had often raided the Jews in their district and whenever bad feeling arose the Jews would say to them: "A prophet will be sent soon. His day is at hand. We shall follow him and kill you by his aid just as [the lost tribes of] `Ad and Iram perished." So when these

SCRIPTURE: A CANON OF AUTHORITY

As a religion becomes successful and grows into an institution, it establishes a canon of authority for itself. Among the scriptural religions, the final and highest authority is scripture, because it represents the word and the will of God. But scripture can be a "wild card" for religion. New revelations of God's will can revise or counter current practice or even the authority of those in charge. The revelation of new scripture therefore always comes to an official end at some point in the process of religious emergence and formation.[1] The Jews, who had canonized their scripture by the emergence of Christianity, naturally would not accept the possibility of new revelations associated with Jesus. And neither Jews nor Christians could remain members of their religious communities and accept the new divine revelations that Muhammad claimed had been revealed to him.

> Arabs heard [Muhammad's] message they said one to another: This must be the very prophet of whom the Jews warned us. Don't let them get to him before us! Thereupon they accepted his teaching and became Muslims.[2]

Many scholars consider some of the special rituals practiced early on by the Muslims as attempts to attract the Medinan Jews to Islam or at least make them more comfortable with it. At first, Islamic prayer seems to have faced the direction of Jerusalem,[3] and before the enactment of the Ramadan fast, the early Muslims engaged in a 24-hour fast on the 10th day of the 7th month called *'Ashūra*, which corresponds to the full-day fast on the 10th day of the Jewish month of Tishre, Yom Kippur.[4] When relations deteriorated with the Medinan Jews, the direction of Islamic prayer was changed to Mecca and the Ramadan fast took the place of the *'Ashūra* fast, which subsequently was no longer required.

But given what seem to be virtually universal laws of relationship between established and emerging religions, it is quite natural that the two communities would not get along. The Jews could not validate Muhammad's prophethood because they observed him reciting revelation that, while certainly reminiscent of and even parallel in many cases to their own scripture, did not conform with the revelations of the Hebrew Bible. Just as important, the canon of Jewish scripture had been closed for centuries and no new revelation had since been accepted. From the honest and authentic standpoint of the Jews, therefore, Muhammad was a false prophet who could not be accepted nor even trusted.[5] But from the honest perspective of Muhammad and his followers, who absolutely believed in his status of prophet, the Jewish rejection was tantamount to the rejection of God. When Jews critiqued him for reciting divine revelation that did not comport with the revelation of the Torah, he responded that the Jews distorted their own revelation. If Muhammad was convinced that his revelation was true, then he must have thought that the Jews were purposefully distorting their own revelation to discredit him publicly. He recites the following verses within a long qur'anic argument against the "People of the Book": "There is a group among them who distort scripture with their tongues so that you would consider that it is from scripture when it is not from scripture; and they say it is from God when it is not from God; and they knowingly tell a lie against God. God would not give scripture and wisdom and prophethood to one person, that the person then say to the people, 'Be devotees of me instead of God.' Rather be devotees of God (*rabbāniyīn*), as you have taught scripture and you have studied" (Q.3:78–79).

The Battle for Survival

The Jews did not simply reject Muhammad, but seem to have campaigned against him actively. This notion is very upsetting to Muslims, who see no reason for even a passive rejection of the truth of Muhammad's mission. Those Medinan Jews thus appear to many Muslims today as contrary and even malicious. Jews, however, become incensed at the accusation that their Jewish brethren might have tried to destroy Muhammad and his new community. According to general Jewish self-perception, Jews do not engage in such behaviors.[6] What both sides often fail to take into account is that the Jews and Muslims of Medina related to one another on an even playing field, and they were all playing by the same set of rules. Both communities engaged in behaviors that would be unacceptable in an enlightened, democratically governed society that supported equal rights and privileges for all religious communities. But 7th-century Medina was not such a place.

The Jews and Muslims of Medina were both culturally Arab. They spoke the same Arabic language (and language is a very powerful determinant of behavior and culture). Both were organized around a combination of kinship and religious expectations, and they seem to have interacted according to the same accepted "rules of engagement." Unfortunately, as is common in history, the only account is told by the victors. There is no Jewish version. But given the conflict described in the oral tellings and verses of the Qur'an, we can piece together a scenario of what might have occurred.

The Jews' rejection of Muhammad, which was necessary, given their position in relation to the emerging Muslim community, probably initiated the conflict. Given the stature of the Jews, rejection was serious, endangering the success of an entire new religious movement. The Jews are depicted in the Qur'an and the early histories as publicly humiliating Muhammad, a common tactic of the time and place: "There are some Jews who change the words from their places by saying: 'we hear and disobey'" (Q.4:46). The Arabic in this text is *sami`nā wa`a-ṣaynā*, which sounds remarkably like the Hebrew *shama`nu ve`asinu*. In Deuteronomy 5:24, *shama`nu ve`asinu* is said by the Israelites as a statement of obedience to the divine will, and it means, literally, "we hear and obey." In Arabic, however, it means the opposite: "We hear and disobey." Within the Jewish community of Medina, the phrase *shama`nu ve`asinu* would have been well known. One can imagine the satirical power of the bilingual double entendre if a Jew were to cite these words when hearing Muhammad preach in Medina. "We hear and obey *our* religious tradition (Hebrew meaning), but we hear and publicly acclaim our *disobedience* to *your* religious preaching (Arabic meaning)!"[7]

The tensions between Muhammad and the Medinan Jews increased, especially with the Meccan attacks of Uḥud and the Khandaq (Battle of the

Trench). In the first battle, the Jews were accused of holding back and not contributing their share to the common defense of Medina as required by the Medina Pact. In the second battle, they were accused of aiding and abetting the enemy, an egregious crime for a community that was being formed for defense. There was also an accusation of a Jewish assassination attempt against the Prophet. Muhammad himself sent assassins to do away with enemies who were humiliating him publicly. None of these behaviors was unusual or outside typical practices of intertribal warfare. What was unusual was the Muslims' anger and indignation against the Jews for engaging in tactics that were common to both sides. The likely explanation for the surprisingly strong Muslim reaction is the power of the Jewish rejection in 7th-century Medina and the great difficulties it caused the new religious community there.

Muhammad successfully divided the Jewish community of Medina and destroyed it. The smallest Jewish tribal community of the Qaynuqā' was isolated first by being accused of publicly humiliating a young Muslim woman; this initiated violence and subsequently a blood feud between Jews and Muslims. When the Qaynuqā' retreated into their fortified area and were besieged by the Muslims, the two larger Jewish tribal communities failed to come to their defense. The Qaynuqā' could not hold out the siege and as a result were exiled from Medina, their property expropriated by the Muslims. Some time later, the second-largest Jewish tribal community of the Naḍīr was isolated for attempting to assassinate Muhammad and with similar results. The largest and most powerful Jewish community again refrained from supporting its religious compatriots.

Finally, after the Battle of the Trench, the largest Jewish tribe, the Qurayẓa, was accused of giving military secrets and aid to the Meccans who were bent on destroying Muhammad and his followers. Like their Jewish brethren, they also retreated to their fortified area and were put to siege for more than three weeks. They considered three strategies that were suggested by an ally. The first was to accept the prophethood of Muhammad, since his victories seemed to confirm the truth of his mission. They responded: "We will never abandon the laws of the Torah and never change it for another." The second suggestion was to "kill our wives and children and send men with their swords drawn to Muhammad and his companions leaving no encumbrances behind us, until God decides between us and Muhammad." They responded: "Should we kill these poor creatures? What would be the good of life when [our wives and children] are dead?" The third suggestion was to attack Muhammad by surprise at the onset of the Sabbath on Friday night when they would not be suspected of engaging in an attack. They responded: "Are we to profane our Sabbath and do on the Sabbath what those before us of whom you well know did and were turned into apes?"[8]

After rejecting these options, they sued for arbitration. It was agreed that the Jews would choose the kinship group from which the arbitrator would be picked. Muhammad would then choose the actual arbitrator. After the Jews narrowed the choice to one kinship group, Muhammad chose a member who was dying of the wound he had sustained in the battle over which the Jews had been accused of treason. The man, Sa`d b. Mu`ādh, was counseled by allies of the Jews to have compassion on them. Both sides had previously agreed that the arbitration was binding. "Sa`d said, 'Then I give judgment that the men should be killed, the property divided, and the women and children taken as captives.'"[9]

According to the sources, the Jews of the Qurayẓa surrendered. Trenches were dug in the marketplace of Medina, and Muhammad had the men's heads struck off in those trenches as they were brought out in batches. Sources put the number of people killed that day between 600 and 900.

Western, non-Muslim thinkers have criticized this act as barbaric and unbecoming of a principled and respectable religious leader, let alone a man representing God's will through his roll as prophet. Muslim critics have considered it a just end determined by the rules of arbitration that were acceptable to both parties. It was not considered unreasonable, taking into account the deceit and treason of the Jews for acting as a fifth column on behalf of Medina's enemies, despite having signed on to the Medina Pact as trustworthy allies. The reader will of course make his or her own judgment, but Jews should keep in mind that biblical patriarchs and kings engaged in massacres of the enemies of Israel in similar numbers.[10] However one decides, it must be kept in mind that in both cases we are observing the behaviors of peoples living in a society with very different norms and expectations than our own.

The stalemate of the Battle of the Trench was a boon to Muhammad and his followers, for it demonstrated that even the combination of the most powerful Arabian forces could not destroy them. The Muslims thus became firmly established and Muhammad was recognized as the most powerful leader in the region. Mecca's standing in Arabia was greatly weakened.

Al-Ḥudaybiyya

It had been common for Medinans to travel to Mecca in order to engage in the religious rituals there, but this practice had ended as the tensions flared up between the two communities. In the spring of 628, shortly after the Battle of the Trench, Muhammad led a group to Mecca to perform the pilgrimage. Muhammad expected trouble with the Meccans who had attacked him only a few months before, and he called for Bedouin and others in the vicinity to join him for protection. Few did, so he traveled with some

700 of his followers in pilgrim garb and with sacrificial animals to demonstrate their peaceful intentions. The Meccans heard he was coming and sent word that he would never be allowed to enter on his own volition: "He may have come not wanting war but by God, he shall never come in here against our will, nor shall the Arabs ever say that we have allowed it."[11] Shortly afterward, his camel knelt stubbornly and would not arise, which Muhammad read as a divine sign that he should not force the pilgrimage against the will of the Meccans.

He encamped where the camel knelt and a number of delegations traveled between him and the Quraysh. Tensions flared on and off until a compromise was reached. Finally, Muhammad had `Alī, his cousin and son-in-law (`Alī was married to Muhammad's daughter Fāṭima), write up a document that expressed the agreement between Muhammad and the Meccan representative, Suhayl.

The treaty of Al-Ḥudaybiyya says:

> This is what Muhammad b. `Abdullah has agreed with Suhayl b. `Amr: they have agreed to lay aside war for 10 years during which men can be safe and refrain from hostilities on condition that if anyone comes to Muhammad without permission of his guardian he will return him to them; and if anyone of those with Muhammad comes to Quraysh they will not return him to him. We will not show enmity one to another and there shall be no secret reservation or bad faith. He who wishes to enter into a bond and agreement with Muhammad may do so and he who wishes to enter into a bond and agreement with Quraysh may do so."[12]

They further resolved the pilgrimage issue by agreeing that Muhammad would return to Medina without performing the pilgrimage against the will of the Quraysh on that occasion. The following year, however, the Quraysh would make way for him and his community to enter Mecca for three nights. After the agreement was witnessed by both sides, Muhammad slaughtered the animals brought for pilgrimage, but he did so in an area outside the sacred precinct of Mecca. He was criticized by some of his followers for not forcing a show-down with the Meccans, but Muhammad was adamant. According to the sources, God sent down His *sakīna* upon Muhammad and the Believers in order to keep them calm in the face of such high tension. According to Muhammad's 8th-century biographer, ibn Isḥāq, the act of confrontation and nonviolent resolution of conflict served as positive witnesses for God's unity and Muhammad's prophethood. "No previous victory in Islam was greater than this. There was nothing but battle when men met; but when there was an armistice and war was abolished and men met in safety and consulted together, none talked about Islam intelligently without entering it. In those two years double as many or more than double as many entered Islam as ever before."[13]

The Poisoning of the Prophet

In 628, some two months after signing the pact at al-Ḥudaybiya, Muhammad marched against Khaybar, which was known as a Jewish settlement made up of many communities and hamlets. The fighting was very difficult and many fighters were killed on both sides, but the Jews of Khaybar eventually capitulated. A special arrangement was made that allowed the Khaybaris to remain in their settlement and continue to farm after agreeing to pay heavy taxes.

As was customary at the time, Muhammad as well as others among his warriors took captured women as wives or as members of their entourage. Muhammad took the beautiful Ṣafīya bt. Ḥuyayy and Zaynab bt. Al-Ḥārith, both Jews. After the battle, Zaynab was assigned to prepare a meal of roast lamb for the Prophet and some of his close companions.

> [She] inquired what joint he preferred. When she learned that it was the shoulder she put a lot of poison in it and poisoned the whole lamb. Then she brought it in and placed it before him. [Muhammad] took hold of the shoulder and chewed a morsel of it, but he did not swallow it. Bishr b. al-Barā' who was with him took some of it as the apostle had done, but he swallowed it, while the apostle spat it out saying, "This bone tells me that it is poisoned." Then he called for the woman and she confessed, and when he asked her what had induced her to do this she answered: "You know what you have done to my people. I said to myself, if he is a king I shall ease myself of him and if he is a prophet he will be informed (of what I have done)." So the apostle let her off. Bishr died from what he had eaten.[14]

This is an interesting passage, since not only was the woman found out in her plot to kill Muhammad, she admitted her deed and explained in a clever and not untypically Jewish fashion why she did it. Her account included a logic that seemed unassailable to those who recorded it. If Muhammad were merely a powerful warlord, he fully deserved the act of vengeance, according the cultural and political context of 7th-century Arabia. But if he was truly a prophet, he would have been protected by God.

Muhammad could easily have had Zaynab killed, but he seemed to have found Zaynab's explanation acceptable. She was not killed. Perhaps the most striking aspect of this story is its conclusion, for Muhammad's death is said to have been caused by the residual effects of Zaynab's poison. Four years after the incident, Muhammad began to suffer from severe head pain before dying a few days later. Among his visitors during those last few days was the mother of Bishr b. al-Barā', Muhammad's companion who died from Zaynab's poison at the victory meal of Khaybar. Muhammad is cited as having said to Bishr's mother on her visit, "O Umm Bishr (Mother of Bishr), I am now feeling a deadly pain from the food that I ate with your son at Khaybar."[15]

According to this tradition, it was a Jew who was responsible for the death of God's last and most beloved prophet. Of course, this is not a new accusation, as Jews have suffered terribly for centuries at the hands of vengeful Christians acting out their rage for their belief that Jews killed Jesus. The precedent was well-known. It would have been easy for Muslims to heap blame on the Jews for killing God's last prophet and find a reason through that libelous accusation for terrible persecution of Jews. Yet nowhere do we find such an accusation used for subjugation and maltreatment.

Mecca Capitulates

In accordance with the agreement between the Quraysh and Muhammad, the Muslims returned to Mecca the following year, 629, and performed the pilgrimage ritual of `Umra, the minor pilgrimage. The Meccans vacated their city for three days and then returned and insisted that the Muslims leave. They complied.

The Muslims continued to engage in raiding, expanding their influence and moving from one victory to another. The Meccans, meanwhile, were losing influence and prestige, and their ability to hold together the necessary tribal confederation to counter the Medinan expansion had become significantly diminished. The exact details of the following episode remain somewhat obscure, but it appears that internal squabbling between some kinship groups allied with Mecca and others allied with the Muslims caused the Meccan allies to violate the terms of the treaty of Al-Ḥudaybiyya. The complexity of the situation and the ambiguous nature of the sources have led to another classic disagreement between some Muslims and non-Muslims. The non-Muslims accuse Muhammad of having found an excuse to break the peace and march against Mecca. The Muslims believe Muhammad's behavior to have been completely acceptable, given the details of the situation.[16]

When those of Muhammad's allies, who were engaged in this conflict with the Meccans, appealed to him for help, he set out against Mecca with an army of some 10,000 warriors. This event took place in early January of 630. There was little resistance to the overwhelming force, and Mecca capitulated.

Muhammad called for a general amnesty and forbade looting. Only a few individuals were excluded from the amnesty, and even most of the ruling polytheistic elite of the city was spared. The idols and figurines of the city, however, were not. The Ka`ba and smaller sacred shrines were emptied of their idols, as were the private homes. The status of the sacred sites of Mecca thus returned to their "original" monotheism, established at the time of Abraham when he and Ishmael raised up the foundations of the Ka`ba. One of the most striking aspects of the results of Mecca's capitulation to Muhammad was the genuine reconciliation that was effected between Muhammad and the Meccan leadership that had opposed him so bitterly.

Mecca was a great victory, but many still opposed Muhammad that year. He engaged in two more major battles, one called the Battle of Ḥunayn (and referenced in Q.9:25), and the other at al-Ṭā'if near Mecca. After these two difficult encounters, there was little resistance to the growing power and number of the Muslims. As the circle of alliances spread, the *umma* became a community that was to transcend the shaky and shifting bonds of tribal confederation. The goal was to create a supertribe, a single community in which the typical raiding between kinship groups would become unacceptable. This unification of Arabian tribes was nothing short of revolutionary. Early on in his career, Muhammad was prepared to make pacts of friendship and nonaggression with non-Muslims. As his following grew stronger, however, he was able to insist on further terms, such as accepting his role of prophet or paying alms or contributions to the "treasury of God."[17] Yet, it is virtually impossible to separate the level of religious commitment from the level of political commitment (or commitment of expediency) among the many groups that joined the *umma*. This became apparent after Muhammad's death, when the confederacy began to crumble and was restored only through force of arms under the leadership of the first caliph, Abū Bakr.

One of Muhammad's primary goals was to transcend the eternal conflicts of tribal factionalism. Ironically, although Islam was a religion of unification that emerged out of an extremely fractious tribal environment, it retained a certain level of tribalism that derived from the very cultural environment out of which it emerged. With the great Arab expansion and conquests that occurred shortly after the death of Muhammad, Arabian tribalism remained embedded in the religious civilization of Islam and was exported far beyond the boundaries of Arabia.

CHAPTER 6

The Death of the Prophet and the Expansion of the Community

The Farewell Pilgrimage

In 632, 10 years after the Hijra, Muhammad led the pilgrimage to Mecca during *dhū al-ḥijja*, the month of pilgrimage. This was the Greater Pilgrimage of the Hajj. It was the first and last time that he would lead the Hajj pilgrimage, and as such it is called the "Farewell Pilgrimage." It became paradigmatic for all subsequent pilgrimage rituals and was a means of Islamizing some of the pre-Islamic polytheistic pilgrimage practices by way of infusing them with monotheistic and Islamic symbolism. Much of the actual ritual was the same as practiced earlier under polytheism, but as with all religions, ancient acts became invested with new meanings and significance.

Muhammad is understood to have made a dramatic speech to his followers in Mecca that was recorded in the sources. In it he reaffirmed the break with pre-Islamic political alliances and the institution of certain social and cultural changes that had already been established through the authority of revelation. It is an oration that is cherished to this day. Only parts can be included here:

> O people, listen to my word. I do not know whether I shall ever meet you in this place again after this year. Your blood and your property are sacrosanct until you meet your Lord, as this day and this month are holy. You will surely meet your Lord and He will ask you of your works. I have told you. He who has a pledge, let him return it to

> the one who entrusted him with it; all usury is abolished, but you have your capital. Wrong not and you shall not be wronged. . . . All blood shed in the pagan period (*jāhiliyya*) is to be left unavenged. . . . You have rights over your wives and they have rights over you. . . . Lay injunctions on women kindly, for they are prisoners with you having no control of their persons. You have taken them only as a trust from God. . . . I have left with you something which if you will hold fast to it you will never fall into error—a plain indication, the book of God and the practice of His prophet, so give good heed to what I say. Know that every Muslim is a Muslim's brother, and that the Muslims are brethren. It is only lawful to take from your brother what he gives you willingly, so do not wrong yourselves. O God, have I not told you?[1]

Death of a Prophet

Muhammad returned to Medina, from which he sent emissaries to distant Arab leaders and to the emperors of the Persian and Byzantine Empires inviting them to Islam. This was during a period when those two empires were exhausting themselves through a generation of invasion and counterinvasion. Soon his followers would engage them in battle, but Muhammad is depicted in the sources as being in weakened health. He developed a severe headache and probably a fever, dying shortly afterward in the arms of his wife, `Ā'isha. It was a major blow to the community. His close companion `Umar remained in denial, but his dear friend Abū Bakr went out to the people and announced, "O people, if anyone worships Muhammad, Muhammad is dead. If anyone worships God, God is alive, immortal."[2]

The Problem of Succession and the First Four Caliphs

The sources and traditions depict the love and respect of Muhammad's followers as overwhelming, and he remains the ultimate role model for Muslims around the world to this day. Multivolume compilations of his words and behaviors have been collected and published from early times, and they form the most important source for Islamic law and ethics after the Qur'an. Yet his death is depicted matter-of-factly, with no hyperbole or heroism. He was buried immediately in the home where he died—as was considered befitting of prophets—rather than in a cemetery. Since the very beginning of Muhammad's prophethood, Islam has carried within it a tension between the inclination among many to adore him to the point of worship and the strict insistence of the religious establishment on a simple and austere form of monotheism in which only God may be the object of adoration.

His leadership within the community was never disputed, but most Muslims believe that Muhammad made no definite provision for the succession of leadership after his death. In fact, the problem of succession lies at the root of many of the most intractable conflicts that would subsequently plague Islam. According to Sunni Islam, Muhammad never named a successor. According to those who count themselves among the Shi`a, he designated his son-in-law and cousin, `Alī ibn Abī Ṭālib as his successor. Sources representing both sides agree that on his return from the Farewell Pilgrimage, Muhammad stopped at a marshy pool called Ghadīr Khumm, where he gathered his companions together and asked them whether he was not closer to the Believers than they were to themselves. They all replied passionately in the affirmative. At that moment he took Ali by the hand and, working in typical Arab literary fashion by using the Arabic root of the same word he used in the previous sentence for "closer" (*awlā*), he said, "To whomever I am a friend/patron (*mawlā*), Ali is [also] his friend/patron (*mawlā*)."[3]

The meaning of this verse is uncertain. Several interpretations and paraphrases are found in the sources, but they tend to support one or other political position that developed later in relation to the succession. Some commentators have understood *mawlā* to mean "friend" (as opposed to enemy), and the sentence as nothing more than affirmation of friendship and support to Muhammad's closest kinsman, who seems to have been engaged in a disagreement with those under his command over the distribution of the spoils on a recent raid. This reading supports the position of Sunni Islam. Other commentators, whose position represents that of Shi`a Islam, have understood *mawlā* to mean "patron," and thus have claimed that Muhammad officially and publicly designated Ali to be his successor shortly before his death. No matter which position is closer to the truth, there is no record that Muhammad left any instructions regarding the governance of the community after the passing of his leadership; as a result, the conflict between Sunni and Shi`i Muslims began to emerge soon after his death.

Abū Bakr

Immediately after Muhammad's death and even before the burial, some of his closest companions moved quickly to decide how to hold the community together. There were plenty of factions within the community based on everything from kinship relationship to ritual practice, and it was critically important to find a consensus maker to take over as head. Abū Bakr was perhaps Muhammad's closest companion. His early conversion brought great respect to the fledgling community in Mecca. He had given one of his daughters to Muhammad in marriage, and he was the only person to accompany the Prophet in his perilous flight from Mecca to Medina. But the decision was made by a small inner circle that went against the old Arabian custom of choosing the leader through a broad consensus. And it caused resentment.

Nevertheless, Abū Bakr was respected, and his position of caliph (*khalīfa*), meaning "deputy" or "successor" to Muhammad at the head of the community, became the title of the leader of the *umma*. As was customary in pre-Islamic Arabia after the demise of a powerful leader, the fractious nature of tribal organization and leadership caused a reassessment of earlier agreements. Tribes near and far began to withdraw from the *umma* in what became known as the wars of the *ridda* (apostasy). Abū Bakr was instrumental in reuniting the community through force of arms. He died two years later and in another decision of the inner circle, `Umar ibn al-Khaṭṭāb became the second caliph. In both cases, Muhammad's closest blood relative, Ali, was passed over.

Ali was not only Muhammad's son-in-law, he was the son of Muhammad's earlier protector and sponsor in Mecca, Abū Ṭālib. He was also the first male convert to Islam (Abū Bakr came shortly afterward) and was clearly part of the program virtually since its inception. He was far younger than either Abū Bakr or `Umar, however, which rendered him a less popular figure in the old Arabian cultural system than either of his elder colleagues.

`Umar

Umar was a more powerful personality than Abū Bakr and was known for both his piety and his explosive anger. When he took over the leadership of the *umma*, he extended the conquest beyond the borders of Arabia begun by Abū Bakr and succeeded within the 10 years of his reign to conquer most of the Persian Empire and take over today's Syria and Lebanon, Egypt, Israel, and Jordan, and parts of North Africa. Legends associate him personally with the conquest of Jerusalem, sometime around 637–638. According to a popular tradition repeated variously in historical sources, when he was guided around Jerusalem by the Christian patriarch, Sophronius, he was shown the Temple Mount area that had been turned into a dung heap by the Byzantine rulers. Its neglect by Christian Rome was purposeful, for the ruins and desecration were considered proof of God's rejection of the "old covenant" with the Jews. The dilapidated state of the Temple Mount was thus a testament to the "new covenant" between God and those who accepted the saving power of Jesus as Christ or messiah.

When Sophronius and Umar reached the Temple Mount, they found the steps and gateway so filled with rubbish that they had to crawl on their hands and knees to get through to the Temple Platform. "Then we arose off our knees and stood upright. And Umar looked around, pondering for a long time. Then said he: 'By Him in whose hands is my soul![4] This is the place described to us by the Apostle of God.' . . . Umar then proceeded to the fore-part of the Sanctuary Area, to the side adjoining the west, and there began to throw the dung by handfuls into his cloak, and we all who were with him did likewise. Then he went with it—and we following him did the same—and threw the dung into the valley. . . . Then we returned to do the same over again, and yet again—he, Umar, and also we who were with him—until we had cleared the whole of the place where the Mosque now stands. And there we all made our prayers, Umar himself praying among us."[5]

Umar is an interesting figure for many reasons. He seems to have had a somewhat messianic aura associated with his unique personality that combined both intense piety and power. He ended Christian rule over Jerusalem and allowed Jews to legally re-enter and live in the holy city for the first time since the failed Bar Kokhba rebellion in the 2nd century. He is associated with receiving the formal submission of the Peoples of the Book to the hegemony of Islam with all the attendant protections and restrictions that were later formally associated with the Jewish and Christian status as *dhimmī*s under Islamic rule.[6] It was under his watch that the rule was first established for conquered peoples to enjoy formal legal protection of their persons and property together with the right to practice their religions without disturbance, though at a lesser status than Muslim believers. The formal details of this arrangement would only be worked out later when Islam became more formalized, but these developments began under the leadership of Umar. Non-Muslims could own deeds to private property, but the conquered lands as a whole came into a kind of trust in perpetuity for the benefit of future generations of Muslims through a theory of land ownership called *fay'*. Umar also ordered the expulsion of the Christian and Jewish communities of Najran and Khaybar and forbade non-Muslims to reside in the Arabian Hijaz for longer than three days.

Umar was assassinated at the height of his powers in 644 and became the first of the next three caliphs to have his career ended in such a manner. The assassin was a Christian slave whose motive is said to have been anger at failure to appeal to the caliph against a tax that was laid upon him. Some modern historians have suggested that the assassin was an instrument of a conspiracy including some of Muhammad's closest companions, including Ali. It is certainly true that the Shi`i tradition has never concealed its antipathy to Umar for having thwarted the claims of Ali and those supporting his leadership. Sunni tradition, on the other hand, holds Umar in the highest esteem and as the epitome of Islamic virtues. He was a brilliant strategist, a bold warrior, and a humble Believer, and he followed a simple and austere lifestyle.

Uthmān

As Umar lay dying, according to the reports, he called for a council to choose a successor. He seems to have favored `Uthmān ibn `Affān, who indeed became the next caliph. Uthmān was a surprising choice, since he was the weakest among those contending for the position—chosen perhaps as a compromise between powerful rivals. By this time, the *umma* controlled great wealth and power through the conquests that were proceeding apace, but it was also becoming increasingly unruly as it spread farther afield. Local governors were already beginning to make assertions of their own independence. Uthmān was one of the few early followers of Muhammad who came from the established Meccan aristocracy. He derived from the clan of Umayya, and he was the first caliph to be interested in pageantry, the finery of royalty, and the splendor of office.

He also angered many Believers for obviously favoring his own kinsmen in choice positions while neglecting those of other tribes and of lesser social and economic background, something that went against the egalitarian ideal of transtribal Islam. He was not particularly admired as a leader, and he lacked the initiative and courage of Abū Bakr and especially Umar.

On the other hand, Uthmān is credited with being responsible for authorizing the collection of the qur'anic revelations. Until then, the divine word remained only in oral form, remembered by those who witnessed Muhammad's recitation, perhaps with the help of notes scratched into masonry or bones or pieces of parchment. Uthmān established a commission headed by Muhammad's last scribe and assistant, Zayd ibn Thābit, to record the revelations. The problems confronted by the collection of the Qur'an will be examined in more detail below, but the initiative is said to have preserved an authentic and authoritative text. In fact, Zayd may have begun this task even before the death of the Prophet. In order to canonize a single text, however, Uthmān collected all variant copies and had them destroyed, which incurred the anger of many in the religious establishment for mutilating or obliterating the divine word. In any case, the final product became known as the "Uthmanic recension" and is considered to be substantially the same as that used by Muslims to this day.

Uthmān had created many enemies and his acts had divided an already divided community. He was supported by the Meccans and hated by many of the Medinans. Finally, after 12 years in leadership in Medina, Uthmān was besieged in his own home and assassinated by a band of dissident Egyptians in 656. His compound was undefended. When those who rushed to his defense learned that he had been murdered, they simply turned around and returned to their base.

The *umma* remained divided forever after. Any political unity among Muslims was over with the end of Uthmān's caliphate, and soon religious schism came out into the open as well. Henceforth, with only a few and short-lived exceptions, the caliphate became merely a seat of power over the *umma* rather than a position associated with leadership, altruism, and a sense of service to all. There were of course outstanding caliphs, but the office and the system would never carry the near-utopian admiration that was reserved for the Prophet and for the first caliphs by most Muslims—excluding, of course, the Shi`a.

`Alī

*Shi`a* is short for *shī`at `alī*, "the party [or faction, followers] of Ali." The Shi`a was merely a sentiment at this time, however, becoming an organized movement only a generation or more later. After the death of Uthmān in 656, Ali finally became caliph, but as in the previous successions, there was a great deal of dissension. The Medinans supported him, but the Meccans had just lost a caliph who was one of their own and who was supportive of the old guard. Ali was accused of failing to protect Uthmān and of not bringing to justice those who had been involved in the assassination. Moreover, Ali replaced many of Uthmān's appointees who, as will be recalled, favored the Meccans and his own tribe and clan. Ali thus alienated powerful people in powerful kinship groups, the most important being the Banū Umayya from which Uthmān derived.

Muhammad's youngest wife `Ā'isha also opposed Ali. She had been slighted by him during the Prophet's lifetime, accused of an impropriety for which she never forgave him. `Ā'isha and two respected accomplices were among those who accused Ali of negligence in the death of Uthmān (though they themselves became implicated in Ali's assassination later on). They organized an army to depose him but failed in the "Battle of the Camel," named after the camel upon which `Ā'isha rode and around which the battle raged. Her accomplices and her camel were killed, but `Ā'isha returned safely to Medina where she lived out her days and became a primary source for the traditions about the Prophet that were collected into the literature known as the *Hadith*.

Ali's problems were not over, however. While most of the expanded provinces of the newly conquered areas recognized Ali as caliph, the powerful governor of Syria did not. Uthmān had appointed his nephew, Mu`āwiya, to rule in Damascus, and Mu`āwiya refused to step down for the new governor appointed by Ali. The issues behind the rivalry are complex; suffice it to say that Mu`āwiya was able to rally a large force of Syrians in 657 to oppose the new caliph, who was backed by a large force of Iraqis. The two opposing armies reflected the two growing centers of power within the expanding empire. The forces of Mu`āwiya and Ali met at Ṣiffīn near the Upper Euphrates River and engaged in the oral accusations and small skirmishes typical of traditional Arabian encounters. These dragged out for weeks, because neither army was eager to engage another Muslim army in battle.

When they finally did engage, Ali seemed to have been gaining the upper hand when Mu`āwiya resorted to a clever trick suggested to him by one of his generals. He had the leading force of his cavalry hoist Qur'ans onto the points of their spears, thus exclaiming symbolically that the Qur'an rather than force of arms should decide. Ali was urged to accept arbitration by many followers, but others felt that agreeing to arbitration demonstrated weakness and a certain parity with Mu`āwiya as an equal contender to office. Ali's agreement to arbitrate thus alienated a substantial following who were called *Khārijites* or "secessionists," who believed that his agreement to arbitrate betrayed the divine authority of his leadership.

Kharijites

The Kharijite motto was "judgment belongs to God alone." This group, the first sect to emerge as a discreet group in Islam, formed their own army to rise up against Ali and justified their attack against the caliph on the grounds that his failure as leader to carry out Islamic principles proved his apostasy. In their view (which became the dominant position in Islamic law), apostasy is a capital crime. Ali attacked the Kharijite camp and nearly annihilated them, but new groups continued to rise up and oppose him.

The Kharijites were no more friendly to Mu`āwiya than they were to Ali. They were principled egalitarians who believed that any pious Muslim of any kinship group—even a slave—could become caliph. They also believed that it is the duty of believers to depose any leader who falls into error—even by means of assassination.

The Kharijites were rejected by medieval Muslim scholars and labeled as heretics, but their often extremist style of opposition to suspect caliphal leadership and their guerrilla style of warfare continued into future generations, and a Kharijite tendency has appeared occasionally in Muslim history to this day. Such "kharijism" has surfaced only among small minorities within the larger *umma*, but they often have had a significant influence over others because of their total commitment to their beliefs and cause, and their atypical willingness to die for them. There is no actual discreet movement or group called Kharijites today, for example, but some contemporary radical ists take on traits and attitudes that have typified the Kharijite groups of history. These include an ethic of perfectionism that requires absolute obedience to the substance and detail of their particular conception of Islamic practice and belief. Only perfect obedience to (their view of) the divine will can bring entrance into paradise, and the corruption of others taints everybody in the community. They therefore tend to seek out sin and corruption in order to eliminate it, and have gone to the extreme of vigilante beatings and even executions of those who refuse to conform to their brand of piety.

This approach has never been the policy of normative Islam, but it has almost always been attractive to certain small, radical ecstatic groups. The commitment of the first Kharijite movement has often drawn a mixed response among Muslims, because while their tactics are usually considered unacceptable, their piety and total commitment have been something of an inspiration. Some groups of militant Muslims in our own day who zealously persist in trying to force their vision of Islam on others are following this Kharijite tradition.

The actual arbitration between Ali and Mu`āwiya took place two years after the battle, allowing for the anger on both sides to fester. Each side appointed a representative and 400 witnesses to engage in the mediation. Although the sources are not in agreement or absolutely clear about what transpired, it seems that both sides were equally invalidated. The two continued to oppose each other, and Mu`āwiya was clearly gaining the upper hand when the stalemate was finally resolved by a Kharajite who assassinated Ali in early 661 with a poisoned sword strike to his forehead.

Ali is considered to be one of the "rightly guided caliphs" by Sunni and well as Shi`i Muslims, and is recognized as a valiant warrior, wise in counsel, honest, and deeply spiritual. After his death, however, many of his party began to regard him as infallible because he was divinely guided, only to be cut down by the enemies of God and of Islam. He was the *imām*, a term that simply means "leader" in Arabic, but which came to take on a special meaning as "true leader" of the Muslim world, especially among the Shi`a.

After the death of Ali, his oldest son, Ḥasan, abdicated, after which Mu`āwiya became recognized as the caliph throughout the Muslim world. Mu`āwiya ruled from Damascus and established a dynasty of caliphs known as the Umayyad Dynasty, named for the clan of Umayya from which they derived.

CHAPTER 7

The Conquests

According to the Islamic point of view, the warriors who engaged in the military expeditions known as the Islamic Conquest were committed Muslims. Historical sources identify them as ethnic Arabs commanded by people who followed the leadership of Muhammad and his deputy successors, the caliphs. But written documentation of the conquest is incomplete. The Qur'an, the authoritative revelation upon which the emerging religion of Islam was based, was not canonized finally until the caliphate of Uthman (644–656), after much of the Middle East had already been conquered. And aside from the Qur'an itself, there were no written Islamic texts until at least three generations after the conquest. Even if the story of hoisting the Qur'ans on Mu`āwiya's lances is true (which would mean that a significant number of handwritten copies of the Qur'an were available to warriors already in 657), they had not been available during the period when Egypt, Syria, Lebanon, Jordan, and much of Iraq had been conquered under Umar.

While one might claim that those engaged in the conquest were committed to Muhammad and the nascent views of Islam—strict ethical monotheism, belief in a Day of Judgment after which humans will enter heaven or hell, obedience to the will of God as articulated in general terms by divine revelation—these views were also common to Judaism and Christianity. It is not clear what the boundaries of identity were that the Muslim community understood or applied to itself. How "Muslim," then, were the Arab warriors who carried out the Islamic Conquest?

In his work on identity in the early Islamic community, Fred Donner suggests that those who engaged in the conquest were not yet "Muslims" in the sense of belonging to a self-defined religious community. Rather than Muslims, he calls this early community "Believers." He says they are made up of those who fulfilled the basic belief requirements of the monotheist *umma* and who joined this pious movement; this included Christians and Jews. The Believers eventually defined themselves as independent of the established monotheisms, just as emerging Christianity had separated itself from Judaism. Later Muslim tradition tried to hide that early unified community and its eventual split into an independent form of monotheism. As Donner puts it:

> [F]or the first few decades of the Islamic era, the Believers may have been quite ready to accept among their number those Christians and Jews who shared their zeal to spread the message of God and the Last Day, and who agreed to live piously by the law, even though the theological implications of some passages in the Qur'an would eventually exclude the *ahl al-kitab* ("People of the Book") from the ranks of Believers. It may have been several decades before [the Qur'anic passages in question] became even known among Believers generally, and several decades more before the full implications of the Qur'an's theological stand for communal self-definition became clear to Believers. Until this had happened, however, some Christians and Jews—those who shared the Believers' insistence on the omnipotence and omnipresence of the one God, the imminence of the Last Day, and the need to lead a life of strenuous piety according to the revealed Law—may have remained part of the community of Believers, particularly within the "colonies" of Believers that were established (initially as garrisons) in newly-subdued provinces of what was becoming a growing empire.[1]

A Christian Nestorian monk named Yohannan bar Penkaye of northern Mesopotamia wrote in the late 680s, at least two generations after the death of Muhammad, that a significant number of Christians were engaged among the followers of Muhammad in the military expeditions.[2] Although there is no hard evidence regarding Jews who were engaged in the conquest, one could surmise the possibility of Jewish involvement as well. Bar Penkaye also notes that "from every person they demanded only tribute, and each one could remain in whatever faith he chose." This and other evidence suggest that the military campaigns were nonconfessional, meaning that they were not intended to bring converts into a religion called Islam, but were more likely part of a process of state formation with roots in a monotheistic revival movement that may have caught the enthusiasm of many non-Muslim monotheists as well.

The Qur'an does not require monotheists, or at least Jews, Christians, and Sabaeans (Q.2:62, 9:29) to become Muslims. Polytheists, however, and especially Arabian polytheists, were another matter. There can be no doubt that, whether or not Muhammad and his followers considered themselves followers of a distinct form of monotheism separate from Judaism and Christianity, the *umma* placed ethical monotheism at its core. Certainly by the time of Muhammad's death, polytheists were not welcome, but it could only be in relation to them that the myth of "the Qur'an or the sword" could be applied (Q.9:5). Forced conversion of polytheists may have been applied outside the confines of Arabia as well, but during the 7th century the Middle East was overwhelmingly Christian, Jewish, and Zoroastrian (which tended to be accepted along with the former two as a form of monotheism). There would therefore have been little opportunity to engage in forced conversion outside Arabia. When India was subdued at least four centuries after the death of Muhammad, even what appeared to Muslims to be obvious polytheism was accommodated within the Mughal Empire, though not without difficulty.

Why Did the Conquests Happen?

Many have tried to understand the motivation and the circumstances that brought forth a mass movement that dismantled the Persian Empire, nearly destroyed the Byzantine Empire, and took on control of the entirety of North Africa, the Middle East, most of South Asia, and much of Central Asia. According to religious Muslim writers, it was the power of the divine will in promoting the true religion as practiced by devout believers that brought about such extraordinary military success. Secular historians, however, have struggled to explain this impressive military campaign, given the overwhelming opposition of organized and trained imperial armies supported by huge populations and economic bases. Many explanations have been given, taking into account military, economic, cultural, sociological, psychological, and even meterological data. But none of these explanations have been satisfactory. Apparently, a combination of factors were at work. Whatever the case, the *umma* that Muhammad formed had become an extremely powerful and attractive social and spiritual movement. It succeeded in attracting a following of exceptionally capable and committed members who were able, in a few short decades, to expand their community into the dominant one in most of the known world.

Whatever the original motivations for the conquest, they continued for generations after the death of Muhammad. It is clear that in the later period, continued conquest became a means of revenue extraction that, along with regular taxation of those within the established borders of the empire, succeeded in bringing in great amounts of wealth needed to develop a great civilization and sustain a successful empire.

Authority to Rule

One of the most persistent problems that confronts any ruler or ruling class is the authority to rule. What gives one individual or group the right to rule over others?

Only a decade or two after the death of the Prophet, the Arabs who identified themselves first as Believers and increasingly as Muslims, took over the palaces of the Byzantines and the Persians. They employed the same well-established taxation structures but collected moneys for their own rule. Uprisings were numerous during the early years, and they were led by members of the old guard or by opportunists. These were put down successfully, but as in any political system, it became necessary to justify the reign of the new leadership.

The Qur'an has little to say about political rule and authority, though it is consistent about the absolute rule of God. It states that God is the supreme ruler of the universe, but does not discuss who should rule the state. During the period in which the Qur'an was revealed, leadership of the *umma* came under the position of God's prophet, Muhammad, who united executive, legislative, judicial, and military leadership in his own person. The record of his life and leadership as recorded in the *Hadith*, along with the revelations sent down to him in the Qur'an, became the two central foundations upon which Muslim rule was justified by religious scholars and jurists, not only over fellow Muslims, but over non-Muslims as well.

The process of working out theories of state and rule, like virtually all of the intellectual contributions in the Muslim world, emerged only after the establishment of a powerful Arab Muslim empire, first under the Umayyads in Damascus, and then under the Abbasids in Baghdad. All the literatures were written after the Conquest, and all the intellectual successes occurred under the political rule of empire. It is therefore natural that theories of state would justify Muslim supremacy, and the interpretive methods and results that engaged that program of authorization can be called "imperialist modes of interpretation." It was a given that Muslims should be politically dominant, and there developed, therefore, a sense of Muslim manifest destiny regarding the domination of other peoples and religions. But it needs to be remembered that this sentiment is not at all clear from the most basic and authoritative source in Islam, the Qur'an, which emerged prior to the imperial period of Islam. Although the Qur'an can be read in such a way that justifies imperialist rule, as it has by those who support the authority of the Muslim empires, it can also be read in a way that supports a world that is independent of Muslim political hegemony. Some Muslims today are revisiting traditional imperialist interpretations that justify Muslim conquest and are reconsidering qur'anic revelation in order to understand a place for Islamic religion and civilization that is on an equal footing with other peoples and religions, rather than being in control of them.

The World of Islam and the World of War

Though it appears nowhere in the Qur'an, a later imperial Islamic theory of state and international politics conceives of the world as divided into two territories: the World of Islam (*dār al-islām*) and the World of War (*dār al-ḥarb*).[3] The World of Islam comprised Muslim and certain non-Muslim communities that accept Islamic sovereignty. Muslims within this territory enjoy full rights of citizenship. The "People of the Book," which is to say, Christians, Jews, and others of tolerated scriptural religions (called *dhimmīs*) enjoyed only partial civil rights; they had second-class status and paid a special poll tax called the *jizya*, based on an interpretation of Q.9:29. However, the People of the Book had full legal status in society. They were protected by due process of law and protected from attack so long as they paid their taxes and accepted their secondary social status in Muslim society.

The state recognized the canon law of each tolerated religious community in relation to matters of personal status, and *dhimmi*s could not be denied access to Islamic courts if they wished to bring their case to the Muslim judge. However, Jews and Christians usually preferred to handle their own affairs internally, and it was considered problematic by Jewish and Christian leadership to revert to Muslim courts.

All areas outside of Muslim political control were known collectively as the World of War. It was the duty of Muslim rulers to bring the World of War into the World of Islam whenever they had the power to do so. The territories of the World of War were considered to be at a lower legal and ethical state than those of the World of Islam (and by many measures of civilization, many surrounding areas at that time would likely be judged as such by neutral outside observers as well). The World of War therefore lacked legal competence to engage in equal and reciprocal relations with the World of Islam, and many jurists considered arrangements made between the two nonbinding, because their status was not recognized by Islamic law.

Some jurists recognized a third category called "World of Peaceful Arrangements" (*dār al-ṣulḥ*) or "World of Pact" (*dār al-`ahd*). It was possible, according to these thinkers, to give qualified recognition to treaty relationships with non-Muslim communities according to stipulated conditions.

The World of Islam was, in theory, in a continuous state of war with the World of War, much like the perpetual theoretical state of war between tribes in pre-Islamic Arabia. The goal was always the absorption of the World of War into the World of Islam. But despite the impossibility of official state recognition of the governments and rulers of the non-Muslim world, Islam "took cognizance" of the authority of those countries outside of its control. A Muslim entering into that territory was obligated to respect the authority of its rulers and the civil laws of the country, and a member of the World of War could be granted legal safe-passage in the World of Islam in order to engage in business or other approved activities.

As is usually the case in the real world, the legal categories could be flexible. Strictly speaking, the World of War failed the legal and ethical standards of divinely guided civilization. Yet the *official* state of nonrecognition did not mean that negotiations could not be conducted in good faith, nor binding treaties concluded. Despite the formal difference in status, therefore, affairs of state were conducted and treaties and agreements with representatives of the World of War were usually respected by Muslim authorities.

Muslim Cultural Imperialism

We in the postmodern world tend to be sensitive to issues such as colonialism and imperialism. During much of the modern period, colonial European powers tried to impose their cultures, worldviews, and religions on indigenous populations, often because they felt that such changes would improve the lives of their captive subjects, sometimes because they felt that it would further the goals of the colonial powers themselves. In many cases, indigenous populations suffered terribly from the purposeful denigration and even destruction of their native cultures, languages, and religions by dominant political powers. "Cultural imperialism" is a term that speaks to the denigration of indigenous cultures and to the forced imposition of colonialist and imperial rule.

But cultural imperialism seems to have been a historical fact of life. The Romans, Greeks, Persians, Babylonians, and other early civilizations perpetrated cultural imperialism. In every case, those who wished to find prestigious jobs in government administration (that is, positions of power and influence) had to speak the language of the rulers and comport themselves according to the cultural norms of the conquerors. And this was no less the case under the imperial rule of Muslims. When the Muslim rulers were Arabs, the language of state quickly became Arabic, as did the language of education and high culture in general. And holders of high and influential office had to be Muslim. This is a natural and unexceptional form of cultural imperialism that was imposed instinctively by the ruling powers of the Arab Islamic empires.

Those Jews and Christians who wished to be a part of the great cultural renaissance that was the Arab Muslim world had to be able to engage in Arabic language and to maneuver in Arab culture. The centers of learning conducted their study and research in Arabic. The scientific texts of the Greeks, Persians, and even Hindus were translated into Arabic, and the new works of science and literature were produced in Arabic. Courts of law were conducted in Arabic and followed norms of Arab-Islamic jurisprudence. Diplomacy and government were conducted in Arabic and followed norms that were infused with Arab culture. Although there were some exceptions, those Jews and Christians who had aspiration for higher education patronized by Muslims or public office had to become Muslim as well.

It is important to remember that until the Arab conquest, Arabic was not spoken outside of Arabia, and Islam was entirely unknown. Shortly after the Conquest, the Middle East and North Africa made a transition from native and previous imperial languages and cultures and the cultural syntheses established by earlier empires to a new synthesis that was the result of an Arabo-Islamic cultural (and religious) imperialism. Even though there seems to have been little actual forced conversion to Islam through violence or threat of violence, those sensitive to issues of cultural imperialism would argue that the fact that prestigious positions required one to become a Muslim is a form of forced conversion. Muslims are often insensitive to such issues, just as European colonialists, Romans, Greeks, and other culturally dominant powers tended to be insensitive to their own role in cultural imperialism.

The Problem of Conversion

There remains some controversy over the rate of conversion to Islam in the wake of the Conquest. It must be remembered that the Qur'an does not require that monotheists become Muslim, though it certainly encourages it. Later Muslim jurists forbade the forced conversion of the People of the Book to Islam, though it is clear that this prohibition was sometimes observed in the breach.

One important early study concludes that the majority population of the Middle East did not become Muslim until at least three centuries after the Arab Conquest.[4] In fact, there are reports in the Islamic historical tradition that provincial governors in the early period (during the Umayyad Caliphate) actively discouraged non-Muslims to convert to Islam. It had been determined that to allow these conversions would dangerously reduce the income to the imperial treasury because *dhimmi* peoples were required to pay a special tax that Muslims were not required to pay. Apparently, a large number of *dhimmi*s had been converting in order to avoid that tax. Later, as the treasury stabilized and as Islam became more established and the rulers more secure in their power, this policy was changed.

The dominant religion of North Africa before the Conquest was Christianity, as was the dominant religion of most of the Middle East. There were also quite sizable Jewish communities throughout the Mediterranean world. Today, there are no indigenous Christians in North Africa, aside from Egypt. Those Christians in Morocco, Algeria, Tunisia, and other modern North African states are almost entirely the product of European colonial influence. Christians are a very small minority in most of the Middle East as well. Although accurate statistics are not available for the Middle East, it is generally thought that Egypt and Syria are approximately 10 percent Christian, while Lebanon may be 30 percent Christian. There are perhaps 5 percent in Iraq and Jordan, less in the Palestinian Territories. What happened to the Christians? Some moved to Christian lands, but it is clear that most became Muslim.

This seems not to have been the case among the Jews of the Muslim world. According to the historian David Wasserstein, the number of Jews in the Muslim world remained basically steady from the Conquest to the modern period.[5] He suggests that the Jews had already lived for centuries as a second-class minority under the dominance of the Christian Byzantine Empire. Those Jews who would convert "out" of their second-class status had probably done so long before the Conquest, so they were already accustomed to such a situation and had incorporated that into their Jewish identity. Christians, on the other hand, because they were accustomed to being the dominant religion, had more difficulty sustaining their communities under the cultural-religious dominance of Islam.

CHAPTER 8

The Caliphal Dynasties

The history of the great caliphates, the dynastic rule of the great empires, takes our journey outward from the emergence of Islam in the Arabian core region to its development under the influence of many cultures and civilizations. These chapters of Islamic history become increasingly complex as they span large geographic areas and long periods of time. The many developments cannot be treated adequately here, though they are of great interest for understanding Jewish history and Jewish-Muslim relations in the medieval period. Time will be taken, therefore, only to point out a few items of interest for the development of some key aspects of Islam and the continuing flow of Jewish-Muslim relations. A far more complex unfolding of Islamic history will be schematized by outlining the history of four caliphal empires: the Umayyad caliphate centered in Damascus, the Abbasid caliphate in Baghdad, the Fatimid caliphate in Fostat/Cairo, and the Spanish Umayyad caliphate centered in Cordoba.

The Umayyad Dynasty (661–750)

The Umayyad caliphate began officially with Mu`āwiya, the third caliph Uthman's nephew, who was appointed to rule Damascus and who opposed the 4th caliph, Ali, when he finally came to power. Mu`āwiya was an extremely adept leader, warrior, and diplomat. He moved the capital to his power base in Damascus, which had only recently been part of the heartland of the Byzantine Empire. The caliphate developed there with the assistance of conquered Christian locals, who were intimately and professionally familiar with the imperial politics, diplomacy, economy, and military arrangements of the Byzantines. Mu`āwiya and his dynasty succeeded, with the assistance of many non-Arabs and non-Muslims in the Umayyad bureaucracy, to project the image of an Arab leader, while ruling an expanding Mediterranean empire as large as that of Rome.

The 90 years of Umayyad rule saw continued expansion of the Conquest. North Africa was taken all the way to today's Morocco, as well as Spain, and with incursions that reached deeply into today's France. On the eastern front, the armies took Kabul in today's Afghanistan and the Central Asian areas of Khurasan and Samarkand. The Umayyad armies even launched several attacks against the Byzantine capital, Constantinople, though they did not succeed in capturing the city.

The great monument in Jerusalem known as the Dome of the Rock was built during this early period (constructed between 685 and 691), and it represents the earliest surviving example of monumental architecture in the Muslim world. The Grand Umayyad Mosque standing to this day in Damascus was also built by the Umayyads (706–715), as was the al-Aqsa Mosque (completed in 715), though it was destroyed in an earthquake—the present mosque is a smaller, rebuilt structure.

As the first expression of Muslim empire commencing only 30 years after the death of Muhammad, the Umayyad caliphate was confronted with the tasks of creating all the institutions of empire at the same time that it had to develop the institutions of a new and rapidly expanding religion. Even with, or perhaps because of, all the institutional stresses, the *dhimmī* communities tended to be treated well.

The tremendous geographical expansion that it inherited and pushed onward created enormous administrative and cultural challenges. The Umayyads established a royal administration and tax system, developed a diplomatic bureaucracy, maintained massive armies and a military system, organized centers and boundaries of governance and administration, and developed the beginnings of a religious bureaucracy. Arabic became the administrative language (replacing Greek, which had been the administrative language of most of the lands taken by the Arabs), and state documents and currency were issued in Arabic. Mass conversions brought a large influx of Muslims into the system.

The Umayyad rulers were criticized for not ruling according to the egalitarian principles associated with Muhammad and the Medinan *umma*. In some later histories, they are depicted much like the imperial rulers that ruled the Byzantine Roman Empire before them. As members of an Arab dynasty, the Umayyad rulers tended to favor the old Arab families and especially those of the Quraysh, and even more, those Quraysh of the clan of the Umayyad caliphs, the Banū Umayya, and all of these over newly converted Muslims. Their cultural attachment to Arabian tribal traditions influenced them to hold to a less universal conception of Islam than did some of their rivals. Just as important, as Islam became more obviously the religion of state and social status, the large number of non-Arab converts to Islam were relegated a secondary status by the Arab Muslim leadership. They were called *mawālī*, which was an old Arabian term used to designate an adopted member of an Arab tribe. The revolution that eventually removed the Umayyads from rule was successful in part because it was able to recruit the large and increasing number of dissatisfied *mawālī* to a cause that was defined as a return to the kind of egalitarian system established under God's prophet, Muhammad.

The Umayyads have met with a largely negative reception from later Islamic historians. They were accused of religious laxity and selfishness, and of promoting a kingship rather than a true caliphate. The implication is that their rule reflected the tyranny of a family; it did not reflect a government that represented religious civilization. It must be remembered, however, that this was a period when the religious institution of Islam was developing its own organic religious structures, and these tended to find themselves in conflict with the structures of state. As "deputies" or "successors" to Muhammad (the meaning of the title, caliph), the Umayyads regarded themselves as God's representatives at the head of the community, but they tended to rule as leaders of state rather than religion. Nevertheless, they seem to have had little interest in sharing religious power or delegating it to any community of religious scholars that was emerging at the time.

While great energies and initiatives were devoted to developing systems of state administration and religious institutional organization (often by competing individuals and powers), few scholarly initiatives were recorded under Umayyad rule. That is to say, the literatures that would become histories, theologies, compendia of *Hadith* and law, Qur'an commentaries, and the writings that would serve to represent the development of imperial Islamic civilization and religious tradition were developing and in process. But with few exceptions their emergence into written forms began in earnest only after the end of the Umayyads. In fact, it was only later, under the patronage of the Abbasid caliphate, the successors to the Umayyads, that Muslim scholars collected and recorded the traditions that form the primary source material for the history of the Umayyads. Not surprising is that these views would be less than complimentary toward the overthrown caliphs and their legacy.

The 'Abbasid Dynasty (750–1258)

The opposition to the Umayyads grew with the successful propaganda and recruitment of the Shi'a and its supporters among other Arab kinship groups and non-Arab converts. It preached a universalism and egalitarianism of "true Islam" that was easy to compare favorably against the hierarchical behaviors and system established by the Umayyads. The core of the movement was in Khurāsān, an eastern province of the old Persian Empire that comprises territories in today's eastern Iran, Afghanistan, Tajikistan, Turkmenistan, and Uzbekistan. The revolution consisted of a coalition of forces and peoples, not the least being an ethnic Persian component that, although Muslim, resented the loss of Persian power to ethnic Arabs who lauded the nobility of their Arabian kinship pedigree.

The leadership that emerged called themselves 'Abbasids (*al-'abbāsiyya*), after al-'Abbās, the paternal uncle of Muhammad. They succeeded in convincing the coalition that only a leader from the house of the Prophet (*ahl al-bayt*) could turn the *umma* back to the path of God, a proposition that clearly resonated with the Shi'a, which revered the line of Muhammad's descendants. The Abbasids, however, managed to undermine the Shi'a, and the leaders that finally emerged after the destruction of the Umayyad armies pushed the Shi'a aside and ruled much as the Umayyads had done before them. They also jettisoned their Persian and other compatriots from positions of significant power and established a second dynasty on the throne that would outlast the Umayyads by centuries. In order to prevent a return of the Umayyads to claim their caliphal heritage, all members of the family were killed, aside from one young man who managed to escape.

The Abbasids learned from the errors of their predecessors, who had projected a bad image, and therefore promoted themselves as pious leaders through successful self-promotion. They took on honorific titles known as *laqab*s, such as Al-Manṣūr (the victorious), Al-Rashīd (the judicious), Al-Ma'mūn (the trustworthy), and al-Mu'taṣim (the one preserved from sin), to demonstrate their upstanding Muslim nature. They also patronized publicists and historians who would paint their rule in bold and positive strokes. It is clear that their rule was not so different from that of their predecessors, but they adopted the oriental style of the old Persian shahs rather than that of the Byzantine emperors. They certainly did not return to the humble style of Muhammad and the first caliphs who ruled from Medina.

Despite the disappointment, especially among the Shi'a who were kept from power, it was the Abbasid caliphate that hosted the greatest advances and glories of Islamic civilization. All the seeds of the various sciences, arts, and literatures that had taken root under the Umayyads blossomed fully under the Abbasids. These included jurisprudence, theology, philosophy, linguistics (philology, grammar, and rhetoric), mathematics, metallurgy, geography, astronomy, Arabic *belle lettres*—virtually every discipline of the arts and sciences.

A new dynasty required a new capital, so the new city of Baghdad was built in 762, strategically on the Tigris River but close to the Euphrates, where it was in an optimal spot to promote trade and communication—and to provide defense. Called the Round City, it was constructed on a circular plan that resembled a *mandala* with symbolism of universal domination and beauty. It was also called City of Peace (*madīnat al-salām*).

It was during the Abbasid centuries that the Babylonian Jewish community became the intellectual, religious, and political center of world Jewry. For two or three centuries prior to the Conquest, the Jews living in Babylon (today's Iraq) had extended the project of the Talmud that had to be abandoned in the Land of Israel under the depredation of the Byzantine Empire. Christianity had based itself theologically on the degradation of Jews and Judaism, so when the Roman Empire Christianized in the 4th century, anti-Jewish discrimination was legalized and the Jewish communities of Byzantium weakened considerably. To the east under the Zoroastrian Sassanid Persians, the Jews of Babylon lived with much less interference and were able to continue the development of Rabbinic Judaism much more successfully. The head of the Jewish community of Babylon was called the *resh galuta,* an Aramaic term meaning "head of the exilic community," and was accorded great respect by the Persian rulers. In addition to the office of the exilarch, the Jews of Babylon established great Jewish academies under the leadership of the *Ge'onim* (singular, *Ga'on*), a title that means "learned" but also conveys something like the title "your majesty." Under the Persians, the Jewish academies in the towns of Sura and Pumbedita continued to develop advanced scholarship in religious studies under the *Ge'onim* after the completion of the Babylonian Talmud. The intellectual and material growth of the Jews of Babylon then took a great leap after the coming of the Abbasids to Baghdad.

Islam enacted discriminatory legislation against Jews, as well as other non-Muslims living in the Muslim world, but the level overall did not reach that of the Christian world. The fact that Jewish learning in so many disciplines blossomed so much more under Muslim rulers attests to the better overall material situation of the Jews under Islam.

As a general rule of Jewish history, the Jewish communities living at or near the seats of greatest Gentile power tend to exhibit a parallel power in relation to the Jewish world. This was most certainly the case in the Muslim world, not only under the Abbasids, but also in Muslim Spain and other regional centers of power. By the 9th century, the exilarch and the academies of Sura and Pumbedita had moved to Baghdad, the center of Abbasid power, though they were still named for the towns of their origin. The greatest medieval rabbi prior to Maimonides, Saadiah Gaon (d.942), presided over Sura when it was in Baghdad, as did the greatest heads of the Pumbedita academy, Sherira Gaon (d. ca. 1000) and his son, Ḥai Gaon (d.1038).

As the Muslim Arab intellectuals cultivated the sciences that were beloved to them under the patronage of the Abbasid caliphate, Jewish leaders and intellectuals found themselves deeply attracted to the same disciplines. The most important from the perspective of Jewish intellectual development were in the fields of systematic thinking (philosophy, theology) and linguistics (especially grammar and lexicography). Of most lasting importance, the Jews discovered a number of linguistic parallels between Arabic (which they knew fluently and spoke daily) and Hebrew. They found that many of the breakthroughs in Arabic linguistic theory and practice that the Muslims employed in order to better understand the Qur'an could be applied also to Hebrew and the study and analysis of the Torah. This Jewish intellectual development occurred under the Abbasids in Baghdad and reached its peak in the competing caliphate of Umayyad Spain.

Although lasting for some five centuries, all was not rosy for the Abbasid Empire. The Abbasid age was the age of the *Arabian Nights* and of Sinbad the sailor who engaged in adventures and fantasy that rivaled those of Odysseus and the fantastic tales of India. These tales tell of the intrigue and plots within plots that are wonderfully engaging to the reader but also indicative of a political system built on absolute power and distrust, and the destabilizing effects of incredible wealth existing beside extreme poverty. The Abbasid caliphate had great periods of excellence along with periods of administrative ineptitude, weakness, and corruption that caused hardship to all the peoples of the realm. The caliphs distanced themselves increasingly from the people, which caused the government to become more aloof and distant in its bureaucracy. The influences that lead to decline of any polity are of course complex and include more than the personality of a leadership or the corruption of a system, but these are indicative of some of the influences that caused the decline of imperial Abbasid rule. Long before the fall of the empire to the Mongol hordes of Hulagu Khan in 1258, the empire had split into minidynasties of governors and factional regional powers, and even competing caliphates, two of which are discussed briefly below.

The Fatimid Dynasty (909–1171)

The Shi`ite Fatimid dynasty was founded in 909 by Sa`īd ibn Ḥusayn who claimed that he descended from Muhammad through his daughter Fāṭima, the wife of `Alī ibn Abī Ṭālib. His direct connection to Muhammad through Fāṭima was the source of the name of the dynasty, *al-fāṭimiyya.* Not only was he a Shi`ite, who therefore supported the rule of the "Party of Ali," he represented a direct descendant of the Prophet through the second son of the 6th Imam, Ja`far. He was extremely successful in carving out an independent rule in northwest Africa and changed his name to `Ubaydallāh Al-Mahdī ("Servant of God, the Guide"). The first capital of the Fatimids was in al-Qayrawān in today's Tunisia. After conquering Egypt, however, the Fatimids established their new and permanent capital in today's Cairo in 969 and called it al-Qāhira, meaning "the Victor," a double entendre that references both the Fatimid conquest of Egypt and the appearance of the planet Mars, which was rising when the capital was founded.

Under the Fatimids, Egypt became the center of an empire that at its peak included all of North Africa, Sicily, the area of today's Israel, Jordan, Syria, the Red Sea coast of Africa, Yemen, and even the holy cities of Mecca and Medina. The empire flourished under an extensive trade network. It also built Al-Azhar, the oldest university in the Muslim world. With the notable exception of one caliph, Al-Ḥākim bi`Amr Allāh, who engaged in such strange behaviors that he is sometimes referred to as mad—he destroyed many churches in the empire and is said to have declared himself the incarnation of God—the Shi`ite Fatimids were quite tolerant, not only of Sunni Islam, but also of Judaism and Christianity. By the mid-12th century, the Fatimid Empire had weakened considerably. It collapsed in 1169 and was taken over by the Kurdish Sunni general Ṣalāḥ al-Dīn (Saladin), who became its governor (sultan). Saladin and the dynasty of rulers after him known as the Ayyubids recognized the Abbasid caliphate, although they were politically and militarily independent of Baghdad. The Abbasids remained in control of Egypt for nearly 90 years, after which they were overthrown by a rule of military commanders known as Mamlukes.

MAIMONIDES

Moses ben Maimon, known as Maimonides, settled with his family in Fatimid Cairo in 1166, after fleeing the repressive and intolerant Muslim regimes that had gained power in Spain and Morocco. He is considered the most brilliant medieval Jewish intellectual, having written the philosophic work, *The Guide for the Perplexed,* the encyclopedic legal compendium called the *Mishneh Torah,* and numerous other important works, including commentaries and medical treatises. He became the personal and court physician to Saladin, and one of his trusted advisers.

The Spanish Umayyads (929–1031)

Spain, known in Arabic as al-Andalus (Andalusia), had been conquered initially by the Umayyads, but like all areas of the Muslim world, came under the rule of the Abbasids after the overthrow of the Umayyad dynasty in 750. The one Umayyad who was not hunted down and killed by the Abbasids managed to find his way to Spain in 755. By the end of the following year, through skillful political acumen, connections, and military support, he managed to become the ruler of Muslim Spain. `Abd al-Raḥmān I did not claim to be caliph, however, and the next century and a half of rule by him and his descendants was the rule of amirs (a lesser title that translates as "commander" or "prince") rather than caliphs. During this period, Spain developed economically, politically, and intellectually, as the Abbasid caliphate in faraway Baghdad weakened and witnessed a level of disintegration. Regions began to break away from Baghdad into independent or semi-independent dynastic rule, and a rival Shi`ite caliph claimed legitimacy in North Africa.

With the weakening of the Abbasids and the threat of a rival to the caliphate in the Fatimids, `Abd al-Raḥmān III, who ruled Muslim Spain from 912 to 961, declared an independent Umayyad caliphate in 929. His caliphate was situated in Cordoba, the traditional Muslim capital of Spain. When Abd al-Rahman III declared himself independent from his Baghdadi overlords, the Jews of Spain (called Sefarad by the Jews) made a parallel move in relation to their Jewish Babylonian leaders, the *Ge'onim.* The strength and influence of the Babylonian Jewish community had been weakening along with the strength and influence of the larger environment in which it lived. Eventually and in parallel with the rise of Muslim Spain, the leaders of the Jewish communities in the Muslim world recognized the Sefaradim, the Spanish Jews, as their religious and intellectual leaders.

The Golden Age in Spain

Abd al-Rahman III symbolizes what has often been called the "Golden Age," or the "Golden Age of Jewish Culture" in Spain. In Spain itself there remains some controversy over the term "Golden Age." It should be pointed out, first of all, that for European history, the Spanish "Golden Age" generally refers to the 150 years after the end of the Spanish *reconquista* in 1492 when Christian Spain, emptied of its Jewish and Muslim inhabitants, became a world power and leader in politics, exploration, trade, and science. For Jewish history, most consider the Golden Age to have taken place between the 10th and the 12th centuries under the Muslims, though a period of tremendous Jewish intellectual and cultural production continued for more than a century in both Muslim and Christian areas of the peninsula.

The major controversy of the Golden Age, however, lies in how golden it really was for the Jews. There is no argument over the tremendous Jewish intellectual, scientific, and cultural development (which everyone acknowledges), but rather in whether it was a time when the relationship between Jews and Muslims was really one of great tolerance and friendship. In other words, all historians would acknowledge the golden age for Spanish Jewish culture, but not necessary a golden age for Spanish Jews. Clearly, the Jews were treated extremely well in some periods, such as during the reigns of Abd al-Rahman III and his son, Al-Ḥakam II (912–976). In fact, a Jew named Hasdai ibn Shaprut (d.970) became the personal physician, adviser, and grand vizier to the caliph Abd al-Rahman III. Other Jews also served the caliphs and Muslim kings of Spain after the caliphate disintegrated in 1031. One of the most distinguished is Shmuel HaNagid (d.1056), who served the Muslim Berber king Badis of Granada as his chief adviser and top military officer for 17 years, beginning in 1038. His son, Joseph, inherited the position and served as grand vizier as well. But for reasons that are still debated, Joseph did not manage to remain in the good graces of his king and populace. It was not uncommon for chief advisers of monarchs of any religious persuasion to be killed for "failing the king," but in the case of Joseph, the Muslim community of Granada rose up and also massacred the Jewish community of the city in 1066 as well. This marked the first case of Muslim mass violence perpetrated against Jews in Spain.

The official position of non-Muslim monotheists as second-class citizens applied officially everywhere in the Muslim world, but when economies were good, the leadership capable, and the Muslim population generally satisfied, the discriminatory laws were enforced with reduced severity. In the many cases where Jews or Christians became personal physicians or advisers to Muslim governors or even caliphs (which was officially forbidden by the laws regarding non-Muslim monotheists), it seems that the rules were obeyed entirely in the breach. Such exceptional situations were not all that common, even in the best of times, but Jews in the Middle Ages tended to fare better under Muslim rule than under Christian rule.

The enlightened and liberal Muslim leaders of Spain, first under the caliphate and then under many of the small Muslim kingdoms after the collapse of the caliphate, were eventually overthrown by waves of fundamentalists from North Africa. As always in such situations, economic, cultural, and political issues were important factors along with religious issues, but the final result was a drastic change from relative tolerance to intolerance toward Jews and Christians. Part of the threat to the Spanish Muslims at this time was the success of the Christian *reconquista* that was bringing northern territories under Christian control. Since the Christians needed to populate the conquered areas from which many Muslims fled, Jews were offered enticing terms and privileges for moving into (or staying in) the captured areas. Jews possessed skills that were needed by the new Christian rulers, including expertise in the management of land holdings. The Golden Age of Jewish development thus continued for a time under Christian Spain. Such famous Spanish Jewish thinkers and intellectuals as Yehudah ha-Levi, Abraham ibn Ezra, and Naḥmanides all lived in Christian regions, though they were products of Muslim Spanish Jewish culture and learning.

POLITICIZATION OF A "GOLDEN AGE"

The notion of a Golden Age where Judaism blossomed and Jews lived happily with Christians and Muslims under a tolerant Muslim government became an image that was manipulated for political purposes in the modern period, but it first emerged in the late 15th century. When the Jews of Christian Spain were violently expelled in 1492, some Jews living in the Muslim Ottoman Empire wrote to their exiled brethren urging them to move to the Ottoman areas where they would be welcomed under a benevolent Islam. Centuries later, influential 19th-century Jewish historians (such as Heinrich Graetz) used the story of the Golden Age to draw contrasts to the increasing oppression of Jews in Eastern Europe. The purpose of modern European Jews calling attention to how much better life was under medieval Muslims was to pressure Christian leaders to improve their treatment of Jews. The image of a Golden Age was thus developed and promoted by European Jewish activists, some of whom were Zionists who used that image to encourage Jews to settle in mostly Muslim Palestine. As waves of Jewish immigrants settled in Palestine, relations between Jews and Arabs deteriorated. The Golden Age vision was then picked up by Muslim Arab intellectuals who blamed the acts of Zionists for ruining what they claimed was the near-utopian generosity and tolerance of the Muslim world toward the Jews. In response to the Arab amplification of the image, some Jewish scholars and historians rejected the utopian image of a Golden Age altogether and published works detailing the many cases of violence and formalized discrimination that were carried out by Muslim powers against Jews. The Golden Age was thus politicized by both sides in ways that simplified and distorted the more complex and nuanced reality of Jewish life in the Muslim world.[1]

CHAPTER 9

The Decline of the Muslim World

The Muslim world was never conquered by a non-Muslim empire. The Mongols sacked Baghdad, but soon became Muslims themselves. Turks became a dominant power, as did Persians, but they were Turkish and Persian Muslims. Territories were gained and then lost to non-Muslim powers, especially along the borders such as in Spain, parts of Eastern Europe, and the Balkans. However, there was never a complete collapse of the Muslim world as there was of the Assyrian Empire, or of the Babylonians, Egyptians, Persians, and western Romans. Already by the 10th century, the Muslim world would no longer be ruled by a single caliph, but it struggled on with periods of great achievements in one region or another until the rise of the European powers in the 17th and 18th centuries.

In 1453, Turkish warriors conquered Constantinople and put a final end to the Byzantine Empire. They continued into southern Europe and some decades later laid siege to Vienna. Thus the Sunni Ottomans came to rule an empire as large as the Byzantine at its height. While the Ottomans were expanding into Europe, a rival Muslim empire was growing in Persia. In 1501, the Safavids established an empire that established a branch of Shi`ism as the official religion of the state. The two states, defined both ethnically and religiously, battled often and persecuted the religious expression of the other. This division divided Sunnis and Shi`is geographically and encouraged a parting of the ways among the two intellectual cultures as well. Shi`ites were vilified by the Ottomans, and popular Shi`ite piety contributed to the hatred of Sunnis as it centered on memory of the Sunni persecution and massacres of Shi`ite imams.

At about the same time, the Mughal Empire was established with its capital in Delhi, eventually expanding to include most of the Indian subcontinent by the turn of the 17th century. This empire embodied periods of great tolerance and of terrible repression. Under Akbar (1556–1605), the special tax on non-Muslims was abolished and the building of Hindu temples was even patronized by the state, but when a Hindu insurrection broke out some decades later, a very hard line was established toward the Hindus. Each case of political and military ascent and development brought economic growth and parallel patronage of the arts and sciences. Internal stresses within and between the many Muslim polities could encourage either development through healthy competition or damage through military engagement. Overall, the Muslim powers declined by the end of the 18th century, though the decline was felt particularly because of the concomitant rise of European trade and power that competed favorably with the Muslim world, eventually overtaking it scientifically, economically, militarily, and politically.

During the early 16th century, as the Ottoman, Safavid, and Mughal powers emerged to become great Muslim states and empires, the early European explorers began to establish the technology and know-how that would culminate in a European monopoly on long-distance trade. The Portuguese first dominated the Indian Ocean and established coastal colonies, but the British overtook them by the 18th century. The Ottomans were driven out of eastern Europe during this period. In 1799 Napoleon conquered Egypt, and though he remained only three years, his action made it clear that the European powers were becoming dominant. France took Algeria in 1830 and remained; Britain seized Aden (in Yemen) in 1839; Serbia and Greece fought wars of independence from the Ottomans during the same time; the French occupied Tunisia in 1881; and the British took control of Egypt and the Sudan in 1882. With the collapse of the Ottoman Empire in the First World War, Britain and France divided most of its Arab territories between themselves. Britain took over Palestine and Iraq, and France took over Syria and Lebanon.

The Muslim world had declined drastically by the end of the First World War, but it never collapsed. Even the great European colonial powers, which nibbled at parts of the Muslim world and then colonized areas for decades or even a century or more, did not "conquer" the areas in the typical fashion of the ancient empires. Traditional religious institutions remained largely intact, as did the traditional languages and social structures. Demographically, there was no overwhelming migration of conquering peoples, and the Muslim world remained overwhelmingly Muslim. At the same time, the political structures changed radically to favor the rule of the colonialists.

Muslim Responses to Modernity

The term "modernity" is generally used to mark a historical watershed or transition that has had a profound impact on most European norms, ranging from technological changes to perspectives on religion, to how the "other" is identified, how polities should be governed, what is private and public, and more. The transition from traditional to what we consider modern modes of thinking and behaving is a Western phenomenon, because modernity emerged in response to natural developments that occurred in the West. This is not to suggest that there were no parallel events outside of what we define as the West, but the core constellation of developments we identify as modern occurred organically only in Western Europe and its closest progeny (such as North America and Australia).

Modernity was not accepted by all Westerners, of course, and there were also countermovements, sometimes quite violent, that represented negative reactions to the anxieties brought about by modernity. But Westerners experienced the transitions as something that emerged from within their own communities rather than having it imposed on them by outsiders.

Although there were certainly contacts and communication between the Western, Christian world and the Muslim world, the two did not share the same core experiences. Whereas the transition to modern notions and expectations was an organic process (even if accompanied by great stresses) in the West, it was imposed by foreign colonial powers on local populations in the Muslim world whose history was quite different. It was therefore received differently, and not fully or without great ambivalence and struggle. Traditional modes of thinking and behaving remained a formidable barrier to the influence of modernity. Nevertheless, modernity has had a tremendous impact on the Muslim world, affecting business, language, governance, economies, science, the arts, and certainly religion. Most Muslims live in areas that were under European colonial control or influence, and all the Islamic movements that have emerged in the last two centuries have been reactions to the dual pulls of tradition and modernity, or to *other* Muslims' reactions to these influences.

One of the most profound changes associated with modernity in the Muslim world is the end of the caliphate and its replacement with secular nation-states. In fact, the caliphate had dissolved long before the emergence of European modernity, but the last great Muslim empire, that of the Ottomans, claimed occasionally to be a caliphate. This was an ironic claim, since most Arabs believed that the caliph must come from (an Arab) kinship group related to Muhammad, and there was general antipathy among many Muslims toward the Ottomans, especially as the empire declined and became riddled with corruption and misrule. In any case, by the time the Ottoman

Empire finally expired in the First World War, most of the Muslim world had come under the direct or indirect rule of European colonial powers (including India, Indonesia, and Malaysia). European governance of these colonies naturally favored removing religious influence from government, and even some indigenous powers such as Turkey secularized their governance. The nation-state became the default political entity under modernizing influences, which countered the universalist notion of the *umma* and the caliphate. Nationalism also became the driving force behind the independence movements. As has been observed, "If the Egyptians, Arabs, Indians, or Indonesians had felt no shared national identity before, they certainly did after the French, British, and Dutch consolidated their control. There is nothing quite like having one's land taken away to elicit a sense of common injury, the need for solidarity, and the development of a shared mythology to support that solidarity."[1]

Religious Modernizers

Throughout the medieval period, the standard of a single unified caliphate was always the ideal, even if it was hardly realized. Where, then, does Islam fit in with the nation-state? The range of responses to this question is broad, but certain general trends may be observed. One is the trend to modernize, by which is meant, adapting Islam to the new phenomenon of a Western-style nation-state. Some Muslim modernizers urged secularization of the nation and the restriction of Islam to a personal practice dissociated from the state and governance. This was the position of Ataturk and was applied forcefully to the Turkish state. Variations of this theme were applied in Syria, Iraq, and Egypt, each through various political systems (one form or another of absolute power in the guise of democracy or socialism). The religious scholars in these countries would be removed from political power or put on the government payroll where they could be controlled.

Another modernizing approach was to reform Islam in modern terms. This was the approach of famous reformers such as Sayyid Aḥmad Khan (d.1898) and Muhammad Iqbāl (d.1938) in India, and Muhammad `Abdū (d.1905) and even Rashīd Riḍā (1935) in Egypt. Although each had a different platform and political and religious philosophy, they tended to reject the blind following of tradition, calling for reinterpretation of Islam to respond to modern life and reorganizing the institutions of religious leadership.

By the middle of the 20th century, the colonial powers had withdrawn or had been forced from their holdings in the Muslim world. As they withdrew, they attempted to remain influential among the rulers of their erstwhile colonies through various means, but the net result of their efforts tended to neglect the most basic needs of the local populations. What remained were independent (at least in name) nation-states that had only partially modernized through their engagement with the West. The various experiments in modernizing the Muslim nation-states were referred to as reformist, democratic, socialist, Arabist, or pan-Arab nationalist. However they were called, they all privileged certain elites and failed to resolve the most pressing problems faced by the majority populations in these countries: poverty, inadequate health care, lack of education, poor economic development, uncontrolled population growth, and massive political corruption. The failures were often identified as a legacy of European colonialism caused by the West and perpetuated by Western-oriented elites who benefited from modernization at the expense of the indigenous masses. Modernization had a tremendous and lasting impact on most of the Muslim world, but by the end of the 20th century, the general approach even of the local Muslim modernizers had been discredited. Modernizing movements are not particularly popular at the time of this writing, but their impact remains strong and new movements may very well emerge again.

Religious Revivalists

The Muslim world experienced revivalist movements at various times in history, including the 18th and 19th centuries as a response to its obvious decline in relation to the West. These movements were generally experienced as responses to internal issues rather than to colonialism or modernization, but their ideologies were similar to current revivalist movements. Islamist revivalist movements agree on the following basics:

1. Islam is the solution to the problems facing the community.
2. A return to the Qur'an and the "authentic" religion of Islam as practiced by the Prophet is the correct method.
3. The community must be governed by God's revealed law.
4. Any who resist these goals, whether Muslim or non-Muslim, are enemies of God.

There are of course many varieties in detail and levels of intensity of expression in the working out of these building blocks of Islamic revivalism. Most Islamic revivalist organizations would claim that, where permitted, they work within the political system and seek change through a gradual process of reform. Some embrace political liberalization and democratization, while others insist that they will only accept the processes of governance espoused by certain medieval religious scholars. Nevertheless, most movements today differ from those of earlier centuries in that they are modern, not traditional, in their leadership, ideology, and organization. Although they may claim to return to the authentic foundations of Islam in the Qur'an and the example of the Prophet, their understanding of what this actually means is inevitably influenced by modern ideas and structures of governance and organization.

There are many groups and movements espousing Islamic revival, and they cannot all be enumerated and studied here. In the broadest terms, Muslim revivalists are referred to as "Islamists," because they hold that Islamic law must be the source for all statutory law in society. They tend to be active advocates of societal reform, the revival of Islamic norms, and their institution in modern society. Many nevertheless resent the term "Islamist" because they believe that their position is the most basic requirement of any Muslim. Other terms for Islamism are "political Islam" and "activist Islam." Two of the most powerful revivalist groups to emerge in the 20th century are the Muslim Brotherhood and Wahhabi Islam.

The Muslim Brotherhood (actually, the name is Muslim Brothers), while officially a worldwide Sunni revivalist (Islamist) organization, has broken into so many subgroups, associations, and parties that it is most accurate to refer to it as a trend rather than a movement. It was founded in 1928 by a Sufi schoolteacher in Egypt named Ḥassan al-Bannā. The official goal of the Muslim Brotherhood is to reestablish the caliphate, worldwide Islamic rule, and unification of the *umma*, and it has experienced many changes in its leadership and direction since its founding. It is regarded by many Western governments and organizations as the source of much terrorism in the Muslim world, but its most basic goal does not require terrorism or violence. Still, some of the most activist expressions of its basic ideology consider violence to be an acceptable means of applying and enforcing God's law. Most Islamist organizations and movements, whether violent or not, are popularly associated with the Muslim Brotherhood.

Although there is some overlap between the Muslim Brotherhood and Wahhabi Islam, they are independent movements. The founder of Wahhabi Islam, Muḥammad ibn `Abd al-Wahhāb (d.1791), preached a strict revivalist doctrine and practice. Together with a local tribal leader named Muḥammad ibn Sa`ūd, he unified much of Arabia through the authority of religion and force of arms. The real power of the synthesis of Wahhabi Islam with Saudi political and military acumen occurred only generations later, after Saudi warriors conquered Mecca and Medina in 1924 and oil was discovered in their area of control in 1938. The vast oil revenues gave an immense impetus to the spread of their conservative Islamic theology and doctrine. Wahhabi has become somewhat of a pejorative term. Those who subscribe to its ideas and practices refer to themselves as *salafi*s, the term for pious ancestors. Like all revivalists, they see their role as restoring Islam from what they perceive to be innovations and deviances from the right path that was clearly defined in the earliest generation. Some of the many practices that they believe are contrary to Islam include celebrating the birthday of the Prophet Muhammad, listening to certain kinds of music, depicting humans in art of any form, praying at the tombs of the righteous, including that of Muhammad (especially for intercession with God for forgiving sins), and any innovation of any kind in matters of religion. They accept the practice of enforcing their understanding of Islam on others, rather than taking the more common Muslim position that each and every individual must take personal responsibility for his or her actions and beliefs.

Muslims in the West and Westerners in the Muslim World

Until the end of the colonial period, very few Muslims lived in the Western world. This has changed significantly with the end of European colonialism. For a variety of reasons, political, religious, and economic, thousands and then millions of Muslims have emigrated to Western countries. Their integration into Western culture has not been easy for both internal and external reasons. Some sought political asylum and had no interest in assimilating Western cultural norms and values. Others wished to do so but were not well accepted by the citizens of their new host-nations. A wide range of responses to the mix of cultures and religions has arisen through the process of emigration, from efforts at successful integration to purposeful cantonization by some Muslims in detached ghetto-like neighborhoods where they can re-create something of the cultures, languages, and religious expressions of their home countries in their new surroundings. The ebb and flow of forces and inclinations will likely continue to be fluid.

Although many Westerners lived in the Muslim world under the colonial powers, most either left or were expelled with colonial withdrawal. Places such as Cairo, Damascus, and Baghdad were extremely cosmopolitan cities. Since the middle of the 20th century, however, the trend has been to detach increasingly from the cultural influence of the larger world. This has been reversed somewhat with the rise of world media and globalization, but the level of internationalism or cosmopolitanism in the Muslim world is far less than in Europe and the West.

PART TWO

GOD,
THE QUR'AN,
AND
ISLAMIC LAW

CHAPTER 10

God

God in the Qur'an

In Islam, the name for God, the one and only God, is Allah, which means, simply, "the God." The word is derived from *al-ilāh*, shortened into *Allāh* (الله) by frequent use. The equivalent in Hebrew would be *ha-el* (האל), and in fact the root of the word is the same in both Hebrew and Arabic. Allah is not a proper name, as is the unpronounceable name of God in Hebrew. Rather, in the Islamic religious formulation, God has no personal name.

Chapter 112 of the Qur'an, called the "Chapter of Sincerity," contains the most basic creedal statement of Islamic theology in the Qur'an, and represents the essential understanding of God in Islam in general.

The Basic Creed: God in Islam:

Say, "It is God! The One!	قُلْ هُوَ اللَّهُ أَحَدٌ
God is eternal	اللَّهُ الصَّمَدُ
neither giving birth nor having been born.	لَمْ يَلِدْ وَلَمْ يُولَدْ
Nothing is comparable to Him."	وَلَمْ يَكُن لَّهُ كُفُوًا أَحَدٌ

The four essential statements of the creed can be understood in the following ways:

Verse 1. *Say, It is God! The One!*

The first two words of the creed could be the answer to virtually any question. Who and what are we referencing when we ask about anything in the cosmos? The answer is, "It is God." The unity of God is absolute in Islam. God is the source of the world and all within it. God is the absolute foundation. All is God, and all is One. God is the only permanent being or essence and the only power in the world because all power and all majesty derive from God. Therefore, it is only God who can be adored and worshiped.

Verse 2. *God is eternal.*

God's limitless nature is certain, but it remained to be worked out in theological discourse exactly what that meant. Various schema were developed by theologians and mystics to make sense of the limitless eternality of God and the relationship between God and nature, matter, the soul, and time, all of which required careful exploration of physics and metaphysics, science and theology.

Verse 3. *Neither giving birth nor having been born.*

Because of God's limitless nature, God *could* give birth if God so willed, but God does not. Having been born assumes a state of deficiency or incompletion that cannot be applied to the perfect and absolute nature of God. Giving birth and sending a corporeal divine power to walk within humanity is absurd in Islamic thinking, because it suggests limitation and division of the divine essence; and dividing the unified nature of God into parts is tantamount to idolatry. The Qur'an is explicit in its condemnation of the Christian trinity: "Those who say God is one third of a trinity certainly blaspheme, for there is no deity except the One God" (Q.5:73).[1]

Verse 4. *Nothing is comparable to Him.*

God is omnipotent and omniscient. No one and no thing resembles God in anything or is equivalent to God in any respect. As we shall observe below, there is a great deal of parallel material to be found between the Qur'an and the prior scriptures of Judaism and Christianity, but nowhere does the

Qur'an suggest that humanity was created "in the image of God" (Gen. 1:27). All images are false images, and to some Muslims even the portrayal of a human in sculpture or painting is a form of idolatry. The iconoclasm of Islam was so great that historically Muslims often defaced the human form in the art of preceding civilizations they encountered, something that is still visible in some of the Pharaonic and Byzantine monumental art that was absorbed into the Muslim world.

The absolute primacy of God is conveyed throughout the Qur'an in its own unique rhetorical style. Hundreds of verses of the Qur'an end with one of many concluding phrases, often repeated in various contexts, referencing the enormity and majesty of God. Among these are: "He is the Hearer, the Seer" (Q.17:1), "the Exalted, the Powerful" (Q.2:255), "the Forgiving, the Merciful" (Q.2:182), "All-encompassing, All-knowing (Q.5:54), "the Benevolent, the Compassionate" (Q.59:22), "the Mighty, the Wise" (Q.62:3), "the Most-high, the Great" (Q.31:30). That God's majesty is beyond human comprehension is one of the most basic creedal messages of Islam. Thus the need for submission to the divine will, which is the meaning of the word "Islam." This has engendered a pious sense of humility in Islam, and it is expected that while one may certainly strive for excellence and may compete with one's fellow, one needs always to understand that one is flesh and blood who will, at the end, meet one's Maker and be judged.

The descriptives listed in the previous paragraph are known as "the most beautiful names," traditionally understood as consisting of 99 divine epithets upon which Islamic theology later based its expositions about the meaning and essence of God. Muslims will often recite the names in a particular order, using what are mistakenly called "worry beads" (the Arabic name is *misbaḥa*, meaning "a device for praising") made up of 33 units as a mnemonic device to work through the 99 names.[2] Other names for God are also found in the Qur'an. One familiar to Jewish tradition that we have already encountered in our examination of pre-Islamic Arabia is the "Merciful" (*al-Raḥmān*), and it is this name as well as *Allah* around which is revealed the verse mentioning the "beautiful names": "Say: Call upon Allah or call upon al-Raḥmān; however you call upon Him, to Him belong the most beautiful names" (Q.17:110).

The second most common term for God in the Qur'an is *rabb*, "Lord." As in Hebrew, the root meaning is "much" or "great." There is evidence that the term was used as a title for pre-Islamic soothsayers, a parallel usage to the Hebrew term *"rav,"* which was applied to Jewish religious scholars.[3] But in Islam, it is used only in reference to God. Even a slave was forbidden to address his master as *rabbī* ("my lord") and was required to use a different term, such as *sayyidī* ("my master"). In Arabic to this day, rabbis are usually called *ḥākhām*, derived from the Hebrew, sometimes *ḥabr*, or rarely *rabbān*,[4] clearly in order to distinguish Jewish religious scholars from the Arabic term for God. A common use of the Arabic *rabb* in everyday speech is found in the frequent expression *al-ḥamdu lillāhi rabb al-`ālamīn*: "praise is to God, the Lord of the worlds."

It is part of the particular rhetorical style of the Qur'an to reference God according to "the most beautiful names." These convey something of the endless majesty and complexity associated with God in the Qur'an, and the repetition of these names or attributes in various combinations and forms functions throughout like a mantra of praise. Not only is God named "wise" nearly 100 times, God is the "justest of judges" (Q.11:45, 95:8) and the "best of judges" (Q.7:87, 10:109, 12:80), "commanding justice" (Q.16:90) and "upholder of justice" (Q.3:18), who will judge humankind on the last day,[5] to determine who will merit a world to come in paradise (*al-janna*) and who will be destined for hell (*al-nār* or *jahannum*).[6]

God is not only the great judge, but also "the forgiver" (Q.7:155), "the oft-forgiving" (Q.2:173) and "the all-forgiving" (Q.38:66), "the pardoner" (Q.4:43) and "the one who turns" to humanity in kindness (Q.2:37), "the loving" (Q.85:14), who accepts humanity's gratitude (Q.35:30). The Qur'an thus understands God through the attributes of justice and mercy. God's complexity is further developed in the qur'anic rhetorical style through a series of many other descriptives: "the comprehensive" (Q.2:247), "the glorious" (Q.85:18), "the dominator" (Q.12:39), "the benevolent" (Q.67:14), "the constant giver" (Q.3:8), "the reckoner" (Q.4:86), "the guardian" (Q.3:173), "the patron" (Q.42:9), "the creator" (Q.59:24) or "unceasing creator" (Q.36:81), "the real (or truth)" (Q.20:114), "possessor or giver of peace" (Q.59:23), and "the guide to those who believe" (Q.22:54). Because of the wide descriptive range found in the Qur'an, readers have construed very different qur'anic images of God, something like the proverbial elephant among the blind men. One individual might mistakenly consider God limited to being harsh, judgmental, and dominating, while another mistakenly considers God limited to being loving, forgiving and nurturing. The extremely broad range of representation is meant to convey the limitlessness of description that must be applied to God and the inexpressible grandeur that is bound up in the divine essence. "The beautiful names" of God are more likely expressions of praise than attempts to express God's nature.

Despite the sublime nature of the divinity conveyed by these references, the Qur'an also ascribes certain qualities that seem to detract from the absolutely transcendent nature of God communicated by "the beautiful names." As in the Hebrew Bible, God does not always seem to be omniscient or omnipotent (compare Gen. 3:8–9, 6:6). God derides (Q.9:79), forgets (Q.9:67), and comes stealthily (Q.7:182). God is depicted as having a face (Q.2:115,272), eyes (Q.11:37, 23:27), and hands (Q.3:73, 5:64), and God is sometimes seated on a throne (Q.7:54, 10:3). Some of these references reflect the style and rhetoric of

Arabic that, like Hebrew, tends toward concrete rather than abstract characterization. These references nevertheless caused not a little consternation to Muslim interpreters, who attempted to maintain the transcendent nature of the divinity in the face of these challenges, not unlike Jewish interpreters who were confronted with similar problems with the biblical depictions of God.

All creation is God's, and God is the creator of all things. In some qur'anic references, creation occurs in six days (Q.7:54). God simply articulates, and the power of that articulation is creative. "'Be!' And it is" (Q.3:47,59, 6:73, etc.). God creates humanity with God's own two hands (Q.38:75), from clay (or mud) (Q.6:2, 37:11, 55:14) or stinking mud (Q.15:28), and breathes spirit into him (Q.15:29, 38:72). The jinn (genies), however, are created from fire (Q.55:15), and all other animals from water (Q.24:45).

Like all expressions of monotheism, Islam is confronted with the problem of juxtaposing good and evil in the world with God's goodness, on the one hand, and the divine role of creator of all things, on the other. How is evil explained in a way that redeems God from the taint of association with it? One solution is provided in the story of the Garden of Eden, repeated in somewhat different variations in the Qur'an. The story of Eden is a complex narrative and found in a number of locations in the Qur'an (Q.2:30–39, 7:11–29, 15:26–48, 17:61–65, 20:115–126). It is Satan's pride that leads to his own and humanity's fall from the Garden. God will exact a final punishment for Satan's sins, but not immediately, thus leaving space for Satan to represent the evil urge that can lead humanity from the right path. Satan thus assumes responsibility for evil, but God provides the means of repentance and, subsequently, forgiveness, by giving Adam words through which he can express regret for sin. One rendering of the story ends with this message: "But if guidance comes from Me to you, anyone who follows My guidance will have no fear and will not grieve. But those who rebel and deny the truth of Our signs are people of hellfire, remaining in it forever" (Q.2:38–39).

A favorite verse that expresses a qur'anic sense of the ineffable God is the "Throne Verse" (Q.2:255):

> **ALLAH!** There is no God but He
> the Living, the Self-subsisting.
> No slumber can seize Him, nor sleep.
> All things in heaven and earth are His.
> Who could intercede in his presence without His permission?
> He knows what is before them and behind them.
> They cannot encompass any of His knowledge except what he wills.
> His throne extends over the heavens and the earth,
> and He feels no fatigue in guarding and preserving them,
> for He is the Highest and Most Exalted.

God and Theology in Post-Qur'anic Literatures

The most powerful expression of the divinity is to be found in the Qur'an, but the Qur'an makes no pretense of being a systematic work; in fact, the rhetorical style of the Qur'an seems to stress a nature of discourse that is beyond human ability to systematize or organize. We have observed a range of descriptives associated with the divinity, along with many of the specific terms used to refer to God. All of these invite speculation, curiosity, inspiration, and even critique. In the wake of the Conquests, a rich and varied tradition of religious literatures developed that contemplated the nature and meaning of God. A massive and diverse library of works has been written, made up of an assortment of genres representing a variety of approaches. These include formal works of philosophy and theology (or systematic thinking), Qur'an interpretation, tradition literature, jurisprudence, and religious poetry. All these contain thinking about God and God's relation to the world, but few works treat theology exclusively.

In fact, Islam is more akin to Judaism than Christianity in that it lays more stress on proper behavior and practice than on proper thinking or conceptualization of the deity. No concept of "original sin," for example, exists in Islam, thus obviating the classical Christian requirement to believe in and accept Jesus's divinely redemptive role in order to merit personal salvation.[7] Yet, despite its emphasis on behavior, Islam tends to privilege theology more than Judaism does. As in Judaism, the unity of God is the core of the religious system of Islam, and it is understood that the only sin for which there is no divine forgiveness is *shirk* (Q.4:48,116)—associating partners with God through a complex godhead or assuming other creative powers. But there are other doctrines of Islamic faith that are basic and required as well, even though theology in general is always secondary to *sharīʿa*, the Muslim equivalent to the Jewish *halakhah* or religious law.

CHAPTER 11

The Five Doctrines or "Pillars of Faith"

Muslim thinkers organize the basic religious doctrines of Islam under five headings that are referred to collectively as *īmān,* or "faith."

1. *Belief in the Unity of God*

The core out of which everything is derived in Islam is the unity of God. God has no partners (Q.6:163). God is not born, nor does God give birth (Q.112:3). This core of Islamic faith is formalized in the first and core section of the "witness" of faith, the *shahāda*: "There is no god but God."[1] The full creed is: "There is no god but God, and Muhammad is prophet of God." According to Muslim jurists, the free and sincere utterance of this statement is all that is required in order to become a Muslim.[2]

According to the interpretive tradition, Muhammad was commanded by God to proclaim the following creed early on in his mission: "Say, 'My Lord guides me to a straight path, an upright religion, the creed of Abraham the upright, who was no idolater.' Say: 'My prayer and my devotion, my life and my death, are for God Lord of the worlds. He has no partners. That is what I am commanded, the first to surrender'" (Q.6:161–163).

2. *Belief in Angels*

The Qur'an often refers to angels (sing. *malak*). In the qur'anic story of the Garden, God created Adam to a status that is in some ways higher than the angels, who were commanded to bow before him (Q.7:11–28). The one that refused was Iblis, who was a genie according to Q.18:50, thereby becoming an evil being who, in post-qur'anic interpretive literature, brought along with him a host of evil followers called "satans" (*shayāṭīn*), who also originated as angels. Some good angels are named in the Qur'an, such as Gabriel (*jibrīl*) and Michael (*mīkāl*) (Q.2:97–98, 66:4), though these seem to be differentiated in some way from other angels, perhaps because they had special roles or are of a different rank. Two other fallen angels are also mentioned in the Qur'an, *Hārūt* and *Mārūt,* along with other "satans" (Q.2:102). While humanity was created from clay (or mud), Islamic tradition understands that the angels were created from light, with the exception of Iblis, who was created from fire (Q.7:12).

Another supernatural creature mentioned in the Qur'an is the genie, also created from fire. Genies are beings that can possess a person, and in the pre-Islamic period they were understood to possess poets, giving them an extraordinary power of creativity. Muhammad himself was accused by his detractors of being possessed by a genie (Q.15:6) and spouting poetry (Q.36:69), probably because of the beauty and complexity of his qur'anic recital. Genies are dangerous troublemakers and associated in the Qur'an with the "satans," but have less power. Genies have limited life spans and are to be judged by God like humans. In fact, they are often associated with humans in the Qur'an (Q.6:112, 128, 130, 7:38, 179). Chapter 72 of the Qur'an is even called "The Genies," and it relates a story of a righteous group of genies that accepts the truth of monotheism and the Qur'an. Because they appear in the Qur'an, genies are subsumed under the more general expectation of "belief in angels."

3. *Belief in Prior Revelations and Prophets*

This is a particularly important issue for Jews to understand. Muslims are expected to accept the divine origin of prior revelation and the holy status of the ancient prophets, but many Muslims feel that Jews (and Christians) do not reciprocate because they deny the divine nature of the Qur'an and the prophecy of Muhammad. According to the Qur'an (and therefore all subsequent Islamic tradition), Muhammad was the last in a long line of divinely inspired prophets. "Say: We believe in God and in what was brought down to us and what was brought down to Abraham and Ishmael and Isaac and Jacob and the Tribes and what was given to Moses and Jesus and what was given to the prophets from their Lord. We do not distinguish between any of them; we are submitters to Him"[3] (Q.2:136).

Some 25 prophets are mentioned in the Qur'an, spanning from Adam to Muhammad. Most of these did not bear written scripture and are thus not considered prophets by Jews and Christians. But in the Islamic perspective, any biblical personage with whom God communicated fits the category of prophet or messenger. Therefore, in addition to Moses and Jesus, Islamic prophets include Noah, Abraham, Ishmael, Isaac, Jacob, David, Solomon, Job, Aaron, and others, including some Arabian prophets such as Hūd and Ṣāliḥ (who are known from pre-Islamic tradition that exists outside of the Bible). The same God that revealed the Qur'an through the prophet Muhammad revealed prior scriptures through the earlier prophets. All divine revelations have equal status. "God brought down the Book to you in truth, verifying what was before it. God brought down the Torah and the Gospel before as a guide to humanity, and He brought down the Furqan.[4] Those who deny the signs of God will have a terrible punishment. God is almighty, able to exact revenge" (Q.3:3–4).

As noted in chapter 5, however, Muhammad and the Jews of Medina both recognized that what was revealed to Muhammad was not exactly the same text or literal scripture that was beloved by the Jews. To take one simple example, the dietary laws of each scripture are similar in a number of ways but also contain significant differences about permitted and forbidden foods. "God has forbidden you only carrion, blood, flesh of the pig, and that over which invocation has been made other than God" (Q.2:173). This clearly resonates with the prohibition of the Torah, but it is significantly less restrictive.[5]

What, then, was the reaction by the Jews and the early Believers in Medina to the discrepancies between the two scriptures and their conflicting truth claims? We can imagine the situation. The Jews had in their possession a scripture that was already ancient and that they deeply revered. It would be extremely difficult and certainly not in their best interest to reconcile this with the claims of a new prophet who recited a message that was different from what they had before them. "When it is said to them, 'Believe in what God has revealed,' they say, 'We believe in what has been revealed to us,' but they reject what [has come] after that, even though it is the truth confirming what they [already] have" (Q.2:91). The Qur'an seems to respond directly to the Jewish claim that the Qur'an is not rigorous enough on the dietary laws. "All food was lawful to the Children of Israel except whatever Israel forbade upon itself before the Torah was revealed. Say: 'Bring the Torah and recite it, if you speak the truth!'" (Q.3:93).

The Jews as a whole simply did not consider Muhammad's revelation authentic. The Qur'an contains a number of verses complaining that listeners did not consider it genuine. With great confidence in its truth, the Qur'an challenges the audience to try to produce something equally sublime. "If you are in doubt about what We have sent down to Our servant, then produce a verse like it!"(Q.2:23; see also 4:153).

To Muhammad, who was confident that he was a prophet of God and believed in the authenticity of his revelation—and who was also convinced that the earlier scriptures were God's work, too—the discrepancies between them could only be explained by errors or purposeful distortions of the earlier scriptures. And the Qur'an accuses the Jews and Christians of purposefully altering their own scriptural texts.

> Remember, We accepted your covenant. . . . But you turned away after that. If not for God's grace and mercy toward you, you would have been lost like the others. . . . you hardened your hearts after that and they became like rocks or even harder. . . . [directed to Muhammad] Do you expect them to believe in you when some of them hear God's words and then knowingly distort it after understanding it? When they meet Believers they say, "We believe," but when they are alone with one another they say, "Are you telling them what God has revealed to you so that they might dispute with you before your Lord? . . . Woe to those who write Scripture with their own hands and then say, "This is from God," so that they might buy some profit from it. (Q.2:63–79)

The Qur'an's language here is angry and seems to express a great sense of frustration. "And there is a party of them who twist their tongues about Scripture so you will think that it is from scripture when it is not from scripture. They say: It is from God when it is not from God, and they speak lies about God, though they know [better]!" (Q.3:78).[6]

These texts clearly represent angry replies to the critiques that were leveled against the new revelations of Islam by the established religions of its day. It is, of course, problematic today, when tolerance and pluralism are so sorely needed, for scriptural texts to denigrate other religions and their believers, but this is a common phenomenon among scriptures. Negative assessments and even condemnation of prior religions and their adherents occur in all three scriptures of Judaism, Christianity, and Islam.[7]

4. *Belief in a Final Judgment*

The fourth fundamental belief of Islam, and one that is expressed repeatedly in the Qur'an, is that all creatures will be brought forth for a final judgment. This theme of a last judgment that will determine eternity in paradise or eternity in hell is extremely common in the Qur'an. It is a complete turnaround from the general pre-Islamic Arabian expectation that a virtually animate "time" (*al-dahr*, sometimes *al-zamān*) would simply overrun and obliterate human lives. Some have suggested that the radical departure from pre-Islamic norms is the reason for the ubiquitous appearance of a final judgment in the Qur'an.

The qur'anic terms for this include "day of judgment" (Ar. *yawm al-dīn* // Heb. *yom ha-din*), "day of resurrection" (Ar. *yawm al-qiyāma*) "the last day"(Ar. *al-yawm al-ākhir* // Heb. *hayom ha-'aḥaron*), "the hour" (Ar. *al-sā'a* // Heb. *ha-sha'ah*), and "the day of reckoning" (*yawm al-ḥisāb*). Although only God knows when the last day will occur (Q.7:187), it may be very soon (Q.21:1) and will occur suddenly (Q.6:31). Many dozens of qur'anic chapters and verses reference the endtime, and these are not systematic. Later commentators attempted to derive a fully consistent system from the qur'anic renderings, but the Qur'an itself seems to intend a poetic expression that would strike deep into the hearts and minds of the listener. Only one of many powerful expressions may be felt from chapter 82, known as "the folding up," a chapter that is formulated in a kind of rhymed prose that is powerful and awesome when heard in formal recitation.

> [1]When the sky splits, [2]and when the stars are scattered, [3]and when
> the oceans are drained out, [4]and when the tombs are overturned, [5]ev-
> ery soul will know everything it has done. [6]O human! What has se-
> duced you from your most beneficent Lord [7]who created you,
> proportioned you and balanced you [8]in whatever way He wished? [9]But
> no! You deny the religion [10]even though there are those to protect you,
> [11]generous recorders, [12]who know what you do! [13]As for the righteous,
> they be in delight [14]and as for the wicked, they will be in the inferno.
> [15]They will roast in it on the Day of Judgment. [16]They will not be absent
> from it. [17]What will inform you of what the Day of Judgment is? [18]Again,
> what will inform you of what the Day of Judgment is? [19]The day that no
> soul can do anything for another. On that day, it is all up to God.[8]

The details of the endtime vary from reference to reference, but the general message may be garnered from chapter 39, known as "The Crowds:"

> [67]They do not assess the measure of God fully, when the entire earth
> is in His grip on the day of resurrection, the heavens rolled up in His
> right hand, God be praised and transcendent beyond any association
> they make. [68]And the trumpet will be blown and all in the heavens and
> on earth will faint except those whom God wills. Then it will be blown
> a second time and now they will be standing, waiting. [69]And the earth
> will shine in the light of its Lord and the Book will be laid out, and the
> prophets and the witness will be brought forth, and true judgment will

> be made among them. They will not be wronged. [70]And every soul will be recompensed for what it did, for God knows best what they do. [71]And those who refused to believe will be driven in crowds to hell. When they arrive, its gates will be opened and its keepers will say to them, "Didn't your own messengers come to you and recite to you the signs of your Lord, warning you of meeting this day?" They will say, "Yes indeed, but the word of punishment for those who refuse to believe is just." [72]It will be said, "Enter the gates of hell forever!" How miserable the dwelling of those who think themselves great. [73]But those who were pious to their Lord will be driven to the garden in crowds until, when they reach it its gates will be opened. Its keepers will say to them, "Peace upon you! You have been good, so enter it forever!" [74]They will say, "Praise be to God who has fulfilled His promise and has bequeathed to us the earth to dwell in the Garden wherever we desire. How wonderful the reward of workers! [75]And you will see angels surrounding the throne, singing out praise of God, judged correctly, and it will be said, "Praise be to God, Lord of the worlds!"

The many details of this and other qur'anic scenarios are carefully considered by commentators and scholars throughout the history of Islam. How the trumpet will be blown, for example, and what is the interval between blasts? How will an incorporeal God hold the world in his hand, who will be gathered and how, how will people bear witness against themselves, and what is the nature and function of the Book? How and where will judgment be rendered? What exactly constitutes sins that determined a negative judgment, and how are sins and righteous deeds balanced against one another?

The Qur'an never mentions the location of the final judgment, so Muslims naturally inquired of Jews and Christians about their views. As a result, it has become a traditional expectation in Islam (as well as in Judaism and Christianity) that Jerusalem will be the place of judgment. Some commentators place Jerusalem as the location in Q.57:13 where a wall will be set up to separate between those receiving mercy and those receiving agony. The pleasures of paradise and the miseries of hell are provided in some detail in the Qur'an (Q.2:24–25, 22:19–24, 44:43–56) and are extended in the exegetical literature.

5. *Belief in Predestination and the Divine Decree*

The question of whether humankind has free will is one that has been discussed and argued in all the monotheistic traditions. Muslims refer to the issue as the issue of God's power and decree (*al-qadar wal-qadā'*). Pre-Islamic

Arabian culture thought that a power or essence, sometimes personified as "time," was the cause of fate. "Time has killed him. . . . Time is relentless. . . . Time is a thief who snatches away friends and relatives."[9] Resistance to such fate is futile. In the Qur'an, however, God controls time and therefore determines the length of the night and the day (Q.73:20). The Qur'an repeatedly stresses the absolute power of God. The fate of all occurrences, good and bad, has been determined to the extent that all has been written in a primordial book even before creation (Q.57:22). "The keys of the unseen are with Him. No one knows them aside from Him, who knows what is on the land and in the sea, and no leaf falls without God knowing it, nor a single grain in the darkness of the earth, nothing verdant and nothing withered that is not in the clear book" (Q.6:59).

God is depicted in the Qur'an as even determining the personal actions of the individual. "God leads astray whom He wishes, and guides whom He wishes" (Q.74:31). Occasionally, however, the Qur'an understands God laying out the choices but allowing humanity to decide what to choose. "Say: 'The truth is from your Lord. Whoever wishes will believe, and whoever wishes will deny. We have prepared a fire for the deniers. . . . As for those who believe and do good works, We do not neglect the reward of anyone who does a good deed'" (Q.18:28–19). In one notable verse, both positions seem to be conflated: "This is the message: whoever wishes may take a path to his Lord. But you will not wish unless God wishes, for God is all-knowing, wise. He brings those whom He wishes into His mercy, and has prepared a painful doom for the wicked" (Q.76:29–31).

This seeming ambivalence or, at the very least, difficult and complex message invited a great deal of discussion among Muslim thinkers. During the 8th and 9th centuries, heated discussions ensued on the issue, and one group of avid proponents of free will became known as the Qadarites (*qadariyya*). They were opposed by those who believed that everything was predestined. Both positions could be supported by the Qur'an, but the predestinarian position eventually won out. Muslims today balance a certain level of individual freedom of choice with a heavy emphasis on God having determined the decisions of humanity.

CHAPTER 12

The Evolution of Formal Theology

Muslims developed a grand theological tradition that was deeply influenced by Greek philosophy and Christian theology, and which in turn profoundly influenced Jewish and later Christian thinking. The motivation for working out complex theological systems emerged from differences between various human perceptions of the meaning of God and His role in the universe. The differences arose not only by way of disputes between Muslims and other monotheists about the meaning of God in the broadest sense, but also by way of arguments among Muslims. In some cases of internal Muslim disputes, proponents of one view or another were able to convince leaders of state to support them, which ultimately resulted in inquisitions and even executions of those insisting on taking what became politically the wrong theological positions. The tide turned back and forth on sometimes subtle issues when one or another faction succeeded in convincing the caliph to enforce their own belief. Eventually compromises were reached and certain acceptable views were recognized. A historical synopsis of some of the main theological developments follows.

Kalām

Theology in Islam is often rendered as the word "*kalām*," which means "speech" or "discourse." *'Ilm al-kalām* is the "science of theology," though often it appears simply as *kalām*. Those engaged in this project are called *mutakallimūn*. As is often the case in the development of religious precepts, crises initiate the need to come to terms systematically with a significant issue. In the case of early Islam, the issue was whether or not a Muslim who had committed a grave sin remains a Muslim. If it were simply a case of anonymous individuals, the problem would not have become a crisis. But the individual in question happened to have been the caliph.

We recall that a faction that had supported Ali for the caliphate had broken off and fought against him. These were the Kharijites, who rebelled against Ali for agreeing to arbitration rather than submitting entirely to God's will by insisting on his position as caliph. Prior to their rebellion against Ali, they had opposed Ali's contender, Mu`āwiya, because Mu`āwiya had revolted against the authority of Ali as successor to the Prophet. According to the Kharijite position, a Muslim must be totally committed to observe God's will. There can be no compromise, so that a Muslim is a "true believer" only if he is thoroughly observant. If not, then that person is simply not a Muslim. When Mu`āwiya refused to acknowledge the properly selected caliph, he proved himself an infidel and apostate. But Ali too, because he agreed to arbitrate with Mu`āwiya over the caliphate, invalidated his own Muslim identity when he failed to insist decisively on his divine authority to rule. That act not only invalidated his candidacy as caliph but revealed that he too was an apostate (whether he agreed with that assessment or not). Both were thus renegades. According to the Kharijites, their respective sins rendered them illegitimate rulers, against whom jihad was a religious requirement (a position derived from Q.9:12).

Most Muslims did not take this view, of course. It was a dangerously destabilizing position, because virtually anyone could declare a leader to be an infidel or apostate, if he carried out a policy that might seem to them "un-Islamic." A counterposition was proffered by a group called the Murji'ites (*murji'a*, "those who defer" judgment). They taught that while a person may or may not appear to be a pious Muslim, only God can truly make that judgment. All Muslims must therefore take the default position of considering all other Muslims to be faithful believers. A final verdict awaits the final judgment. This theology allowed caliphs to rule even if they were not absolutely righteous individuals. It also brought a certain level of peace between Muslim factions and a tolerance toward those converts who might appear to be less than totally committed in their observance. The Murji'ite position came to dominate that of the Kharijites, but eventually it fell out of favor when Murji'ites extended the logic to claim that no Muslim would enter hell, since traditional Sunni belief (supported by the Qur'an) has it that some Muslims will enter hell temporarily, after which they will be purified and enter into heaven.

The Murji'ites validated Umayyad rule for Sunni Islam despite the general acknowledgment that the Umayyad caliphs were less than fully devout and pious. The Umayyads claimed, against the view of the Kharijites, that even if they sinned, they remained Muslims and ruled by divine decree. This claim raised the theological issue of determinism versus free will. Those who opposed the Umayyads claimed that human beings alone were responsible for their acts. Others held that the omniscient and omnipotent God predetermined all acts. We have seen that verses from the Qur'an may be cited in support of both positions. The battle between the two positions resulted eventually in an inquisition that endangered the unity of the empire. The chief advocates of the free will position was a group called the Mu`tazila.

The Mu`tazila

The Mu`tazila means "those who stand apart," and tradition has it that the name came from one Wāṣil ibn `Atā', who withdrew from studying with the famous early traditionist scholar Al-Ḥasan Al-Baṣrī (d.728 or 737) because of theological differences with the great master. Wāṣil and his followers began to develop views that employed rational Greek methods of thinking that countered the methodology and results of the traditionists, who relied only on the Qur'an and the sayings of Muhammad. This development eventuated in the complex theology of the Mu`tazila.

The Mu`tazila referred to themselves as the "people of (divine) justice and unity." They employed a Greek-inspired rational dialectic to formulate a theology that was meant to preserve both the just nature of God and the absolute unity of God, despite the tendency to break up the sense of God's unity based either on the problem of how God relates to evil, or on the problem of divine attributes as articulated in the Qur'an.

The Mu`tazila focused on five principles:

- The absolute unity of God
- The absolute justice of God (despite the existence of evil in the world)
- That God will not go back on his word, nor can he act contrary to his promise (this is in reference to the Day of Judgment and the threats and promises about that day as explicated in the Qur'an)
- An "intermediate position" between Kharijites and Murji`ites on the status of those who are not fully believers but not fully unbelievers or apostates
- "Commanding the good and forbidding evil," derived from Qur'an 3:110 (and many other verses), which is developed in some detail regarding the meaning of obligation, command, etc.

While all five principles raise interesting issues, the two that became of particular concern were the problematics of God's unity (#1) and God's justice (#2). In order to preserve God's unity (theologically speaking), the divine attributes articulated in the Qur'an, such as God having sight, hearing, knowledge, and power, could not be literal descriptions of God, because they would thus anthropomorphize the transcendent essence. Anthropomorphism is the application of human characteristics to God, which would make God into something like a human or an idol, thus leading to polytheism. Consequently, the qur'anic language must be taken metaphorically. Therefore, concrete terms referring to God are used in the Qur'an only to convey to humanity important messages about the deity. God is depicted as having hands because we are limited by the inadequacy of human language and concepts to understand God's power or beneficence otherwise. Similarly, the doctrine that the Qur'an was the actual speech or word of God cannot be taken literally. We know that the Qur'an is a separate entity. If it is the actual words of God, then it is a part of God, which would mean that both God and God's speech were eternal and uncreated. If two entities are eternal and uncreated, they would actually be two entities—two divinities, which is impossible. Therefore, although the Qur'an seems to refer to itself as preexisting (Q.13:39, 43:4), it was actually a *creation* of God, who is an uncreated being. This view was a minority position and opposed by many others.

The second major issue was that of God's justice and human free will. How could God judge people justly if people are not free to act as they will? If all human action were predetermined, how could people be punished by a just God? But insisting on the justice of God required limiting God (theologically), because then God would not be responsible for all acts such as acts of evil and injustice. God could command only that which is just and good, therefore limiting God's power. The logic required that God either be absolutely all-powerful but then also responsible for evil, or absolutely just but then not all-powerful. The Mu`tazila held that humanity bore responsibility for human injustice. Incidentally, this position countered the position of the Murji`a: that one could not judge the behavior of other Muslims. According to the Mu`tazila, since people are responsible for their acts, one could criticize the behavior of the caliphs. By the time the Mu`tazila developed their views, the controversial Umayyad caliphate had been overthrown by the Abbasids, whose ruling dynasty was considered more pious than that of the Umayyads.

By the 830s, the Mu`tazilite doctrine had the support of the caliph, Al-Ma'mūn (d.833). He instituted a test of judges and other high state officials concerning their view of whether the Qur'an was created or not. All Muslim thinkers agreed that the Qur'an is the direct and unadulterated speech of God, but they did not agree about whether it was created or preexistent. Those who rejected the Mu`tazilite doctrine of the createdness of the Qur'an were removed from office, and some were imprisoned or flogged. This was a kind of religious inquisition that lasted from 833 until 848. But the pendulum eventually swung the other way. Traditional thinkers reacted strongly to the Mu`tazilite doctrine because it seemed to restrict God's power, and traditional forces eventually gained the ear of the caliph. As a result, the teaching that the Qur'an had been created later became forbidden, and violations on this ban could result in imprisonment or even death.

The Ashariyya

Muslim theology was thus pulled in two seemingly irreconcilable directions. One side insisted in the unqualified absolute power of God, which raised the dual problem of God's justice and human free will. The other side insisted that God's actions follow from God's just and reasonable nature, making humans responsible for the nature of their actions but limiting the power of God. If the debate took place only in the academies, it would have centered among a group of rarified academics. However, it became a public debate that had managed to harness the power of the state, with dire consequences resulting for those holding the wrong position at the wrong time.

A solution had to be found, and it arrived through a new synthesis provided by a Mu`tazilite thinker named Abūl-Ḥasan `Alī al-Ash`arī (d.935). Al-Ash`ari broke with the Mu`tazila over what he considered to be the Mu`tazilite overemphasis on human reason and human concepts of justice in explaining the nature of God. To al-Ash`ari, the extraordinary and unfathomable essence and character of God easily transcend all human categories of thought and experience. Human reason is simply unable to explain the problematic of divine justice. This is an ignorance-based (not "ignorant") view that assumes human reason is incapable of discerning the morality of God. Humanity has free will, but God nevertheless knows all things. Humanity can act and think independently, but nevertheless does not create.

One of the particularly interesting aspects of al-Ash`ari's system is that he employs the methods of Greek thinking in order to subvert the rationalists' conclusions. This was an approach that was shared by later Muslims and their Jewish counterparts, such as Muhammad al-Ghazzālī (d.111) and Yehudah ha-Levi (d.1141). In order to preserve human free will along with the absolute omnipotence of God, for example, al-Ash`ari established, by way of the Qur'an, a doctrine of "acquisition." According to this thinking, all acts are created and produced by God. They then attach themselves to the will of humans who thus "acquire" them. Because humans have a consciousness through which they own their own acts, they must act responsibly; yet that very consciousness is created by God. Al-Ash`ari also resolved other problems, such as the unity of God in light of the divine attributes, the question of reward and punishment, and the question of divine speech. Although not all thinkers agreed with his positions, he and his followers developed a school of thought called *al-ash'ariyya* (or sometimes *al-ashā'ira*) that became extremely influential. New schools of theology continued to develop, however, in response to developments in thinking, interaction with other religions and cultures, and changes in science. This process has never ceased and continues into the present.

Philosophy

Wherever the Arabs conquered, they acquired the learning and science of the peoples and civilizations that came under their political control. When they conquered the Greek-speaking areas of the Byzantine Empire, entire libraries of knowledge came under their control along with the communities of thinkers that were associated with them. A movement soon emerged to translate the classical Greek texts of these great libraries into Arabic, and these included texts of science, medicine, and philosophy. The Muslims were thus introduced to Plato, Aristotle, Plotinus, and the Stoics, along with many commentaries and responses to the systems that the philosophers developed. The Muslims then advanced their own responses to these in a complex and extraordinarily rich literature that influenced the development of philosophical thinking also among Christians and Jews into the modern age. This discipline is called *falsafa* in Arabic.

There is clear overlap between the project of the philosophers and the project of the theologians mentioned above. Both were *mutakallimūn*, meaning that both groups engaged the same general world of thought. Both groups engaged in rational methodologies to arrive at an understanding of the universe. Both intended to harmonize philosophical thinking with the received tradition found in the Qur'an and the traditions of the Prophet (*Hadith*). In short, the Muslim theologians and philosophers engaged in a parallel program to harmonize *reason* with *revelation*. And some of the great names who engaged in this project are referred to sometimes as theologians, sometimes as philosophers. Even the most philosophical, such as Ibn Rushd (Averroes) or his Jewish counterpart, Maimonides, wrote tracts treating religious law that presume the absolute truth of the divine word. The major difference between pure philosophy and theology lies in the extent to which the thinker is willing to go to follow the possible outcome of an argument.

According to the purist forms of philosophy, one must accept the possibility of truth from any source and follow the argument wherever it leads. Religious believers, on the other hand, have a set of religious principles that they hold to be unchallengeable. Muslim, Christian, and Jewish philosophers agreed that there are certain religious principles that are absolutely true, the most basic of which is divine revelation. Their major challenge was to understand the particular claims set out by revelation in rational terms. Some thinkers claimed that this is impossible, meaning that one cannot be both a pure philosopher and believer in a revealed religion. That is, one cannot be both a Muslim (or Jew or Christian) *and* a philosopher. But others think that such a synthesis is possible. We have observed that Muslim theologians used philosophical arguments to prove that a dogma is true. But another way of operating is to test religious principles through independent philosophical analysis before accepting them as true. Yet a third, rarer, and more difficult approach is to systematically apply philosophical analysis to religion as a system.

Some of the most common and troubling questions about religion that were subjected to philosophical analysis are the following:

- What is the nature of God? How do we know that God exists?
- What is the nature of revelation? How do we know that God reveals the divine will to humankind?
- What is the nature of divinely guided messengers in relation to philosophers?
- What is the nature of human leadership on earth?
- Which of our individual religious traditions must be interpreted literally?
- Which of our individual religious traditions must be interpreted metaphorically or allegorically?
- What must one actually believe to be considered a true adherent of our religion?
- How can one reconcile the findings of philosophy and science with religion?

Some of the great Muslim thinkers who worked on these issues include Abū Yūsuf al-Kindī (d.873), Abū Naṣr Muhammad al-Farābī (d.950), Abū `Alī Al-Ḥussayn ibn Sīnā (Avicenna, d.1037), and Abūl-Walīd Muhammad ibn Rushd (Averroes, d.1198); some of their Jewish counterparts include Sa`īd ibn Yūsuf al-Fayyūmī (Saadiah Gaon, d.942), Yehudah ha-Levi (d.1141), Abū `Imrān Mūsā Ibn Maymūn (Maimonides, d.1204), and Levi Ben Gershom (Gersonides, d. 1344). All the Jewish philosophical works written by these thinkers, aside from Gersonides who lived in Southern France, were written in Arabic, and all were profoundly influenced by the Arab philosophical tradition.

Despite the genius of their thinking, the works of the great philosophers had little real impact on religious thought, which was dominated in the Muslim world by the theologians. In premodern Muslim and Jewish circles and in religious circles to this day it is the great philosophers' *other* writings on religious law that have had lasting impact. Ironically, perhaps, their major influence has been on the development of Western philosophy. They transmitted Greek philosophy through their translations and commentaries to medieval Europe, where it influenced the curricula of its universities.

To point out a fascinating example of this irony, for many centuries European scholastics and philosophers attributed a famous Latin philosophical work called the *Fonz Vitae*, the "Fountain of Life," to a Christian philosopher known as Avicebron. But in the middle of the 19th century, a Jewish scholar named Solomon Munk discovered a Hebrew manuscript in the Bibliothèque Nationale in Paris that was the same as the Latin *Fonz Vitae*. The Hebrew proved to be a collection of excerpts from an Arabic original written by the Jewish poet and scholar Abū Ayyūb Sulaymān ibn Jabrī'ūl (Solomon ibn Gabirol, d.1058) that had been translated first into Hebrew, then into Latin. Perhaps the most ironic aspect of this discovery was that the text itself was so thoroughly philosophical that it had no particular religious aspects of Judaism that would have identified it as a "non-Christian" philosophical work. At the peak of the philosophical project, Jews, Christians, and Muslims were working on the same issues and could read and share each other's works fully.

CHAPTER 13

The Qur'an

To Muslims, the Qur'an is the literal and inimitable word of God. The voice of the Qur'an is that of God, not Muhammad, who was only a prophet and messenger of God and whose major role was only to convey the divine word of God to the people. Muhammad's recitations of the Qur'an in the public square were therefore nothing less than the precise and literal recital of the divine word that was revealed to him. He was not a messiah and had no supernatural power of his own. The Qur'an is the product of God and God alone. The "omniscient narrator" of the Qur'an, therefore, *is* God, and God is often referred to in the plural, the "majestic form," *We*. Such phrases as the following are quite common: Thus do We reward the righteous . . . , So when Our commandment came to pass . . . , We revealed to Moses . . . , and so on.

As noted earlier, "Qur'an" literally means "recitation." The Hebrew parallel that Jews apply to their own scripture is *Miqra'*, "a thing that is read or recited," from the Hebrew root *q-r-'*, "to read." In the ancient world, very few specialized individuals were trained to read, so reading was almost by necessity an oral act, a means of communicating information through recitation of the inscribed words, like the proverbial town crier who would recite or call out a written message so that the community would receive it. The Hebrew root therefore also means "to cry out, call, invite, proclaim" as well as to read.

The Qur'an came into history many centuries after the Torah, and its appearance reflects the changes in writing technology of the time. Rather than appearing in the form of scrolls, as in the case of the Torah, the Qur'an appears in the form of a codex. "Codex" refers to the specific "book-form" that we associate with books today: a central binding and pages laid out flat. The physical book-form of the Qur'an is usually called *muṣḥaf* in Arabic. Other terms for divine scripture found in the Qur'an itself are "the writing" (*al-kitāb*), "what has been sent down" (*al-tanzīl*), the guidance (*al-hudā*), and "the criterion" (*al-furqān*) for dividing between truth and falsehood, though it probably derives from the Aramaic word for redemption because of its redemptive nature.[1] The most common term used today and printed on most Arabic texts of the Qur'an is "The Noble Qur'an" (*al-qur'ān al-karīm*).

According to Muslim consensus, only the Arabic language text qualifies to be called the Qur'an. A translation of the Qur'an is therefore not the same as the Arabic-language Qur'an. The process of translation requires that the translator choose among a variety of words and styles of prose to convey meaning from one language to another. Even the most literal translations require that translators decide how to convey what they think is the meaning, and that process is inevitably interpretive. Technically speaking, therefore, translations of the Qur'an are interpretations, and are therefore not considered the true al-Qur'ān al-Karīm.

Each of the three great monotheistic scriptures is revealed in its own unique manner. The core of the Hebrew Bible is the Torah, which was revealed in one grand revelation before the Israelites at Mount Sinai. The core of the New Testament is revealed through the personification of God in the person of Jesus, whose very speech was divine revelation and recorded in the Gospels. The Qur'an was revealed in serial form by God to Muhammad through the archangel Gabriel, who served as an intermediary between the perfection of the divinity and the imperfect reality that is the created flesh and blood of humanity, including the humanity Muhammad.

The Qur'an, therefore, reflects the history of the mission of Muhammad from the moment he received his first revelation at the age of 40 to the last revelation shortly before his death at 62. Despite its serial nature, however, it is not organized chronologically and has extremely few references to historical or geographical context.

Meccan and Medinan Revelations

As noted in Part 1, universally accepted Islamic tradition understands that Muhammad received his first revelation while he was meditating in a shady spot on Mount Hira, a short walk from the urban area of Mecca. There is some disagreement regarding which of two chapters was the first to be sent down to Muhammad (96 or 74), but both are written in the same semi-poetic and exhortatory style known as *saj`* that is considered typical of the early revelations. This style is associated with Muhammad's period in Mecca, and the chapters that Muslims believe reflect this period are called the "Meccan chapters."

The Meccan material is rhetorically powerful and often refers to an impending day of judgment that is near at hand. It reflects an urgent "fire and brimstone" style of preaching and moralizing that drives in the message of ethical monotheism, and it references the fate of doomed peoples and communities that refused to listen to their prophets (e.g., Q.7:59–99, 11:25–95). The poetic prose of this material is audially as well as literarily powerful and appealing. Typical to these sections is an assonance or actual rhyme that does not depend on a particular meter, though one can often note a kind of rhythm in the versification.

It is impossible to convey the power of this Arabic style in English. Nevertheless, one well-known attempt by Arthur Jeffrey, the great English scholar of the Qur'an, is reproduced here.

> I swear by the splendour of the light
> And by the silence of the night
> That the Lord shall never forsake you
> Nor in his hatred take you;
> Truly, for you shall be winning,
> Better than all beginning.
> Soon shall the lord console you, grief no longer overwhelm you
> And fear no longer cajole you.
> You were an orphan boy, yet the Lord found room for your head
> When your feet went astray, were they not to the right path led?
> Did he not find you poor, yet riches around you spread?
> Then on the orphan boy, let your proud foot never tread
> And never turn away the beggar who asks for bread.
> But of your Lord's bounty, ever let praises be sung and said. (Q.93)[2]

This style of exhortation and the citation of various occasions for divine reward and punishment seems congruent with the mission of a prophet engaging a doubtful community. And it is typical of Muhammad's period in Mecca as portrayed in the sources. Muhammad would virtually stand up on the proverbial soapbox at the city center and call the people to abandon their errant ways, leave their idolatrous and unethical practices, and devote themselves to the One Great God who is merciful to the upright believers and unrelenting to the wicked idolaters. After moving to Medina, however, the context changed radically, and so did the style and content of the revelations.

In Medina, Muhammad encountered a divided community that nevertheless agreed as a whole and in principle to accept his leadership and guidance. The tone in the chapters ascribed to this period is far less exhortative than the Meccan material, the rhymed prose less prominent, and the style more legalistic, concentrating more on prescribing social duties and norms of behavior than on proving the imminence of divine judgment. A typical example of a "Medinan chapter" is chapter 4, known as "The Women." The first 10 verses are cited here.

> [1]O humankind! Revere your Lord, who created you from a single soul, and created its mate from it, and disseminated many men and women from the two. Revere God through whom you beseech one another and of relations, for God is watching you. [2]Give orphans their property. Do not exchange the bad for the good and do not absorb their wealth into your own, for that is great sin. [3]If you fear that you will not be just to the orphans, then marry the women who seem good to you, two, three or four. But if you fear that you will not be equitable, then one, or someone whom you possess, for that is best so you will not go wrong. [4]Give the women their dowries as their own, but if they bestow some of it upon you personally, then enjoy it in good health. [5]Do not give to the feeble-minded your property that God has made to sustain you, but provide for them with it, clothe them, and speak to them kindly. [6]Test orphans until they reach marriageable age. If you know that they are reasonable, then pay over to them their property and do not consume it excessively or in haste before they reach their majority. The rich should abstain, while the poor may use it fairly. Then, when you turn their property over to them, have it witnessed for them, for God is sufficient in accounting. [7]Men may have a portion of what parents and close relatives leave behind, and women may have a portion of what parents and close relatives leave behind, whether little or great, an assigned portion. [8]And if relatives or orphans and the needy are present for the division, then provide for them from it and speak to them kindly. [9]And let those be anxious who, if they left behind helpless children, they would fear for them. Let them fear God and speak kindly. [10]Those who consume the property of orphans unjustly only consume fire in their bellies. They will be exposed to a blaze.

These verses are interesting for a number of reasons, not the least being their concern for fairness and the clear sensitivity they exhibit toward providing for the needy of the community. These verses provide the basis for the ruling that Muslim men may take more than a single wife, rationalized as it is in a section that treats the needs of orphans. It has been explained that in a strongly patriarchal and warlike society such as pre-Islamic Arabia, the male population tended to be reduced numerically because of war, thereby causing girls and young women to become vulnerable in two ways. When male heads of household die, their female children become at risk, because their ability to produce a dowry (or trousseau) when they enter marriage is drastically reduced. In addition, the reduction of the number of males in general leaves women at risk of remaining unmarried and therefore vulnerable in a harsh physical environment dominated by patriarchy. Note from verse 3 that in the case of multiple wives, they must be treated equally, and if that is impossible, only one wife may be taken.

This system may be compared with the traditional Jewish polygamous marriage system that was based on the observation that biblical patriarchs had multiple wives. As the stories of the patriarchs clearly convey, polygamy is a system that is rife with tensions and difficulties. Note also that in the biblical system, no limit in the number of wives is imposed. The rule of monogamy in contemporary Judaism was based on a *takkanah* or legal ruling that was formulated by the authority of rabbis and not through the authority of the text of the Torah. It was the 10th-century rabbi Gershom ben Yehudah of Mainz (in today's Germany) who determined, most likely under pressure exerted by Christian leaders in his region, that the Ashkenazic Jewish community would be forbidden from engaging in polygamy for 1,000 years. The term of the decision passed, according to many authorities, in 2004, but has remained effectively in force.

A second item of interest for comparison with Judaism is the issue of female inheritance. Note here that the text of the Qur'an requires that women inherit just as men, and the language in the verse is equal. In contrast, the Torah does not require that women inherit, as the case of the daughters of Zelophehad so poignantly conveys in the book of Numbers, chapter 27. In the following verse of our section (Q.4:11), the text requires that women inherit only half the amount of men: "God directs you regarding your children: to the male belongs the equivalent portion of two females. But if there are more than two daughters, to them belong two thirds of what one leaves." Nevertheless, the fact that women inherit at all would appear to be a progressive position in relation to the position of the Hebrew Bible.

The "Medinan chapters" include a number of categories of instruction ranging from cultural norms (dietary laws, family law, health and purity laws) to religious norms (ritual requirements and prohibitions, theological expectations), civil law (property and damages, taxes, weights and measures, lending) and criminal law (assault in various forms, punishments) to ethical instruction. These are more akin to the instruction that is found in the Torah than in Western legal systems, and the types of rules that are enumerated do not fall within the usual categories that have evolved in the West. It is therefore easier to compare them with biblical law than with Western norms. One apt verse that demonstrates these observations may be found in the following:

> Righteousness is not turning your faces to the east and the west. Rather, the righteous are those who believe in God and the last day, the angels and scripture and prophets, who out of love for God give resources to relatives, orphans, the poor, travelers, those who are in need, and for the sake of [freeing] slaves; who pray regularly and give alms, who fulfill their promise when they make one; and those who are patient in misfortune, affliction, and bad times. These are the ones who confirm the truth, who are truly pious. (Q.2:177)

A sophisticated legal system soon emerged in Islam that carefully systematized and fleshed out many nuances that are imbedded in such complex verses. As will be observed below, it based its authority on the foundation of the Qur'an quite in parallel to the sophisticated legal system in Judaism, which is based on the Torah.

The Organization of the Qur'an

It is not at all clear what organizing principles may have been operative in the actual layout of the Qur'an. According to Islamic sources, the Qur'an was not officially collected until some 20 years after Muhammad's death, and the thousands of parts that were remembered or recorded by listeners to Muhammad's recitations seem not to have been kept in any particular order until the official redaction of the Qur'an occurred.

To the uninitiated reader, the Qur'an may appear to be a jumble of chapters and verses. We have observed earlier how the story of the Garden of Eden is told or referred to in the Qur'an seven times in seven different and widely separated chapters. There is no obvious topical or chronological order, no discursive structure, and no systematic separation of narrative sections from poetic sections or legal sections as there is in the Hebrew Bible and the New Testament. In fact, it is quite possible that this particular nature of the Qur'an was intentional, perhaps to make a statement about the unique nature of this revelation.

The basic themes of the Qur'an are repeated in various ways in different parts of the book, usually with slight variations or nuances in their renderings. To non-Muslims this may feel repetitive and disorganized. It may seem like a weakness or blemish that makes it appear as if it could not be a sublime text. To Muslims, however, the artistry of its articulation lies in its repeated themes coupled with unceasing linguistic and creatively nuanced variation. As Frederick Denny has pointed out, "The Qur'an is entirely self-consistent and harmonious on the level of its basic teachings, but it is discontinuous and unlike other writings, especially the Bible, which it only faintly and superficially resembles at points. This is another dimension of [its sublime nature]."[3]

The Qur'an is nevertheless divided into chapters and verses, and the chapters are designated by name or title, and by a number. Muslims know the chapters by their names, which do not relate to the subject matter as a whole but, rather, often to a single word within it that has come informally to typify the chapter as a whole. The first chapter is known as the "Opening" (*al-fātiḥa* // Hebrew: *ha-petiḥah*), and is a short prayer used frequently and in most prayer services. Some chapters are known by more than one name, such as chapter 9, which is usually called "Repentance" (*al-tawba* // Heb. *ha-teshuvah*) for a typical qur'anic theme that is relatively common there. But chapter 9 is also known as "Disavowal" or "Renunciation" after the first word that occurs in it. Similarly, chapter 17 is usually called "The Night Journey" because it opens with a verse that is understood by Islamic tradition to reference Muhammad's night journey from Mecca to Jerusalem. But it is also known as "the Children of Israel" (*banū isrā'īl*) because of reference to the Children of Israel in the following few verses. After the opening chapter, the chapters are said to decrease in length from the longest (chapter 2), with 286 verses, to the shortest (chapter 114), with 6.

A chapter is called a *sūra*, and the term for "verse" is *āya*, which also means "sign," "mark," or even "miracle." Whereas the entire Torah is recited publicly each year in the synagogue by reading one section every week, the entire Qur'an is to be read privately by Muslims each year during the month of Ramadan by reading one section every day (based on Q.17:105–106). The Qur'an therefore has an additional division into 30 parts for the Ramadan recitation. The size of the Qur'an is roughly equivalent to that of the Torah (the first five books of the Hebrew Bible) or the New Testament.

Each chapter of the Qur'an is designated "Meccan" or "Medinan," but not every single verse within these chapters fits its chapter designation; some verses in Medinan chapters are considered to be Meccan and vice versa. Muslim scholars have always known that, aside from the shortest, the chapters are composite and made of smaller segments of material that were edited together. It is clear that some of these segments were intentionally placed in proximity, such as the material that treats warring in chapter 8 ("Spoils of War"), though other important verses about war are found in other chapters such as chapter 2 ("The Cow") and chapter 9 ("Repentance"). So too, can one find many segments treating pre-Islamic prophets in such chapters as chapter 21 ("The Prophets"), but they may be found in dozens of other chapters as well, including some with relevant names such as "Jonah" (chapter 10), "Hūd" (chapter 11), "Joseph" (chapter 12), "Abraham" (chapter 14), and "Mary" (chapter 19). In order to learn what the Qur'an has to convey about any single topic or narrative, therefore, one must turn to a concordance or index in order to find the relevant material that may be spread across a number of chapters. It is difficult for the uninitiated to simply pick up a Qur'an and begin reading. The nature of the text is such that it must be studied.

The Problem of Apparent Contradiction

Because of the difficulty in making sense of the complicated and sometimes obscure qur'anic Arabic, the lack of comprehensible organization of the Qur'an, the appearance of categories of material in widely separated contexts, and the occasional repetition or near repetition of phrases, verses, and ideas, early Muslim readers of the Qur'an began to express an interest in systematizing the revelations in a way that would not interfere with the physical arrangement of the verses in the canonized version. Another motivation for finding a way to organize the revelations was the observation that some verses seemed to contradict others. Given the assumption of God's omniscience and ethical nature, actual contradiction was considered impossible because God would never contradict himself, forget what had been revealed previously, or confuse people by providing conflicting revelations. The task of the interpreters was to find a way to explain the apparent contradictions, for there could be no actual contradictions in real divine scripture.

There developed various approaches that utilized methodologies ranging from grammatical analysis to attempts to discover a chronology of revelation that might explain why God revealed what sometimes appear to be different messages to the believers. Grammarians studied the language of Arabic in great detail and applied their knowledge to the meaning of the qur'anic verses. Historians attempted to correlate the revelations to the history of Muhammad's prophetic career by analyzing contextual data in the Qur'an and matching it up with knowledge about Muhammad's life.

The method of the grammarians expanded the knowledge of Arabic tremendously. Jews living in the Muslim world observed this interest and were influenced by the growing and exciting intellectual climate. Some scholars of the Hebrew Bible noticed many similarities between Arabic and Hebrew, and they applied grammatical developments in Arabic to their study of Hebrew, thereby opening up a great range of technical approaches to the study of the Hebrew Scriptures. The most famous medieval biblical commentator to synthesize the learning of generations of Arabic and Hebrew grammarians was Abraham ibn Ezra, whose extremely sophisticated education derived from an environment highly influenced by what is called the religious sciences, developed by generations of Muslim scholars.

The method of the Muslim historians was to contextualize the revelations according to the history of Muhammad's prophetic career. This was done by developing a genre of Qur'an analysis called "Occasions of Revelation." Because every revelation occurred at some point during the last 23 years of Muhammad's life, the goal was to match up the verses with actual occasions. If they knew what might have caused a specific revelation, they would better understand its meaning and significance. Some revelations were easy to contextualize because they contained information that appeared obvious to the readers. One example of this is Q.3:123, which actually references a particular event in the history of the early community: "God made you victorious at [the Battle of] Badr when you were lowly, so be pious to God and be thankful."

Most parts of the Qur'an, however, had little obvious contextualizing information that could locate them unambiguously within the biography of Muhammad, so the interpreters were required to find hints of information with which they could place them. They also needed to have a coherent biography of the Prophet upon which they would attach the revelations. This was being developed by some scholars out of the oral tradition about the deeds and sayings of Muhammad that was passed down through the generations. Once a system was developed to organize the revelations chronologically and according to an accepted history, interpreters were able to discern patterns through which they arrived at certain principles of relationship between repeated verses or verses that seem to be contradictory.

Some observed that in many cases of apparent contradiction, earlier verses seemed to have been revealed to Muhammad to treat specific and immediate issues that needed to be resolved for the good of the community. These were "verses of the hour" that were brought down in order to solve specific problems rather than to serve as universal and eternal statements. Later verses, however, tended to be more universal in nature. It was assumed, therefore, that later verses on any given topic were expected to abrogate earlier verses. This solved the problem of apparent contradiction, because God intended the earlier verses to apply only to specific, narrow situations, while the later verses would apply universally.

A classic example of this is the case of the many verses in the Qur'an that deal with the ongoing conflict with those who were antagonistic to the Believers. Some verses treated the tension and conflict by advising Muhammad to avoid conflict altogether, even with obvious idolaters. "Profess openly what you have been commanded, and turn away from the idolaters, for We are sufficient for you against the scoffers" (Q.15:94). Others advocate absolute and ruthless war against the idolaters: "When the sacred months have passed, kill the idolaters wherever you find them, and seize them, beset them, watch for them everywhere; if they repent and establish the prayers and pay alms, then let them go their way, for God is forgiving, compassionate" (Q.9:5).

The apparent discrepancy was resolved by assuming that the verses that urged avoiding conflict or solving conflict through quietist means were formulated earlier and were therefore temporary. God commanded patience and forbearance when Muhammad and the young community were weak and unable even to defend themselves. Later, as the community grew in numbers and strength, they were commanded to defend themselves but not to initiate physical violence against their enemies. "Those who are fought are given license because they have been oppressed, and God is powerful in their aid, those unjustly expelled from their homes simply because they say, 'Our Lord is God'" (Q.22:39–40). "Fight in the path of God those who fight you, but do not transgress limits, for God does not love transgressors" (Q.2:190). As they grew stronger the Believers were allowed to initiate hostilities, but with certain limits. "They ask you about fighting in the Sacred Month. Say: Fighting therein is a grave [offense], but far worse to God is blocking the way from the path of God, denying Him, and expelling His people from the Sacred Mosque. Religious persecution (*fitna*) is worse than killing. They will not stop fighting you until they turn you away from your religion, if they can" (Q.2:217). Finally, when the community was able, God commanded absolute dominion over non-Muslims. Idolaters were to be killed, but People of the Book were allowed to live as long as they paid a special tax and submitted to second-class status in the Muslim world. "Kill the idolaters wherever you find them, and seize them, beset them, watch for them everywhere; if they repent and establish the prayers and pay alms, then let them go their way, for God is forgiving, compassionate" (Q.9:5). "Fight those given scripture who do not believe in God and the last day, who do not forbid what God and His messenger have forbidden, and who do not profess the religion of truth, until they pay tribute willingly and are humbled (or humiliated)" (Q.9:29).

This schema solves the problem of abrogation, but it does so at the expense of historical consistency. The problem is that it assumes a general consensus regarding the contexts in which the various verses examined here were revealed. However, if one reads the many attempts to contextualize these verses by the earliest generations of Qur'an scholars whose "Occasions of Revelation" works survive, one finds that there is wide disagreement over when and under what conditions they were revealed. Many actually cancel each other out.[4] What the Qur'an reveals in this case may actually be something quite different.

After the Conquests, when the Arabs had conquered huge territories and taken many peoples under their control, they were confronted with the age-old problem of how to legitimize their rule over others. The Qur'an, revealed before the Conquests had even begun, has little to say about controlling land or people beyond the vicinity of Mecca and Medina. But the interpreters who developed the schema outlined above understood it to represent divine authorization for empire. This is an "imperialist" interpretation, and like most scriptural interpretation, it is strongly influenced by historical (and cultural, economic, political, and religious) context.

What the wide variety of verses treating conflict resolution most likely represents is different opinions about fighting within the early community of Believers. Some Believers were probably quietist, perhaps even pacifist. Others believed that they had the right and the responsibility to defend themselves against their accusers and their attackers but no more. Still others believed that if they had the means, they had the license to attack their enemies and to dominate them. The success of the Conquest suggests that the more militant factions won the day, and the winners, as is common knowledge, write history. On the other hand, all the other positions regarding conflict resolution remain within the framework of divine scripture, because scripture can never be erased. But it can be "managed" by interpreters who compete with one another for influence. Nevertheless, when the historical context is appropriate, other verses might speak to interpreters and opinion makers, and those verses that were considered abrogated might reappear as valid exemplars of the divine will.

We observe the same phenomenon in Judaism. The militant warrior verses of the Bible were influential during periods when Israelites and Jews believed they could defeat their enemies, and they provided inspiration and motivation for warring. After the catastrophes resulting from the Jewish rebellions against the Roman Empire during which tens or hundreds of thousands of Jews were killed, the rabbis of the Talmud found that the militant verses no longer spoke to them. In this case, Rabbinic interpreters managed the situation by developing interpretive techniques that would remove the option of engaging in war from the real-time repertoire of Judaism. But because the verses always remain a part of scripture and can never be deleted from the corpus of holy writ, they are always potentially available to be reinterpreted.[5]

The Qur'an in Relation to Other Scriptures

The Qur'an contains a great deal of material that is parallel to the scriptures of Judaism and Christianity. The most obvious is the appearance of many biblical characters from Adam and Eve (though she is not named in the Qur'an) to Noah, Abraham, Isaac, Ishmael, Jacob, Joseph and the tribes, Moses, Aaron, Miriam, Saul, David, Solomon, Jonah, Elijah, Job, John the Baptist, Zakariah, Mary, and Jesus. Many narratives known from prior scriptures are referenced or related in the Qur'an, but in forms that clearly differ from earlier narrations, and some material may be found in the Qur'an that finds direct parallels with the Rabbinic literature of the Talmud and Midrash (Q.2:93, 5:27–32).

The natural reaction among Jews and Christians to the differences in the new revelation was to believe that it was an inaccurate or poor attempt to mimic their own "true" revelation. We have examined this natural response earlier in the context of Muhammad's confrontation with the Jews of Medina, and we have noted how the Qur'an itself explains the differences by accusing the People of the Book of being untrustworthy regarding scripture and of even distorting their own. That episode was only one example of the conflict and competition between scriptures. The Qur'an records some of the arguments that were made against it, such as the critique that it was not revealed all at once as was the Torah (Q.25:32), or that it is only the ravings of a man possessed (Q.16:6). Five times, God is depicted in the Qur'an as commanding Muhammad to challenge his detractors to produce verses or chapters equal to those of the Qur'an. "If you are in doubt about what We have brought down to Our servant, then bring a verse like it, and call on your mortal witnesses if you are truthful. But if you do not—and you will not—then get ready for the fire whose fuel is humans and stones, some who will not believe" (Q.2:23–24).[6]

These verses, known in later Islamic tradition as the "challenge verses," were taken a century or so later as proofs that the Qur'an is matchless and inimitable. The absolutely perfect, miraculous nature of the Qur'an thus emerged as a religious dogma in Islam in response to challenges to its authority and authenticity. Today, and for well over 1,000 years, the perfect nature of the Qur'an is a sine qua non of Islamic belief. Its miraculous nature applies not only to its unsurpassed language and style, but also to its perceived truth in every detail.

Because of the arguments over the accuracy and general status of the Qur'an between the early Muslims and adherents of previous religions, it was necessary to understand its historical and theoretical relationship with the earlier revelations of Jews and Christians. A theory of universal revelation emerged already in the Qur'an that made sense of the similarities and differences, but it was elaborated considerably in post-qur'anic literatures. The basic position is that God, in God's great love and compassion, sent prophets with instruction and revelation to all human communities (not only Jews and Christians) throughout history (Q.2:136, 21:25, 43:2–8). All divine revelation originates in the "Mother of Books" (*umm al-kitāb*—Q.13:39, 43:4) that is found on the "preserved tablet" (Q.85:21–22), which is, in turn, located in heaven at the divine throne. Although there may be differences in the details, there is no difference in the essential moral message of the revelations (Q.3:3, 26:192–197).

This theory of universal revelation allows for an open attitude toward previous scriptures. Every prior scripture originates with God. The Qur'an emphasizes that the scripture revealed to the Arabs is in clear Arabic language (Q.12:2, 26:192–197, 39:28), which presumes that the scriptures revealed to other peoples were given in different languages. Later thinkers understood that the differences were not only linguistic, but were also cultural, thus making sense of the obvious parallels and no less obvious differences.

As explained in our earlier discussion of the natural tensions that arise between newly emerging religions and establishment religions, such a position makes sense for a new religion that is trying to gain a foothold in a world dominated by well-established religions. It says, in essence, "We are as legitimate as you are!" Established religions, however, are not interested in welcoming communities that would threaten their position. Jews and Christians believed that any new claims of divine revelation must be false. They therefore rejected any such new claims.

The natural reaction of those who believe in the new revelations is to be suspicious of the criticisms of those representing establishment positions. The new prophet is only acting like the biblical prophets when he responds to God's command to go out and preach to the community. Why not welcome another prophet who is only confirming the monotheism that they already practice? The reason for not admitting the new prophet may be that those representing the establishment religions are arrogant or are jealous and care only for themselves. They are rebelling against God's will by refusing to heed the message of a true prophet. The Qur'an therefore condemns the positions of the People of the Book and accuses them of going so far as to distort their own revelation in order to defame the new prophet. "Woe to those who write Scripture with their own hands and then say it is from God in order to make some profit from it. Woe to them for what their hands have written, and woe to them for what they earn" (Q.2:79). "When a messenger of God comes to them affirming what they have, some of those who were given Scripture throw the Book of God behind their backs as if they do not know" (Q.2:101). "O People of Scripture! Why do you deny the revelations [or signs] of God even as you witness?" (Q.3:70).

The problem of working out the relationship between the Qur'an and prior monotheistic scriptures was never resolved. After the success of the Conquests, Jews largely dropped out of the polemical arena, but Christians, under the protection and competition of the Byzantine Empire and later, Christian Europe, continued to challenge the authenticity of qur'anic revelation. Scriptural differences became symbolic of larger issues when most of the known world was divided between the Christian Byzantine Empire and Europe, on the one hand, and the caliphate and the Muslim world, on the other. The contest for prestige and the political and economic competition between the two worlds were often articulated through religious terminology and polemic, and the polemical literatures in both communities made a deep and lasting impact. The current tensions and antagonism between "the

West" and the Muslim World is not new, of course. Part of the difficulty in overcoming it results from the deep-seated prejudices on both sides, perpetuated in the polemical literatures for many centuries.

However, the complex relationship between the Qur'an and the Bible was not always articulated through heated polemics. Muslim, Jewish, and Christian scholars were also intrigued by the many similarities in form, content, and style, and this has stimulated much thinking and writing among both Muslims and non-Muslims from medieval times to the present. Today dozens of comparative studies of the Qur'an and the Bible are available in libraries and for purchase, and scholars continue to study the fascinating relationship between them.

But even conscientious contemporary scholars tend to retain a basic religious or cultural affiliation with their own scriptural tradition, and this maintains a certain low-level tension that continues to feed old arguments between the faiths. Jewish and Christian scholars tend to assume that the Qur'an represents a significant "borrowing" of data and style from preexisting literatures. Muslim scholars are inclined to view the differences as errors and attrition among the older scriptures that have been associated with the copying and passing down of ancient texts.

It is not really necessary to bridge the divide. The Qur'an and the Bible are different texts and they represent different revelations. They employ distinct languages and styles to convey similar but somewhat different messages. Both secular and religious scholars would do well to remain modest in response to the tremendous depth and complexity of relationship. It is likely that no solution to the issue will ever be suggested that will satisfy all the parties. As the Qur'an itself articulates: "We have appointed a divine law and custom. If God had wished, He would have made you all one nation but [the intent is] to test you by what He has given you. So compete together in doing good works! You will all return to God and He will then inform you of how you differ" (Q.5:48).

CHAPTER 14

The Interpretive Tradition

The Qur'an proclaims repeatedly that it is clear and understandable: "These are the verses of the Book and a comprehensible recitation" (Q.15:1); "This is clear Arabic language" (Q.16:103); ". . . this is a reminder and a clear recitation" (Q.36:69).[1] But anyone who reads the Qur'an, including native Arabic speakers, knows that it is an extremely complex and difficult text. Many words are obscure, the syntax of many verses complex, and allusions ambiguous and difficult to understand. I have noted earlier that nearly complete lack of contextualization of chapter and verse adds greatly to the difficulty in understanding.

Given the fact that Islam is a scriptural religion basing its entire authority on the will of God, and that the only direct conduit to the divinity is through the record of God's communication to humanity through Muhammad, the importance of making sense of the Qur'an became critical. The Qur'an was the ultimate source for the resolution of disagreements over any issue associated in any way with Islam. It is true that secondary sources of authority emerged as well, such as the *Hadith*, the recorded sayings and acts of God's last prophet Muhammad. But the accuracy of many of these was called into question, and they could in any case be trumped by citing a text from the Qur'an itself. The Qur'an, therefore, is the ultimate and most important authority for all aspects of Islamic practice and theology. Because it is such a difficult text, making sense of it through interpretation became an extremely important endeavor.

Early Qur'an Interpretation

Despite the obvious need to explicate the text, there was initial resistance to doing so. The major problem of any scriptural interpretation is that uninformed or unregulated readings can suggest that God is requiring behaviors or beliefs that may be problematic. The earliest written interpretations of the Qur'an began only a century or more after Muhammad's death, and these claim to cite the Prophet or his respected companions as their sources. But popular preachers soon offered personal opinions about the meaning of the divine word that were considered irresponsible and even subversive. In order to control the possible destabilization of interpretation, therefore, a general consensus emerged that rejected interpretations that could not be traced to Muhammad or his trusted companions and their followers. Subsequently, commentaries are sometimes divided into two categories: those based on the sayings of Muhammad and his companions and their successors (sometimes called "traditional commentary") and those based on personal opinion. Only the former are consistently allowed, though in truth even the most traditional commentators managed to include their own opinions. The extraordinary traditionist, Muhammad ibn Jarīr al-Ṭabarī (d.923), for example, after carefully citing many pages of opinions of respected traditionists, would then frequently offer his own personal opinion about the issue in question.

The most common term used for Qur'an interpretation is *tafsīr*, which comes from *fassara*, "to explain." A related term is found in the Hebrew, *pesher*, and some of the commentaries discovered in the cache of ancient manuscripts called the Dead Sea Scrolls are called *pesharim*, such as *Pesher Naḥum* and *Pesher Ḥabakkuk*.[2] The term occurs in the Qur'an only once: "We give you the truth and the best explanation" (Q.25:33). A more common qur'anic term is *ta'wīl*, which appears most often in the qur'anic story of Joseph in relation to his divinely inspired ability to interpret dreams.[3] Both terms were used interchangeably during the early years after Muhammad's death, though they were sometimes used without consistency to distinguish between different modes of interpretation. Eventually, they were used to represent two different general approaches to interpretation. *Tafsīr* became the term to denote philological interpretations and explanations of the contextual or "literal" meanings, while *ta'wīl* became a technical term to identify allegorical interpretation. *Tafsīr* became the generic term for Qur'an interpretation in general, while *ta'wīl* became narrowed to mostly to Sufi and Shi`i interpretations. We refer to all interpretation here as *tafsīr*.

As one can imagine, Islam produced a huge library of commentary on the Qur'an, and these reflect the various methodologies, theologies, legal schools, linguistic approaches, and religious affiliations of the Muslim communities. Categories of *tafsīr* can be divided in a number of different ways based on different approaches to their division. I cannot hope to do justice here to the breadth and depth of the exegetical tradition, so I will restrict my discussion to only a few aspects of the discipline.

One of the earliest types of commentary in the formative period of Islamic exegesis is the employment of narrative traditions to fill out the many details that are lacking from brief qur'anic references to ancient legends. The Qur'an often references stories that the audience is expected to have already heard or known. A common introductory word that alerts the audience to what is coming is "remember," meaning roughly, "remember the following story, when . . ."[4] The reference is usually to a tale that occurs also in the Bible or one that is known from old Arabian traditions, and the story is often cited in order to make a particular point, so it does not include many details. These details are then sometimes provided in the commentaries in explanations that take the form of short narratives.

Such narrative interpretations occur also in Judaism in relation to terse or spare biblical stories. In the Jewish context it is called "midrash," and it makes up one of the very earliest forms of Jewish exegesis on the Bible. Qur'anic narrative exegesis sometimes reproduces whole midrashim that can be found in Jewish texts written before Muhammad. In other cases, the parallels occur in Islamic interpretive collections that predate the parallel stories found in midrash. The intertextual relationship clearly proves that Muslims and Jews were in communication and knew each other's stories. They freely borrowed material from one another and did not consider the interpretive story to be "owned" by either community. Such stories about biblical and other ancient characters were common cultural information that was shared by Jews, Muslims, Christians, and pre-Islamic polytheists alike.

As time went on, however, the early arguments between Jews and Muslims (and Christians) over which form of monotheism truly represented the divine will continued, and quarrels and disagreements between monotheists never ceased. When Islam became the dominant religious and political system in the region, a sentiment emerged among some Muslim thinkers to rid Islam of accretions that might be traced to other religious traditions. In the meantime, the general category of midrash-style narrative interpretation that originated with Jews (and Christians and Persians as well) had become known as "Israelite stories" (*isrā'īliyāt*). They were well respected in the early generations, but they eventually were branded as foreign and were excluded from the most respected commentaries. Today, "Israelite stories" are condemned by most religious scholars, yet they have never disappeared. Some have dropped out of the most prestigious commentaries, but they may be found among many collections of stories that are called "Stories of the Prophets," and such collections continue to be popular in many Muslim languages to this day.

Another important genre of Islamic exegesis is legal exegesis, which sorts out the meanings of qur'anic material in terms of the juridical principles and legal schools. There is no specific term for this category, but one popular title found among the collections is "Statues (or judgments) of the Qur'an." As with many categories of interpretation, jurists approached the Qur'an as a source for deriving legal decisions. Some, however, read the Qur'an in order to validate legal decisions that had already been made and promulgated. The first endeavor is purely exegetical, because it attempts to learn something from careful study of the text. The second approach is often referred to as eisegetical, meaning that it attempts to read a conclusion already arrived at into scripture in order to prove that the position is correct.

The same critique of eisegesis was leveled against many commentators who were accused of interpreting according to their personal opinion (*tafsīr bil-ra'y*). The problem is of course much more complicated. *Ra'y* does indeed mean "view" or "opinion," but it became a negative label for any kind of independent interpretation that did not rely on what came to be considered the authoritative statements of Muhammad as conveyed by his companions and successors. But traditional commentaries cited companions of the Prophet who held widely different views about the interpretation of some words or verses. Conflicting traditions would not likely derive from the same source in the Prophet, so at least some of their interpretations must be considered their own.

This conveys a sense of subjectivity. But many commentators were attempting to engage the texts of scripture through methods that had not been established during the first generations. These included new insights into the sciences of logic, grammar and lexicography, rhetoric and history. "Free-thinkers," and especially the Mu`tazila, regarded reasoned personal engagement with the text to be a fundamental source of knowledge.

Despite the pressure against it, independent reasoning remained a part of all the religious disciplines of Islam, from Qur'an interpretation to jurisprudence and theology. In the field of legal studies, independent reasoning is called *ijtihād*, which derives from the same root as *jihad* ("striving"). *Ijtihād* means something like "self-struggle," and it is used to differentiate from *taqlīd*, meaning imitation or the unquestioning adoption of previous tradition. *Ijtihād* was a common practice in law and also in theology and philosophy. It was also an acceptable means to interpret the Qur'an. But as the community expanded exponentially under the Empire and as it absorbed many foreign peoples with their foreign ideas and manners and expectations, there was a natural inclination to narrow the parameters of interpretation in law, religious practice, and the Qur'an in general. The proverbial "gates of *ijtihād*" were declared closed sometime in the 8th and 9th centuries. What this meant was not the cessation of any independent thinking, though that was certainly the goal of some leaders. Rather, the closing of the gates of *ijtihād* meant a narrowing of the parameters of what could be accepted by the political and intellectual establishment.

There always remained individuals and groups that maintained independent reasoning in relation to all fields of Islamic tradition. But they were pressured and sometimes persecuted for their nonconformism.

More genres of Qur'an exegesis emerged in addition to the narrative and legal categories discussed above. Some concentrated on the variant readings of the text of the Qur'an. Interest in this topic encouraged the development of linguistics, including lexicography, morphology, and dialectology. Others were interested in the rhetoric of the Qur'an.

Two additional categories of interpretation considered above include the "occasions of revelation" and "abrogation," more commonly, "the abrogating and the abrogated." The first attempted to contextualize the revelations in the life history of Muhammad. The second attempted to resolve the problem of apparent contradiction by contending that some later verses abrogated some earlier ones, based on an interpretation of Q.2:106: "We do not abrogate [or cancel] any revelation or cause it to be forgotten without bringing a better one or its equivalent."

Parallels to most of the approaches in Qur'an interpretation may be found in Jewish interpretation of the Bible, including the attempt to resolve problems of apparent contradiction (among Jews this remained a goal but did not become an interpretive genre). Rationalist, allegorical, grammatical, narrative exegetical, and mystical approaches are found in both religious communities. Some of the commonalities simply arose from engaging in similar activities, but especially with the grammatical, rationalist, and allegorical approaches, it is clear that Jews learned some of their most effective tools and methods from their Muslim colleagues.

Modern Qur'an Interpretation

Some modern Qur'an interpretation continues the classical tradition of interpretation, but important new developments have emerged from the meeting between Islam and modernity. Two issues have tended to focus the direction of modern interpretation: the compatibility of the qur'anic worldview with the findings of modern science, and the question of an appropriate political and social order based on qur'anic principles.[5] The first issue is self-explanatory. The second emerged from reactions to colonial control of Muslim lands but has since taken on a new focus with the persistence of local dictatorships that continue to plague the Muslim world. Related to both is new thinking about how the legal status of women can be understood in view of modern aspirations toward equal rights for both sexes.

One of the earlier modern developments has been the attempt to engage Enlightenment rationalism in the project of Qur'an interpretation. It should be remembered that Mu`tazilite interpretation engaged rational approaches to the Qur'an a millennium ago (see above, "Formal Theology"), but the encroachment of Enlightenment ideas presented a new challenge that was picked up both in India by Sayyid Ahmad Khan (d.1898) and Egypt by Muhammad `Abdū (d.1905). Both in their own ways attempted to demonstrate that there need be no necessary contradiction between modern natural science and Islamic revelation. This general approach paralleled similar engagement by modernizing Christians and Jews, such as Rabbi Joseph Hertz (d.1946), whose Torah interpretation commonly known as *The Hertz Commentary* was a standard feature of many American Conservative synagogues until the late 20th century. Related to this is the so-called scientific exegesis of the Qur'an. This general approach assumes that most or all the great scientific findings of the modern era were already anticipated in the Qur'an. "Scientific exegesis" is a highly eisegetical program, however, that reads things into the text that would not naturally be seen within it. We also find parallels of this kind of interpretation in neoscientific Jewish and Christian interpretations of scripture, some that continue to be produced in the West today.

Much more interesting are the interpretations that approach the Qur'an from the perspective of literary studies. The most famous advocate of this approach is the Egyptian intellectual, Ṭaha Ḥusayn (d.1973), who taught that Muslims should study the Qur'an as a work of literary art, just as Christians and Jews have engaged the "Bible as literature." Although still a small minority, Muslim women such as the Egyptian `Ā'isha `Abd al-Raḥmān (pen name, Bint al-Shāṭī') have also written commentaries or have otherwise engaged in such interpretive inquiries. Just as conservative Jews and Christians initially objected to subjecting the Holy Book to literary readings, Ṭaha Ḥusayn and similarly minded scholars have been subject to criticism and even legal proceedings. This has forced some Muslims such as Fazlur Rahman (d.1988), Daud Rahbar, and Naṣr Ḥāmid Abū Zayd to take their qur'anic studies to Western universities.

Indeed, since the last decade of the 20th century, a large compliment of young Muslim scholars has taken positions in American and European universities where they can engage in highly critical study of the Qur'an without interference from government or religious establishments. They work with Jews, Christians, and Muslims in textual reasoning and all the other current methodologies of the academy. This is a new development, and the impact of their research has yet to be felt much beyond the academic environment, but it is clear that with the increase in international academic conferences and the Internet, their scholarship will have an impact on thinking about the Qur'an in the Muslim world.

One of the more interesting modern historical approaches carried out by such scholars as Fathi Osman and Mohammed Arkoun insists that the Qur'an must be contextualized in the history of 7th-century Arabia. According to this approach, one must be careful before drawing broad universal conclusions from the Qur'an, since much of its sentiment and legislation was intended for a specific cultural and historical context. All these modern approaches exhibit an awareness of the cultural distance between the modern world and the world in which the qur'anic message was primarily communicated. This awareness parallels that of critical Jewish biblical scholarship.

A different approach that might be called postmodern neofundamentalist takes the position that it is possible for Muslims today to regain immediate access to the original meaning of the qur'anic text by returning to the beliefs of the first Muslims, thereby actively struggling for the restoration of the pristine Islamic social order. These are expressions of what today is called "Islamist" exegesis first suggested by Sayyid Qutb (d.1966) in his major work, *In the Shade of the Qur'an*. According to this approach, which is popular especially among politically active Islamists who strive to reestablish the caliphate, the Qur'an remains entirely accessible and relevant, but only to those who return to what they claim is the original and authentic practice of the earliest Muslims. This approach tends to reject even much traditional *tafsīr* because it is suspect as being under the influence of foreign Greek ideas and the *Israelite Stories* mentioned above. It tends to rely, rather, mostly on the *Hadith* literature, which purports to convey only the authentic views of Muhammad and his closest coterie of companions. This methodology can bring one into a certain intimate, contextual understanding of the Qur'an, but it cannot be harmonized with modern pluralistic ideas.

The Meaning of the Qur'an in the Life of the Muslim

The Qur'an is far more than a scriptural text for most Muslims. It is almost like a living thing (some will not undress in a bedroom in which a Qur'an is laying). Its oral nature has been retained powerfully even in the modern period and many centuries after the culture of the earliest Muslims, the Arabs, shifted from an almost entirely oral society to a highly literate one. Children learn the Qur'an through recitation from a very early age, and one of the highest honors for any Muslim, female or male, is to know the Qur'an by heart. In fact, the very word for this kind of knowledge, *ḥāfiẓ*, is an honorific epithet that conveys the meaning of safeguarding or preserving, as well as remembering, even defending.

The audial nature of the Qur'an is immediately evident when visiting a Muslim country. Formal Qur'an recitation is blasted loudly from tape recorders and CD players in the markets and on the radio in taxis, and one can find an evening program of live Qur'an recitation open to the public in most neighborhoods. Television programs air competitions that are judged by experts, and some will draw crowds of people to a television set up in front of a store as large as the crowds drawn to the soccer finals of the World Cup. Some of the most famous persons in the Muslim world are the most beloved Qur'an reciters.

The recitation of the Qur'an is both a religious and a spiritual act. The religious nature of recitation is the articulation (and also personal absorption) of God's message, thereby inculcating a deep religious sensibility powered by the words of God. The spiritual nature of recitation is apprehended as a transcendental taking in of the sound, conveyed in a kind of rhythmic and tonal emotionality that for believers is moving even to tears. This sentiment is not only reserved for mystics or the particularly devout. Even Christian Copts in Egypt have expressed their appreciation for the deep and spiritual nature of qur'anic recitation. Judaism also values a beautiful and articulate public reading of the Torah, but the appreciation for it rarely reaches the level of adoration that one finds among Muslims.

Preserving Scripture

As in Judaism, the recitation of the Qur'an is meant not only to convey the divine message and to evoke a sense of awe in the words of God, but also to preserve the accuracy of the text. In the Jewish system, the actual Torah scroll that is recited in the synagogue today is written in its most traditional form—on vellum sheets rolled together on wooden rods, which was the custom of producing "books" before the invention of the codex, the common book form that we have today. The Hebrew alphabet is consonantal only, and the vowel signs were only developed centuries after the canonization of the Bible. To this day, the writing in the Torah scroll retains the ancient pre-vocalic alphabetic tradition. It lacks the vowels that would ensure a clear and consistent rendering for the text. For all those many years before the invention of the vowel signs, the vocalic accuracy of Hebrew scripture was preserved by oral recitation, and it was critical that Torah "readers" (reciters, actually) pronounce all the words correctly. Although Hebrew Bibles in book form usually include those vowel markings today, the official Torah scrolls do not, and in the synagogue to this day, one or two persons must attend the reciter in order to make corrections if any errors are made in the public rendering of the text.

The Arabic alphabet, like the Hebrew, also lacks vowels, and the development of the vowel signs for Arabic occurred around the same time as for Hebrew (the process began in about the 7th century). But unlike Torah scrolls, it became the custom in the Muslim world for qur'anic codices, called *muṣḥaf*s, to include the later addition of vowel markings. Nevertheless, the great emphasis on exact oral recitation was never relaxed in Islam. In fact, it became an art form. Qur'an reciters follow a complex and strict formula of rules that ensures the proper pronunciation of words and the correct preservation of the syntax of sentences, but they are free to engage creatively in the musicality of recitation. There continues to be a mild debate in the Muslim word over whether this recitation should be considered musical. In some extremely conservative sectors of the Muslim world, "music" is forbidden. But Qur'an recitation is nevertheless cherished.

Importantly, Jewish communities throughout the world do not agree exactly on the proper pronunciation of the Hebrew, and a few slightly different ways of reciting the Torah have become acceptable. The Muslim world is somewhat more consistent in its determination of proper pronunciation of the Qur'an, but it also has a number of acceptable recitations. Despite the relative consistency in the Hebrew pronunciation, the musicality of the Hebrew recitation varies considerably, and it usually reflects the musical styles and trends of the lands and periods in which it emerged. The musicality of Torah recitation among Jewish communities that derive from the Muslim world reflects the same musicality that influenced Qur'an recitation. One can immediately recognize the "eastern" tonality of Torah recitation among Syrian, Egyptian, Moroccan, Persian, and Turkish communities.

Although it is not required that the Qur'an be recited publicly in the mosque as the Torah must in the synagogue, every act of Muslim prayer must include selections from the Qur'an. In the required daily prayers, the opening chapter is always recited, as well as at least one additional selection that is the worshiper's choice. Qur'an recitation is a cherished evening activity, and Sufi groups may choose a short qur'anic phrase or word for meditative group recitation.

According to the oral tradition (*Hadith*), Muhammad considered knowing the Qur'an and reciting it to be of utmost importance, not only for personal religious development, but also in order to preserve the divine word. Prophets who could recite God's word beautifully were favored by God, and Muhammad himself loved to hear his followers recite it to him. "Abū Hurayra said that he heard the messenger of God say, 'There are only two types that may be envied: those who recite the Qur'an during the night and during the day . . . and those who have acquired wealth through God and who spend it justly.'"[6]

The written words of the Qur'an also play a major role in the daily life of Muslims. They serve as amulets for protection and as reminders that God is never far away. Buses and trucks as well as private autos may display on their windshields Noah's words when entering the Ark, "Ride in it in the name of God, whether it is going or not, for God is forgiving, merciful" (Q.11:41). One may often find a segment of the story of Solomon and the Queen of Sheba in the kitchen or dining room of a home as an acknowledgment of thanks: "This is from the bounty of God" (Q.27:40).

The written word of the Qur'an thus carries its own sanctity. As with Hebrew scriptures, an Arabic Qur'an may not be discarded even if it is worn out and no longer usable. In such cases, texts are saved until enough have been collected to dispose of properly. While in the case of the Hebrew Bible such disposal is burial, the Qur'an is typically disposed of through burning.

Because the Qur'an was revealed in Arabic, both the language and its script carry a certain sanctity, and Qur'an calligraphy has been raised to the finest art in the Muslim world. The representation of the human form and even animals has often been forbidden by Muslim legalists, so Qur'an calligraphy became the single most important form of Islamic visual representation. Calligraphy in "arabesque" floral and geometric designs is the only form of art permitted in mosque decoration. Complex designs sometimes convey equally complex meaning by forming abstract renderings of nature that require experts to decipher, and entire scenes may be portrayed through the stylistic calligraphy of only a word or phrase from the Qur'an. Ironically, these may even render the figures that might otherwise be forbidden, but their representation in qur'anic verse renders them not only permissible, but highly desirable, such as the intricate design and bird images depicted below.

In the *muthanna* or "doubled" style of calligraphy shown on the left, each half of the design is a mirror image of the other. The *basmalah* in the *thuluth* script on the right has been written in the shape of an ostrich. (*Aramco and Its World: Arabia and the Middle East.* Dhahran, Saudi Arabia, 1980.)

CHAPTER 15

The Prophetic Record

The Sunna

While Muhammad was alive, he was the obvious authority to whom his followers would turn for guidance and interpretation of the revelations that he recited. He was the Prophet, and his authority was paramount. The Qur'an commands the people to refer disputes to Muhammad, who is placed almost on a par with God in a verse treating mediation and adjudication: "O you Believers! Obey God and obey the messenger and those with authority among you. If you dispute anything, refer it to God and the messenger if you believe in God and the Last Day. That is the best and most excellent explanation" (Q.4:59). Already mentioned is how the behavior (*sunna*) of respected tribal elders was emulated in pre-Islamic Arabian culture. This cultural feature naturally continued as the religious culture of Islam began to dominate in the area of Mecca and Medina; however, in place of the tribal elder stood the religious leader who was naturally emulated by his followers. As the overall leader, Muhammad's own *sunna*—his words and deeds—were scrutinized and remembered. Muhammad was the Prophet and the definitive leader, but some of his closest companions assisted him and gained a great amount of respect and, therefore, a certain level of emulation as well.

Muhammad's death marked the end of revelation. It also clearly marked the end of his powerful leadership and his role of interpreter of the revelations. This was a double blow to the community, because the Prophet and the revelation were so intimately bound together. The Qur'an itself taught that Muhammad was an example to be followed: "You have an excellent example in the messenger of God for whoever looks forward to God and the Last Day and who frequently refers to God" (Q.33:21).

In the earliest period after his death, Muslims emulated the *sunna* of both Muhammad and his closest companions, but soon the sense of *sunna* was narrowed only to that of the Prophet and became known as the Prophetic *Sunna* (*al-sunna al-nabawiyya*). It filled out broad areas of life that were not treated directly in the Qur'an, and it became an important instruction about how to live a pious and just life as a member of the community of Muslims.

The *sunna* was fluid in the early period because it was based on the memory of Muhammad's deeds and conversations among his companions and followers. The memories remained in oral form and were retained in the minds and hearts of his companions and followers who told and retold portions of what they remembered as best they could recall them. Those who never knew Muhammad heard and learned the tales from those who did or from others who heard the *sunna* from companions who personally witnessed the behaviors of the Prophet.

The Hadīth

Sunna is an abstract reference to behavior in general. The Prophet had a *sunna*. But that *sunna* was conveyed by recounting brief, concrete descriptions of his behavior or short reports that portrayed what he said or did in a very specific context. Each paragraph of information about Muhammad's *sunna* is called a *ḥadīth* (written in lower case here), which in Arabic means both a short conversation or statement, and a report of something that has occurred. A *hadith* is a segment of information about the Prophet and is sometimes referred to in English as a tradition.

When uncertainty or a disagreement would arise over any aspect of how to conduct one's life in the early community, people would ask what Muhammad did or would have done in relation to it. Naturally, people remembered things somewhat differently and sometimes two or more conflicting *hadith*s would surface that answered questions in substantially different ways. As a result, there developed differences of opinion as to which *hadith*s were more accurate. After a while it had become clear that people had begun inventing *hadith*s in order to authenticate their own opinion of proper behaviors or even personal innovation. In this way, a great deal of fascinating information began entering Islam that clearly could not have come directly from Muhammad, such as aphorisms from Greek philosophy, verses or paraphrases from Jewish, Christian, and Zoroastrian scriptures, maxims of Buddhist wisdom, and social and customary traditions from many of the lands into which Islam spread under the Conquests.

Eventually, methods were devised for sifting through the various *hadith*s and evaluating which were more authentic, and which needed to be considered with caution or even rejected outright. The major criteria for determining the value of *hadith*s centered on the reliability of the people who related them. One was required to know not only who related the *hadith* itself, but also from whom he heard it and from where he received it. Eventually the human chain of transmitters had to go all the way back to one of Muhammad's known companions who personally witnessed his words or actions. The term *sanad* or *isnād* was used to refer to the chain of transmitters of the *hadith*s, and only certain ones were considered authentic. Each person who made up the links of the chain had to be known as reliable, and each had to live in chronological and geographic proximity to one another such that they could have actually passed the information between them. Every proper *hadith* is therefore composed of two necessary parts: The actual body of text that reports the behavior or speech of the Prophet is called *matn*; it is useless without an acceptable chain of transmitters, called *isnad*.

A typical *hadith* might appear as follows: "It was told to us by . . . who received it from . . . who got it from . . . on the authority of . . . to whom it was related by . . . that the Prophet said. . . ."

Because of the problem of authenticity, a classification system was developed to differentiate between the levels of reliability, from "sound" to "acceptable" to "weak" and even "forged." Many other technical terms evolved to describe the specific ways in which a *hadith* could be considered unreliable. The record of Prophetic *Sunna* in the form of the many *hadith*s, each containing an *isnād* and a *matn*, is often referred to in general as the *Hadith* or the *Hadith* Literature. In English it is often referred to as the "Tradition" or the "Prophetic Tradition."

The *sunna* of the Prophet remained in oral form for generations. As in the case of Judaism, the division of the Written Law from the Oral Law meant that the oral nature of the Prophetic *Sunna* ensured that its value would not attain that of written revelation. The fluid nature of oral literature, however, not only allows for variations that are much more difficult to control than in written texts, it also allows for growth and expansion. As might be expected, the *sunna* expanded and grew as the number of transmitters increased with each generation and became increasingly spread geographically throughout the empire. Pious scholars would go in search of *hadith*s and would travel great distances to collect (in oral form), learn, and memorize the *hadith*s of esteemed teachers. The mass of information eventually grew to such an extent that it became extremely difficult to retain the enormous volume of information by memory and to sift out the reliable ones from the weak.

By the 9th century, the number of *hadith* reports had risen to hundreds of thousands, and it was clear that something had to be done or the growth and spread of unreliable reports about Muhammad would endanger the stability of the religion itself. Finally in the same century, the hundreds of thousands of *hadiths* began to be collected, evaluated, and formally written down in collections (many had been informally written down probably for a long time previously). In the middle of the century, two great scholars of *sunna* known as Al-Bukhārī and Muslim composed separate collections of many thousands of *hadiths*. Ismā`īl Al-Bukhārī (d. 870) was said to have collected some 200,000 out of 600,000 that he heard, after which he finally selected 7,300 to appear in his collection. Because a single *hadith* may reappear in the collection under different topics, the actual number of separate and independent traditions is his work is about 2,760. The collection of Muslim ibn al-Ḥajjāj (d. 875) contains about 3,000. These are the most respected *hadith* collections and are referred to as "The Two Sound Collections." Four other slightly later collections were also accepted into the canon of "sound" traditions that are universally accepted in the Sunni world, though they also accepted some *hadith*s that were not at the same level of reliability.[1] Together they are called "The Six Books," and they are used along with the Qur'an for determining the law of Islam.

Each of the six major collections is organized topically, and in modern printings by book, section, chapter, and number. They are not difficult to read or to use, and *hadith* commentaries soon emerged to provide detailed opinions about the reliability and contextualization of the many thousands of traditions collected. Although this is all considered "Prophetic *Sunna*," some *hadith*s in these collections relate information about Muhammad's close companions. Therefore, despite the general recognition that *sunna* refers to the deeds, sayings, and behaviors of the Prophet—his companions known as the *ṣaḥāba* are also considered to be authoritative examples of proper Islamic behavior as they appear within "The Six Books."

Sunni Islam is named as such because it purports to epitomize proper Islamic practice as articulated in the *sunna* of the Prophet. While all Muslims, including those who refer to themselves as Shi`is or Sufis, regulate their lives through the *sunna*, not all Muslims agree that "The Six Books" are accurate representations of what Muhammad really said and did. The Shi`a has a separate compilation of *hadith*s in five collections that reflect its own practice and beliefs. Some *hadith*s appear in the collections of both branches, but the Shi`a generally accept only those that were transmitted by Ali, his followers, and subsequent generations that counted themselves among the Shi`a, or "Partisans of Ali." Among the authentic *hadith*s according to the Shi`a is the tradition that Muhammad explicitly designated Ali and his descendants to govern the community.

Because of the acknowledged problem of authenticity, many Western scholars dismiss the reliability of the *Hadith* in general. Whether or not it represents the exact words and deeds of the Prophet, however, the *Hadith* has served as an authority for determining Muslim behavior from the earliest times that is second only to the Qur'an itself.

The following examples of *Hadith* demonstrate some of the wide variety of *hadiths* related to the act of prayer.

> Muhammad b. al-Muthannā reported to us that Yaḥyā reported that Hishām said: My father told me on the authority of `Ā'isha that the prophet came to her one day when a woman was with her. He said: "Who is this?" `Ā'isha said: "She is so-and-so" and mentioned her [probably excessive] praying. Muhammad said: "You must do what is tolerable. God does not tire as you do. The best deed in relation to Him is what is done him regularly. (Bukhari, Book of Belief, Ch. 33 [Kazi 1:36])

Although the Qur'an often refers to prayer and regular prayer is stipulated in it (Q.4:103, 7:204–206, 24:58), the actual number of prayers is not determined there. The requirement of five daily prayers, one of the most basic and firmly expected aspects of daily Islamic ritual, derives from the *Hadith*, which also provides some of the details relating to their practice and the merit gained by engaging in them.

> Ibrahim b. Ḥamza related to us that Ibn Abū Ḥāzim and Al-Darāwrdī related to him on the authority of Yazīd b. `Abdallah [who said] on the authority of Muhammad b. Ibrahim [who said] on the authority of Abū Salama b. Abd al-Raḥmān on the authority of Abū Hurayra that he heard the messenger of God say: "If there was a river at the door of any one of you who bathed in it five times every day, would you see any filth remaining on him?" They answered, "Not a bit of dirt would remain on him." [The Prophet] responded: "That is an example of the five prayers through which God blots out sins." (Bukhari, Book of the Times of Prayer, Ch. 5 [Kazi 1:301])

Already mentioned is that Jerusalem was considered the proper direction for prayer in the early day of the Prophet. The Qur'an itself is understood to authorize a change of direction from Jerusalem to Mecca. This theme is treated in the following *hadith*.

> Abdallah b. Rajā' related to us, saying that Isrā'īl related on the authority of Abū Isḥāq, on the authority of Al-Barā' b. `Āzib who said: The messenger of God prayed toward Jerusalem (*bayt al-maqdis*)

> sixteen or seventeen months, but the messenger of God loved to turn toward the Ka`ba [in Mecca]. So God revealed [the verse], *We have seen the turning of your face to the sky* (Q.2:144). Then he turned toward the Ka`ba. And said *the foolish people* (Q.2:142)—these are the Jews—[will say] *"What has turned them from the direction of prayer to which they were accustomed? Say: To God belongs the east and the west. He will guide those he wishes to a straight path* (Q.2:142). A [certain] man was praying with the Prophet [when this incident with the accompanying revelation occurred] and went out after he prayed. He passed a group of Medinan believers ["Helpers"] praying the afternoon prayer toward Jerusalem. So he said that he witnessed the Messenger of God praying while facing the Ka`ba. So the group broke off and turned their faces toward the Ka`ba. (Bukhari, Book of Prayers, Ch. 31 [Kazi 1:237–238])

The variety of topics reflected in the *Hadith* is vast and ranges from hygiene associated with using the toilet or which foot is best for taking the first step to the making of wills, the merits of the prophets, emancipating slaves, engaging in jihad, proper slaughter of animals, responsibility associated with making vows, pilgrimage rituals, and even descriptions of the seven heavens as seen by Muhammad during his Night Journey to Jerusalem, from where he made his ascension to God. Despite the number, variety, and detail of the traditions, they are not systematic. They were organized according to a variety of schema in the collections, but they were narrated and recorded as moments of "witnessing" of the life of the Prophet. They thus served more as a model or guide for proper conduct than a legal formulation of what is forbidden, permitted, or recommended in the way of ritual, ethics, and other modes of behavior. Out of this mass of tradition, and in conjunction with the revelations of the Qur'an, Muslim scholars and jurists would develop a complex system of law that parallels in many ways the legal thinking and processes of Judaism. We will examine this development below, but first we need to examine how the traditions relating to the life of Muhammad were organized chronologically in the form of prophetic biography.

The Sīra

Given Muhammad's foundational role as leader, prophet, and role model for proper behavior, it was natural for subsequent generations to want to know about his biography. During the first generations, it was enough to hear the stories in oral form. Later, however, some became interested in knowing his life in a more organized fashion. Interest in the details of his life story grew in relation to the interest in understanding the contexts in which the various verses and chapters of the Qur'an were revealed, which in turn could shed light on the exact meanings of the revelations themselves.

Some Muslims who were interested in the early stories of the new community collected traditions that related to it and joined them together to form longer narratives. Thus was born the stories that are called "raids" (*maghāzī*) because they are organized around the expeditions or military campaigns of the early community. The traditions that treated the life of Muhammad, however, were arranged by those who transmitted them or by topic rather than by chronology, so it was necessary to reorganize them into narrative form according to what was understood to be his life story.

These are called *sīra*, which root meaning derives from a sense of setting out on a journey, but has come to mean "biography." The most famous is *al-sīra al-nabawiyya*, the Prophetic Biography of Abū Muhammad 'Abd al-Mālik ibn Hishām (d.834), who edited an earlier biography by Muhammad ibn Isḥāq that was subsequently lost and is now known only in the recension edited and preserved by Ibn Hisham.[2]

Ibn Isḥāq is the source of most of this work, and he derived his information from the *hadith*, from old poetry, and from the Qur'an and early commentaries on it. He placed them together to form a coherent narrative of Muhammad's life, which is read and studied today by Muslims throughout the world. The tremendous love and affection for Muhammad is evident from the many different versions of the Prophetic Biography written for all ages and found virtually in all languages spoken by Muslims and literally in all corners of the Muslim world. It is recited to children from infancy, taught in the lower grades, and studied with commentary in the upper grades of Islamic schools. The purpose is to instill a deep and personal sense of relation to the person of Muhammad, who remains a role model for Believers throughout the world to this day.

The Status of Muhammad in Islam

Muslims consider Muhammad to have been fully and only human. He is described in the religious literatures of Islam as a man with a sense of humor, who enjoyed eating certain foods and observing children at play, and who personally experienced divine revelation while remaining accessible, modest, and humble. He was wise but not all-knowing, and a famous story mentions that he did not know where his camel had wandered until God intervened and told him. He was generally happy but also able to become angry or melancholy. He suffered pain and enjoyed pleasure, but bore the duties of leadership and the difficulties of life equitably.

But with all his humanness, he was also the founder of a community that developed into one of the most successful civilizations of human history. It was quite normal that he became bigger in death than he was in life. Because of his foundational role in the community and the custom of emulation of his *sunna*, Muhammad eventually became exalted above ordinary mortals, and a doctrine of virtuousness to the level of infallibility emerged in relation to him that is known as *`iṣma*, meaning "protected sinlessness."

This doctrine cannot be found in the Qur'an or in the Sunni *Hadith*, for it developed later in a manner typical of human groups that create hagiographies—stories and literatures that idealize heroes by attributing to them wondrous deeds, exemplary characteristics, and even miracles. According to the general perspective reflected by this doctrine, Muhammad's immunity from error was part of his nature, for he was, after all, exceptional enough that God would choose him above other mortals to be his prophet and messenger. God then provided additional protection, which all prophets enjoy according to Islam. Among the Shi`a, *`iṣma* applies not only to Muhammad and the ancient prophets, but also to the Imams, the descendants of Muhammad through the line of Ali.

This doctrine of prophetic infallibility was opposed by traditionalists, who upheld the literal meaning of passages in the Qur'an and *Hadith* that depict the prophets in general and Muhammad in particular as being fully human, and the tension between the two views of Muhammad is sometimes reflected in the tension between official religious dogma and popular religion. The fear of the traditionalists was that Muhammad himself would be worshiped. The modern traditionalist movement known as the Wahhabis razed virtually all of the buildings and mosques in Medina in the early 19th century because they were associated with the veneration of Muhammad and his family. The Wahhabi perspective condemns acts that they believe can lead to the diminution of the unity of God, such as praying at saints' tombs and at graves, and any prayer ritual in which the suppliant appeals to a third party for intercession with God. Consequently, the Wahhabis forbid grave markers or tombs in burial sites and the building of any shrines that could become a locus of "association."

Shi`is, on the other hand, freely and openly venerate Muhammad's family, and it is likely that the docrine of *`iṣma* originally developed through this group. They regularly pray at the graves of the Shi`ite imams and hold the family of Muhammad, known as the *ahl al-bayt*,[3] with special reverence. This difference in perspective and practice has led to significant tension and occasional violence between these two communities.

A classic example of the tension between official and popular religion may be observed around the time of Muhammad's birthday. There is no official religious holiday to commemorate the birthday of the Prophet, and traditionalists find the merriment associated with the Prophet's birth particularly objectionable. Nevertheless, special *mawlid* festivals are often celebrated on his birthday in many parts of the Muslim world.[4] As part of these celebrations, parades and processions are held, homes and mosques are decorated, special foods are prepared, and exemplary stories about the life of the Prophet are narrated by experts. These celebrations are a basic part of Shi`a Islam, and although less universal among Sunnis, they are also popular among them as well. The trend over the past few decades in the Sunni Muslim world, under the influence of strict traditionalist Islam, has been to forbid or discredit such festivals. The famous colorful processions in Egypt at the birthday of Muhammad and others who are revered as saints (both men and women) have been reduced drastically in recent years as a result.

The Meaning of Muhammad in the Life of Muslims

Muhammad is regarded as the most exemplary model of what human life can and should be, and Muslims identify with him by learning his *sunna* and by doing the best they can to emulate his behaviors. Today, especially among those engaged in the resurgence of traditional Islam, one can observe how men increasingly dress according to the way tradition describes the dress of the Prophet. Many grow beards and wear their hair as similarly as possible to the way in which they imagine that the Prophet did. One may observe a similar sentiment among some sectors of the American Christian community in the popular idiom *WWJD*—"What would Jesus do?" It became particularly popular in the 1990s among many who used the phrase to remind themselves that Jesus is the supreme model for moral behavior. In the case of Jesus, the basic sentiment is *imitatio Dei*, imitating God. In the case of Muhammad, it is emulating the most perfect and divinely protected model of fully human behavior. It is truly impossible to overemphasize how much inspiration Muhammad provides to Muslims, among women as well as men. Cultivating his behavior is assumed to bring success, and tremendous joy as well as inspiration comes with learning about the details of his life and striving to emulate his *sunna*. In Egypt today, it would appear that half the males are named Muhammad or one of its derivatives, Ahmad or Mahmoud. It is thought that anyone given Muhammad's name will possess an extra portion of his *baraka* or "blessing."

The Qur'an itself praises him effusively: "God and his angels pray for the Prophet. O Believers! Pray for him and greet him with peace" (Q.33:56). As a result of this qur'anic injunction, devout Muslims follow every mention of Muhammad's name with the phrase, "May God bless him and grant him peace." The names of other prophets are often followed with a similar but shorter phrase, "peace upon him," but the special statement of praise for Muhammad is unique in Islam. The eulogistic formula associated with Muhammad's name is also found in writing, sometimes written in abbreviation in four Arabic letters following his name and sometimes following the designation "prophet" in relation to him as well. It also appears occasionally in English, with the letters PBUH, "peace be upon him."

CHAPTER 16

Islamic Law

Islam, like Judaism, is far more than a faith system. It is a religious civilization that encompasses all aspects of life. And Islamic law, like Jewish law, is a complex system that has emerged to treat norms of individual and communal behavior. Cultural conventions and behavioral expectations were of course normative in Arabian society even before the emergence of Islam, but these were not formal legal formulations. They were, rather, informal (but no less important) norms, expectations and rules of behavior that regulated virtually all aspects of human relationships. These carried over into the period of emerging Islam and were modified to fit the changing ritual, ethical, and social expectations that emerged along with the developing religious community. Muhammad received revelation that radically altered many of the pre-Islamic Arabian norms. He then conveyed that revelation to the people. He is therefore seen as a "lawgiver" in a manner that parallels the role of Moses in relation to the Torah, but neither Moses nor Muhammad was the source of the law. The source in both systems is deemed to be God. Also like Moses, Muhammad was not a legal expert. The "science of law" in Islam emerged later as a human effort to make sense of the divine command in relation to the developing culture and technologies of a nascent religious civilization.

Sharī`a

The term that best conveys the full behavioral system of Islam is *sharī`a*, which means "the way," and in its most basic sense means "the way to the water hole."[1] Like the Hebrew word *halakhah*, which conveys the sense of "going" or "walking," *sharīʿa* expresses a sense of direction for humanity to follow in order to do the right thing before God. Although the two words are unrelated linguistically, they both convey the sense of "the right way."

Sharīʿa refers to a system whose legislative authority derives directly and immediately from God. God is the sole legislator of *sharīʿa*. Jurisprudence, on the other hand, is the human endeavor to make sense of the *sharīʿa*. It is the "science of law," and it consists of the study and interpretive methodologies employed to understand and apply the divine imperative in the lives of the community. In Arabic and in general Islamic discourse, the word for jurisprudence is *fiqh*.

Fiqh

The basic meaning of *fiqh* is understanding or comprehension. Although the human intellect cannot fully understand the divinely authored *sharīʿa*, it can and must be applied to the lives of Believers through human engagement in jurisprudence.

During the lifetime of the Prophet, the *sharīʿa* was learned from the ongoing revelation of the Qur'an and the advice and direction provided by Muhammad. The community at that time was highly centralized around Medina and, toward the end of his life, Medina and Mecca. In such a localized situation, all questions could be referred directly to the Prophet. Muhammad's death marked the end of both the revelation and his personal guidance. Almost immediately thereafter, the conquests moved the community out of Arabia, where it became dispersed among the many conquered peoples. The Muslims continued to appeal to the personal guidance of the first four caliphs, who rendered decisions with the assistance of their companions and advisers as new questions arose. But upon the establishment of the Umayyad caliphate in 661 with its capital in Damascus, judges called *qāḍī*s were appointed by the caliph as his delegates to provincial governors.

The Qāḍīs

The job of the *qāḍī* ("judge") was to arbitrate disputes based on his knowledge of the Qur'an and the tradition and to see that government decrees were properly carried out. The social, political, economic, and religious developments during this period of conquest and consolidation were enormous, and the *qāḍī*s were expected to rely on their own best judgment as they rendered their pronouncements. The Qur'an was the ultimate source of authority, and no judgment could overrule divine revelation. But the Qur'an is not a legal code and does not treat many aspects of life that required consideration. Personal judgment therefore became a necessary tool for problem-solving, and this type of interpretative endeavor, as noted earlier, took on the name *ra`y*, meaning "opinion."

The rulings of the early *qāḍīs* were also influenced by their own Arabian tribal customs and local laws and customs in the various provinces where they were stationed. The resultant rulings tended to be pragmatic and flexible, and mixed Islamic norms with local ones that would not compromise the Qur'an and the directives of Muhammad. The rudimentary legal tradition that began to develop, therefore, differed from one locale to another. It was at once tolerant and unsystemized. The Qur'an served as a centralizing institution as far as it went, but since the Prophetic *Sunna* was expanding at this time, there was a natural tendency toward fragmentation.

The Umayyad dynasty ruled from 661 to 750, and during the period was criticized for allowing Islamic practice to become confused among the differing customary laws, regional variations, the personal opinions of the *qāḍīs* and the decrees promulgated by the caliphs. The result was a system with contradictory laws and expectations, arguments between various factions, and a decided lack of a systematic process for determining proper behaviors, laws, and ritual. Critics argued that God's law should be defined clearly and applied equally to all Muslims, and a call emerged for a clearly defined and unified system of behavioral law. There was also a desire among many to limit the autonomy of Muslim political rulers.

Some extremely able individuals began to work on the problem systematically by reviewing the developing customs and the rulings promulgated under the Umayyad caliphs in light of qur'anic teachings. They worked out of Medina, Damascus, Baghdad, and some other urban areas. The most influential jurists came to be viewed as the founders or leaders of schools (or legal systems) of law in the Sunni world. Only four survived, though other schools were popular at one time or another before they died out by the 13th century.

The four current Sunni schools are:

- The Ḥanafi school associated with Abū Ḥanīfa from Kufa (d.767)
- The Maliki school associated with Mālik ibn Anās from Medina (d.796)
- The Shafi`i school associated with Muhammad al-Shāfi`ī from Gaza (d.820)
- The Ḥanbali school of Aḥmad ibn Ḥanbal from Khurasan in Central Asia (d.855).

The Shi`a also have schools of jurisprudence, the most important of which is the Ja`farī school, associated with Ja`far al-Ṣādiq (d.765), who was one of the imams in the line of Ali.

The Umayyad caliphate was overthrown in 750 by a coalition of opposition groups that produced the Abbasid caliphate centered in Baghdad. Conscious of the criticism leveled against their predecessors, the Abbasids became great patrons of *fiqh* along with most of the known disciplines of learning in general. Under the Abbasids, the *qāḍī*s were not authorized to determine law, but only to apply it. The development of *fiqh* then came into the hands of a class of specially trained scholars called *fuqahā'* (those engaged in the *fiqh*), a subgroup of the scholar class known as "those with knowledge" (the *`ulamā'*), who worked independently on discovering, interpreting, and applying the divine will to everyday life. The classic scholars of this program worked from about 750 to 900 to develop a comprehensive legal system. These theoretical scholars are sometimes referred to as jurists, to distinguish them from the judges who engaged, under salary from the state, in applying the work of the jurists to individual cases.

The "Roots of Law"

It was not a simple task to create a unified legal system, because the major authority of the Qur'an tends to convey its position on human behavior in broad and general terms: compassion for the weaker members of society (Q.2:215, 107:1–7), fairness and good faith in commercial dealings (Q.6:152, 17:35), incorruptibility in the administration of justice (Q.4:58,135, 5:8), etc. Even in specific prohibitions, such as the imbibing of intoxicants and gambling (Q.5:90–91) or the taking of interest (Q.2:278–279), the definitions of what exactly constitutes these acts, the conditions under which errant individuals engage in them, and the consequences for doing so all needed to be worked out. Among the 6,000 verses of the Qur'an, only about one tenth touch on legislative issues, and these tend to center on ritual practices such as prayer, fasting, and pilgrimage. No more than 80 verses treat legal topics in the strict sense.[2]

The jurists were required, therefore, to rely on other sources in addition to the Qur'an. We have noted that the most authoritative source after divine revelation became the *sunna* of the Prophet, but there remained controversies over the authenticity of the *hadith*s. It was decided in general that only the Prophetic *Sunna* that was consistent with the Qur'an could be accepted in Islamic jurisprudence. Some authorities also took into consideration other sources such as local custom, customary Arabian tradition that predated Islam, and personal opinion, as long as these did not conflict with the Qur'an.

As a result of the different approaches and the local customs and expectations that influenced the legal scholars, consistency tended to elude the jurists.

Two contending methodological positions on determining law emerged that still exist to a certain extent to this day. One wished to bring uniformity to the system by restricting the use of independent reason and by relying almost entirely on precedent from the Prophetic *Sunna*. This camp is known as the "People of the *Sunna*." Adherents of the other school vigorously asserted their right to reason for themselves according to criteria of human conceptualization that transcended the limits of the traditions found in the *Hadith*. These were called the "People of [personal] Opinion." A great deal of argument and debate ensued between the two positions until the legal sentiment swung in favor of the People of the *Sunna*, who advocated restricting legal analysis to precedent. The person who is associated with this result was Muhammad ibn Idrīs al-Shāfi`ī, the founder of the Shafi`i legal school.

According to al-Shāfi`ī, there are only two sources from which one may derive a legal decision: the Qur'an and the Prophetic *Sunna*. It was also Shāfi`i who narrowed the sense of acceptable *sunna* to that of the Prophet. Although Muhammad's companions were righteous and capable persons, only Muhammad was seen as divinely inspired, and only his *sunna* could be used to determine divinely authorized law. Tribal and local custom henceforth also had to be excluded, and personal opinion would have no authority. Shāfi`ī reduced the power of the individual schools of interpretation by transferring the authority for legal interpretation to the consensus of the community, basing it on a prophetic *hadith*, "My community will not agree upon error." This principle of community consensus is called *ijmā`*.

These restrictions narrowed the possible range of interpretation and therefore the range of possible results, but without some form of interpretive flexibility it would also severely restrict the possibility for deriving relevant rulings. One important principle of interpretation was allowed in order to resolve the problem, and this was analogical reasoning, called *qiyās*.[3] Through analogy, jurists could seek out similar situations to the question at hand within Qur'an and *sunna* from which they could derive new rulings. This approach was intended to remove any arbitrary human reasoning from the process of interpreting the divine *Sharī`a* and applying it to daily life. Shāfi`i thus was able to establish what became the four basic sources or "roots of law," which are, in order of importance: Qur'an, *sunna*, consensus, and analogy.

Legal Reasoning in History

It is one thing to resolve a dispute within the context of one's own generation. It is another to resolve complex issues forever. In every generation, new situations arise that could not have been anticipated and for which no clear, explicit, revealed text, Prophetic *Sunna*, consensus, or obvious analogy exists. The interpretive enterprise therefore continued to develop. Personal opinion was no longer an acceptable hermeneutic, but jurists could not help but engage their own personalities and histories in their analysis and employment of analogical reasoning. Moreover, the rule of consensus was becoming virtually impossible as the community of believers reached the millions and then tens of millions.

Jurists therefore narrowed the meaning of the rule of consensus to the community of legal scholars who act on the behalf of the larger community, but even that did not eliminate the independent reasoning of individual scholars. They simply had no choice but to apply their own reasoning to interpret the law, and this inevitably resulted in different legal opinions. Often these differed only in detail, but sometimes they were substantial. No overarching authority ever emerged in Islam to parallel the authority of the pope to overrule those with conflicting opinions. On the other hand, over many generations, certain interpretations became more widespread and accepted while others tended to be forgotten and to disappear. Thus developed a kind of de facto consensus of history.

By the 10th century, the general consensus among the jurists was that the principles of Islamic law had been successfully established and preserved in the literatures that were produced by the four major schools of law. While the four schools differed in some details, the consensus among them was that more independent reasoning was no longer necessary. The *umma* had no more need of individual, independent legal interpretation. Henceforth, all that was required was to follow precedent and imitate the past by relying on earlier rulings. This is known as "imitation" (*taqlīd*), as we noted above in relation to qur'anic interpretation. The term has also come to mean "tradition" or "convention."

Through this process, the previously dynamic and creative process of problem-solving became increasingly restricted until the process was essentially stopped entirely. Jurists were expected to study the law books and manuals of their predecessors but were not to seek new solutions or produce new laws. This cessation of legal development is known as the "closing of the gates of *ijtihād*," and it was justified by the assertion that the work of applying the *Sharī`a* to the life of the community was finished. Innovation became a negative appellation and understood as deviation from the proper, established norms of tradition. The accusation of engaging in innovation (*bid`a*) became not only an insult but virtually an accusation of heresy.

The actual situation, however, was more complex. Innovation continued despite its condemnation, but it had to be couched in the traditional language and images of "imitation." Even (or especially) some of those who claim to be the most extreme traditionalists engage in their own innovation.[4]

It should also be noted that religious scholars never entirely eliminated local custom or ancient tribal expectations from their thinking and writings. Circumcision, for example (including female circumcision among some groups), was a pre-Islamic Arabian custom.[5] Although the source for the Islamic rule of male circumcision is found in the *sunna* (not in the Qur'an), there is no legal requirement for circumcising females. Nevertheless, it is practiced in some areas on the strength of custom. Other customs that non-Muslims (and some Muslims as well) often associate with religious practice similarly have no authority from the religious tradition of Islam. These include some abhorrent customs, such as so-called honor killings, which are cultural norms and not sanctioned by Islam.

Law Courts

The judiciary has never been independent in Islam because the *qāḍī*s have always been appointed by the government (to this day), receive salaries from the government, and serve at the pleasure of the government. As mentioned above, they began as interpreters of the law, but interpretation became the prerogative of the jurists, leaving the judges only to apply the law, as they do in *Sharī'a* courts. Case law (the precedent of actual court cases) is not recognized in *Sharī'a* courts, so each case must be judged according to the theoretical rulings of the jurists in the manuals. This aspect of Islamic law is quite different from Jewish law, where case law is paramount. Judges were assisted in their work by legal consultants called *mufti*s, who were also employed by the government.

There developed a natural tension between the judges, who were under the employ of the government, and the jurists, who were independent of government and were not infrequently critical of it. The judges were obligated to carry out their legal conclusions based on the theory of the jurists, but they also felt pressure from government officers to render decisions favorable to them. The caliphs, whose official title as deputy to the Prophet was "commander of the faithful," also established separate caliphal courts that would enforce laws promulgated by them. The jurists tried, in general, to limit the power of the caliphs, particularly autocratic rulers, based on the belief that only God was the lawgiver. And the jurists naturally considered themselves most capable and qualified to determine the meaning and application of *Sharī'a* for the people. This exemplifies a tension between the political needs (and desires) of the rulers of the empire and the religious expectations that were the domain of the religious scholars.

The tension is exemplified by the development of two largely separate judicial systems. The caliph claimed, as deputy to the Prophet, the obligation to implement good government according to *Sharīʿa*. In order to do that they claimed the need for broad administrative and judicial powers and created what were called "grievance courts." These grievance courts were initially established to enable the caliph or his representative to hear complaints against senior officials, whose status or power over the judges might have inhibited them from free engagement to bring charges against them. These courts eventually became a full system that functioned under the jurisdiction of the ruler. The result was a dual system of laws and courts to uphold them. The caliphal court system tended toward issues of government and other "secular" matters such as criminal law, taxation, and commercial regulations, while the *Sharīʿa* courts became increasingly restricted to family law (marriage, divorce, and inheritance) and the handling of religious endowments.

The dual system has survived to this day, even among countries like Saudi Arabia that claim to be Islamic States where the law of Islam is the law of the land. The system allows governments to introduce modern ordinances for administering the nation, despite the official legal rule outlawing innovation. When Sunni jurists tried to counter the force of particularly tyrannical caliphs, they tended to lose, and lose quite badly through imprisonment and even death. As a result, they came to the conclusion that even tyrannical government was better than no government at all. Therefore, they ceased judging the moral character of the ruler as long as he acknowledged the *Sharīʿa* as the official law of the land, even if restricted to the truncated jurisdiction of family and religious law.

Muslim Law Today

In the Muslim world today, all the positions described here continue to exist except that of caliph. There is no more caliphate, so rule is imposed through the structures of the modern nation-state. The *Sharīʿa* courts continue to function alongside a system of state courts, and the quality and nature of relationship between the two depends on the relationship between the secular rulers of state and the religious leaders. Among the religious scholars are certain individual experts recognized for their learning who are consulted in order to render formal legal opinions. These legal consultants are known as *mufti*s, and the opinions they give are called *fatwā*s. The equivalent in the Jewish system is a rabbi who is known as a legal scholar to whom a question is posed. The answer is given in the form of a legal opinion. In both cases, the opinion is supposed to be arrived at very carefully by consulting earlier scholars and scholarship on the topic as well as scripture and tradition.

CHAPTER 17

The Workings of the Sharī`a

The *Sharī`a* portrays itself as universal and egalitarian. According to all Muslims, God is the judge of all humanity and the source of the *Sharī`a*. Because God is, by definition, good, then the products of divine creation are also good. The *Sharī`a* is therefore considered by Muslims to be an absolutely ethical system, and as such is considered a system of ethics as well as law. Working out that system by the jurists through *fiqh* is a human endeavor. According to some on the more progressive or liberal end of the spectrum, this system may not always reflect the perfection and goodness of God. But according to the traditionalists, it most certainly does.

The Five Categories of Behavior

One of the ways in which the ethical nature of the system is articulated is in the categorizing of behaviors by the schools of law. Modern legal systems usually classify behaviors in three categories: required, forbidden, or neutral. In Islam, five categories are provided to evaluate and legislate human acts. These are called "the Five Norms" (or categories). The terminology varies somewhat, but the categories are consistent.

1. Required acts: obligatory duties whose performance is rewarded and omission punished. Examples include ritual requirements such as prayer and fasting, and requirements that have both religious and civic aspects, such as the giving of alms and providing a

minimum bridal gift. Some acts in this category are further broken down into those required of the community as a whole but not of every single member, or those incumbent on each individual.

2. Recommended acts: behaviors or even duties that are expected but not required. Performance of such acts is rewarded, but omission is not punished. Examples of these include certain nonobligatory prayers, visiting Medina after the Hajj to Mecca, or keeping inheritance within the family rather than allowing it to be directed to nonfamily members.
3. Permissible acts: acts whose performance or mission is neither rewarded nor punished.
4. Disapproved or not recommended acts: acts that are censured but not forbidden (there are significant differences of opinion regarding these, but one example is divorcing one's wife unilaterally and against her will, which is considered by most to be reprehensible but not actually forbidden).
5. Forbidden acts: acts punishable for their commission. Examples of these are stealing, consuming alcohol, lending on interest, murder, and so on.

The ethical nature of this system is evident from the fivefold nature of the categorization. Modern legal systems generally omit the two categories that we might call "judgment calls" and content themselves with what is absolutely forbidden and absolutely required, allowing all other behaviors to exist in a neutral category to which no moral judgment is implied. In the Islamic system, problematic behaviors that could not be fairly forbidden are nevertheless condemned, and behaviors that cannot be required but are of benefit are strongly encouraged. This might be considered by some to be an encroachment on individual freedoms, but it also provides ethical guidance that is generally beyond the bounds of modern legal systems.

A parallel to the fivefold taxonomy may be found in Jewish law as well as Islamic law, though in less developed form. The categories and their terminology as found in Rabbinic literature are:

1. Required—*ḥayyav*
2. Recommended—*meshubbaḥ*
3. Neutral—*muttar* (lit. "permitted")
4. Condemned—*megunneh*
5. Forbidden—*asur*[1]

A second parallel between the *Sharīʿa* and the *halakhah* is the division between duties to God and duties to other people. The former category treats ritual observance, and the latter category, social transactions. The quintessential requirements of the first category are laid out in the "Five Pillars of Islam," which treats prayer, fasting, almsgiving, and pilgrimage. The second category officially treats civil and criminal law, commercial law, and family law.

Sharī`a Family Law

Family Law is one category of human relations that has always remained under the jurisdiction of *Sharī`a* courts. It worked out family relations and responsibilities in response to the needs of the community during the early centuries, so it is reflective of a worldview that in many ways finds more parallels with traditional Jewish law and customs than with modern secular sensibilities.

The primary social unit of the decidedly patriarchal Arabian culture was (and is) the extended family headed by one male leader, the most senior, who guides and controls the family. The basic unit consisted of the father, his wife or wives, unmarried sons and daughters, and married sons with their wives and children. All had specific roles within the family structure, which served their basic social and economic needs. In the pre-Islamic period, a woman seems to have had little autonomy. She could not inherit and could be divorced at will, and if sustenance stretched the resources of the family unit,

SHEIKH YŪSUF AL-QARADĀWI

One of the most respected and influential spokespersons for Islam in this generation is Sheikh Yūsuf Al-Qaradāwi,[2] an Egyptian-born religious scholar who moved to Qatar and, in addition to his extensive writings, has become extremely popular through his television program, "Sharī`a and Life" and his website, "Islam Online," founded in 1997. He is a controversial figure, as are most public religious personages in the Muslim world, and is considered by many to be a "moderate conservative." His views, which will be cited occasionally below, would be a reasonably fair indicator of the sensibilities of the large middle, located between the radicals, on the one hand, and highly Westernized types, on the other. He articulates general principles upon which relational behaviors are based: awareness of the strong bond of brotherhood that links one individual to another and the protection of the rights of the individual and the sanctity of life, honor, and property.[3]

female newborns could be left to die so as not to use up valuable assets. The Qur'an made substantial changes in the status of women. While not granting the same level of rights as to men, some verses articulate the spiritual equality of women before God: "Men who surrender unto God and women who surrender, men who believe and women who believe, men who obey and women who obey, men who speak the truth and women who speak the truth . . .—God has prepared for them forgiveness and a vast reward" (Q.33:35).

The Qur'an forbids female infanticide (Q.81:8–9), women have the right to offer legal testimony though not at the same level of men (Q.2:282), and they have the right to inherit, though also at a reduced level from men (Q.4:11). Women receive material sustenance as part of the marriage contract (Q.4:4), and according to some interpretations of Q.2:229: (" . . . it is no sin for either of [the husband or wife] if the woman ransom herself"), women may initiate divorce. The work of both women and men is valued (Q.3:195), and both may retain what they have personally earned (Q.4:32). Women are thus considered independent individuals economically in *Sharīʿa*. They may generate their own income and own their own property.

These are generally considered progressive developments according to modern observers, but the Qur'an, like the Torah, is not a modern text. Both scriptures reflect cultural values and expectations from a different time and context, and as such they also contain material that would be considered problematic by most moderns. As noted above, the rights of women remain at a level that is below that of men and they are sometimes objectified in the Qur'an in relation to men. The classic example cited by many non-Muslim critics is that young females become one category of the "rewards" for men in the hereafter (Q.44:51–54, 52:17–20). And while modesty and modest dress applies to both men and women (Q.7:26), women's modesty is specified in greater detail than that of men, one classic example being Q.33:59: "O Prophet, tell your wives, your daughters and the believing women to put on their outer garments. That is most suitable so that they will be recognized and not molested."

It is of course possible to collect only those verses of the Qur'an, or any scripture for that matter, that reflect our own current values, and it is possible to collect verses that would appear anathema to our current values. As students of a religious system that is not our own, we must be careful to use the same criteria of judgment that we would apply to our own religious system. One can easily find objectionable verses and commendable verses on similar topics in the Torah or in the New Testament.

Arguably, one has the right to be critical of the religion of the other only as long as one is willing to apply the same criteria of judgment to one's own religious system. Our natural human tendency, however, is to judge our own system with more leniency than we judge a system that is foreign to us. We must be ever aware of that tendency if we are to overcome the barriers that divide people against one another. The great Jewish sage, Rabbi Yehoshua Ben Perachia, is known for having uttered the famous maxim, "Procure a teacher for yourself, acquire for yourself a study partner, and judge all people charitably."[4] The term for "all people" in this dictum is the Hebrew phrase, *kol ha-'adam*. That term refers not only to Jews but to all human beings.

Islam is confronted with a similar situation as Judaism in that its primary sources are ancient and reflect ideas and sensibilities that are often very different and problematic to many readers. On the other hand, many Muslims (and certainly some Jews reading this book) do not necessarily find the theoretical assumptions underlying many of these rulings to be problematic. We refer here to the assumption that certain societal values are grounded in the permanence of the divine essence as reflected authoritatively in scripture. This sense of necessary, absolute groundedness in divine writ is often considered problematic to moderns, but even with such a position, traditional interpretive modes applied to scripture and post-scriptural religious literatures and practices can and often do manage to renew the meanings and the practices of religious people.

Religions such as Islam and Judaism have a breadth of interpretive strategies and processes that can convey divinely authored scripture and tradition in a meaningful way to people with modern sensibilities about the role of women, the meaning of ritual, and so forth. Those strategies and processes do not inevitably move in a single direction, however, either toward liberalism or toward traditionalism. Rather, they reflect the complex ways in which humans interact between their traditional beliefs and values, on the one hand, and ever-changing social and technical realities, on the other. The net result is a multiplicity of interpretations of religion and, therefore, modes of practice, each reflecting a unique combination of issues with which populations and subpopulations, groups and subgroups, grapple in their attempts to find meaning in the universe in which they live.

PART THREE

THE *UMMA*: ISLAM IN PRACTICE

CHAPTER 18

The *Umma* and the Caliphate

The *umma* is the term that is most frequently used to describe the entire community of Muslims throughout the world. In the Qur'an, all of humankind was once part of a single *umma* (Q.2:213) to which God graciously sent prophets and scriptures. After the division of humankind into peoples or nations, *umma* is the reference for the individual ethnic or religious communities to whom God sent prophets (Q.10:47, 16:36), such as an *umma* in Arabia to which God sent Muhammad (Q.13:30). The people of Moses are referred to as *umma* (Q.7:59), as are some of the People of the Book (Q.3:113).

The Pact of Medina discussed in Part 1 created an inclusive *umma* in which Believers, Jews, and even polytheist Medinans were initially included, but over the years of Muhammad's mission in Medina it became increasingly Muslim in character and membership.

With the expansion of Islam through the conquests, the Arab rulers found themselves in control of a great multiethnic and multireligious empire made up of many different peoples. Sometimes this entire empire is referred to as the *umma*, but sometimes *umma* refers only to the Muslims within that empire. The *umma* as a whole enjoyed a centralized government under the caliphs, the leaders at the very top of the pyramid of rule whose name signified that they were the lieutenants or replacements of Muhammad in all but prophethood. The non-Muslim religious communities who came under Muslim rule governed their own internal affairs according to their traditional systems, but always under the overall rule of the caliph. The caliphs, also known as "commanders of the faithful," governed in theory if not always in reality from the death of the Prophet in 632 until the conquest of the Mongols in the 13th century. The caliphate, ruled by the caliph, was the political system for governing the *umma*. While it was an ideal institution in theory, it is recognized that the caliphate did not maintain anything near the integrity of the *umma* under Muhammad's leadership.

Few contemporary governments in the Muslim world are beloved or even much respected by their constituencies today, and there are movements, particularly among the more radically activist Islamists, to unify the Muslim world through the reestablishment of the caliphate. Returning the caliphate through force of arms is not a priority except among a small fringe, although the notion of the caliphate ideal remains important for most Muslims. The inclination to reestablish the caliphate is nevertheless only one expression of the desire among many to revive the stature of the Muslim world. The notion of a united *umma* has remained a part of the Muslim self-concept throughout history to this day, but there is little agreement about what that united *umma* should look like in reality. They do agree, however, that when the *umma* is governed properly by *Sharī'a*, it is an eminently ethical system and egalitarian, protecting the rights of Muslim and non-Muslim alike, and that it does not distinguish among race, class, or ethnicity.

Non-Muslims

The Qur'an has a number of designations for those within and outside the community of Believers, and the meaning of these is somewhat fluid. The terms "Muslim" and "Believer" and "*ḥanīf*" were discussed in Part 1. The most important terms for those outside the community range from idolater (*mushrik*) to disbeliever (*kāfir*).

Idolaters

A *mushrik* is one who associates other powers with divinity. The polytheism of pre-Islamic Arabia is simply called *shirk*, meaning "associationism," that is, assigning associates to God. Those associates take the form of idols. Abraham is cited in the Qur'an as articulating the essence of the problem: "You are only worshiping idols rather than God, and you manufacture falsehood. But what you worship in place of God cannot sustain you, so seek the sustenance of God, worship Him and thank Him, for to Him you shall be returned" (Q.29:17). *Shirk* is the worst possible sin, and the only sin for which there can be no divine forgiveness (Q.4:48). The act of *shirk* is not only a travesty in relation to God, it is a distortion and falsification of reality. It is an act of stupidity and ignorance reflected in the very term for the pre-Islamic period in Arabic: *jāhiliyya*, meaning "ignorance" and suggesting something akin to simple and complete lack of civilization.

Idolaters, therefore, are an absolute enemy to the most basic and defining aspect of monotheism, the unity of God. As mentioned, idolatry has both religious and sociopolitical meaning, since it is intimately associated with evil behavior. Ethics and *shirk* are as opposite as are night and day. Idolaters, therefore, represent the enemy, those who persist in the dual evil of idolatry and immorality.

Unbelievers

The word *"kāfir"* derives from a root meaning "to cover" or "to conceal." The word has a near-exact equivalent in the Hebrew verb, *kafar*, meaning "to deny," and it is the operative term in Judaism for those who would deny the existence of God. In Judaism, one who is *kofer be`ikar* is an atheist. The Arabic term *kāfir*, as articulated in the Qur'an, references one whose stubborn refusal to acknowledge the truths of Islam and the prophethood of Muhammad serves to conceal those truths. This denial of the truth of Islam is called *kufr*, and the term may be found in its various forms hundreds of times in the Qur'an. The old standard translation into English used to be "infidel," meaning one who practices infidelity to the truth, but today it is often translated as "unbeliever."

"INFIDELS" OR "UNBELIEVERS"?

> We brought down the Torah in which is guidance and light. The prophets who submitted judged the Jews by it, as did the rabbis and the learned, according to what was entrusted to them from the book of God, of which they were witnesses. So do not fear people. Rather, fear Me! And do not sell My signs for a petty price. Whoever does not judge by what God has revealed are the unbelievers. (Q.5:44)

As may be observed from this verse and many others, the unbelievers are not necessarily idolaters, though they may be idolaters as well. Whether idolaters, Jews, or Christians, they refuse to acknowledge the divine nature of qur'anic revelation articulated by the prophet Muhammad.

Jews

We have observed the ambivalent position of the Qur'an regarding the Jews. On the one hand, they represent an ancient and respected tradition of monotheism. On the other, they refused to accept the true prophetic mission of God's messenger in Muhammad. The clash between the ideal of a fellow monotheistic people and the reality of a community that refused to accept Muhammad resulted in a conflict that has never been adequately resolved. Here and in the following section we leave the particulars of history in order to consider the position of Jews and Christians as paradigmatic of the monotheistic religious "other."

The Jews are referenced in the Qur'an both as Jews (*yahūd* or *alladhīna hādū*) and as Israelites (*banū isrā'īl*). The second reference for Jews, *alladhīna hādū*, means literally "those who judaized," and probably refers to the fact that the Jewish community of Arabia was made up of many indigenous Arabs who had converted to Judaism. *Banū isrā'īl* refers to the Israelites of the Bible, but they serve a double role in the Qur'an. On the one hand, they represent an ancient monotheistic people that was redeemed from Egyptian slavery, given the Torah in the desert, and experienced the miracles of the parting of the sea, the manna and quail, and the entrance to the Holy Land promised to them by God. That is to say, they represent a historical example of how God rewards monotheistic peoples. On the other hand, the *banū isrā'īl* serve as a metaphor for the local Jews of Arabia in their stiff-necked nature and backsliding away from obedience to the divine word. In the actual historical context of 7th-century Arabia, where two monotheistic communities vied with each other over potential supporters among polytheistic peoples in the region, one powerful advantage held by the Jews was their ancient history and venerable customs and traditions as the earliest representation of monotheism. The newly emerging community of Believers could counter this claim by pointing out how the ancestors of these very Jews were punished by God for their continuous habit of disobeying the divine word, rejecting their own prophets, and even violating the very scripture that their God had personally revealed to them. All these accusations are fully rehearsed in the Jewish Torah! What more could be expected from their children and descendants who publicly refute the claims of God's final prophet and refuse to accept God's last and most perfect revelation?

Jews are specifically and repeatedly condemned in the Qur'an for having distorted or corrupted parts of their own scripture. "Some of the Jews pervert words away from their proper usage . . ." (Q.4:46). "Since they broke their covenant We cursed them and made their hearts hard. They pervert words from their places . . ." (Q.5:13). "The Jews, those who listen to lies, who listen to other people who have not come to you. They pervert words from their proper order . . ." (Q.5:41, and see also 2:79). These accusations reflect upon the discrepancy between the revelations that Muhammad received and the claims of the Jews with whom he came into contact that the Qur'an does not conform to their scripture and is therefore incorrect.

The disconnect between the Jewish and Muslim views and representations of common scriptural heroes can be better understood when we examine the expectations and meaning of scripture within the two religious systems. The literary nature of the Hebrew Bible allows for a great deal of criticism of its heroes. There is no single protagonist in the Bible that is not without error, without problems or selfishness that makes him or her fully human and recognizable to those who would relate personally to the difficulties of life. In the Qur'an, however, the same "biblical" personages appear as divinely guided prophets who exhibit little of the frailty of the human condition that is so emphasized in the biblical stories. The Qur'an is less a literary work than it is a self-conscious scripture. It is more straightforwardly didactic than the Hebrew Bible, which conveys its lessons in a more nuanced and less direct manner. The Abraham of the Qur'an, for example, has a more straightforward image as one who surrenders entirely to God's will in all of its depictions, serving as an ideal role model of the kind of human behavior that monotheists should strive for. In the Bible, however, Abraham sometimes doubts God's ability and hedges his bets (Gen. 12:10–20, 17:15–21, 18:22–32). He epitomizes the human struggle to surrender to the divine demands at the same time that he sometimes doubts the ability of God to carry them out. Each style accomplishes a similar goal, but each one fits the particular cultural context to which it was designed to reach out.

According to the Qur'an, the Jews of Muhammad's generation were a mixed community, just like their Israelite forebears. While some quarreled and were stiff-necked, others were upright and true believers (Q.2:83, 3:110–114). It is likely that the quarrelsome and stubborn group represented the overall Jewish community that refused to accept the prophethood and the revelation of Muhammad, while those considered upright and true believers were the individuals who accepted Muhammad's role of prophet and religious leader.

Christians

Like the Jews, the Christians in the Qur'an are portrayed as unfaithful to their covenant with God, thus providing an opening for the newly emerging expression of monotheism represented by Muhammad and the Qur'an (Q.5:18,72). That said, the general qur'anic position regarding Christians is less harsh than its view of Jews (Q.57:27). This most likely reflects the fact that Muhammad and his generation had less conflict and competition with

Christians than with the Jews. No organized Christian community lived in either Mecca or Medina, so Muhammad did not have the same unhappy experience of being rejected by them. "You will find the people most hostile to the believers to be the Jews and polytheists, and you will find the closest in love to believers to be those who say: 'We are Christians'" (Q.5:82).

While the sentiment toward Christians is milder, the qur'anic view of Christianity is much harsher than its view of Judaism. It condemns what it considers the Christian doctrine that God is one of three (Q.4:171, 5:73), that Jesus and his mother Mary are gods (Q.5:116), that they associate other powers with God (Q.9:31, 17:111, 25:2), that God has a son or child (Q.19:35, 23:91, 25:2), and that the messiah is the son of God (Q.9:30).

To summarize, the Qur'an condemns Jews more than Christians (the people), but Christianity more than Judaism (the religion). The pristine expressions of both Judaism and Christianity in their original and unsullied state are assumed to have been accurate reflections of the divine will because of their authentic prophetic origin. But over the generations and ages they became corrupted. The authentic revelation of the Qur'an was meant to be a corrective to the deep flaws in the older systems. This is not a supercessionist revelation, but rather a *corrective* revelation. The earlier systems are not canceled, but they are also not fully acceptable because of their corruption. The peoples who follow the flawed religious systems therefore enjoy a legal status in the Muslim world, but they are not equals to those who follow the unspoiled revelation articulated by Muhammad. The Qur'an and prophetic mission of Muhammad thus find a most honored place in the sacred history of humankind.

People of the Book

While Jews are proud to refer to themselves as "People of the Book," most are unaware that the origin for this term is likely the Qur'an. The qur'anic use of the term refers not only to the Jews, but to all communities that had received revelation prior to the revelation of the Qur'an. These earlier revelations are all considered divine and the God that revealed them is identical to the God of Islam. "Do not argue with the People of the Book except with what is better, aside from those of them who have been unjust. Say: 'We believe in what has been revealed to us and in what has been revealed to you. Our God and your God is one. We surrender to Him'" (Q.21:46). We have observed how Muhammad assumed that the People of the Book would naturally recognize the truth of Muhammad's revelation. When they are called upon to accept the completion of revelation through the Qur'an, however, at least a faction refused to do so. "Have you seen those who have been given a portion of the Book and are called to the Book of God to judge among them; and then a part of them turn away, avoiding?" (Q.3:23).

The People of the Book include Jews, Christians, and Sabeans (Q.2:62, 5:69). Among these, "any who believe in God and the Last Day and who do good have their reward with their Lord. They need have no fear, nor should they grieve." Qur'an 22:17 seems to add Zoroastrians to the list, and later commentators cite this verse as a proof text for including Zoroastrianism among the protected religions.[1] All will be judged by God on the day of resurrection, but those at the top of the list in the verse seem to stand in contrast to the last community, the idolaters who associate others with God. "As for the Believers and Jews, the Sabeans, Christians and Zoroastrians, and the idolaters, God will decide between them on the Day of Resurrection, for God is witness to all things" (Q.22:17). That God is the final arbiter of Judgment and that the religious and moral-ethical merit of all individuals will be judged by God is a repeated theme in the Qur'an (Q.2:113, 5:48, 6:108, 16:93, 42:15, 88:21–26). As long as they "believe in God and the Last Day and do good," they have no need to fear. And because it is impossible to judge the internal beliefs of one's fellows, one must be satisfied to judge only their actions. This message allows and encourages Muslims to live together with non-Muslims who are not idolaters without being required to take responsibility for or meddle in their internal religious affairs.

The Qur'an states quite clearly that the scriptures of the People of the Book are divinely revealed (Q.2:89, 3:3, 6:89). Muhammad is even advised in one revelation to consult the People of the Book about any uncertainties in his own divine revelation. "And if you are uncertain about what We have sent down to you, ask those who read the Book [that was] before you. The truth has come to you from your Lord, so do not be one of those who doubt" (Q.10:94).

The Dhimma

The People of the Book are defined in *Sharī'a* as being People of the *dhimma* or *dhimmīs*, usually translated as "People of the Pact" or "protected people." The term *"dhimma"* occurs only occasionally in the Qur'an, and it implies "pact" or "treaty" (Q.9:8,10). In a slightly different form, the root means "condemned" or "disgraced" (Q.68:49, 17:18,22). It is the term that has come to define the legal status of the People of the Book in Muslim society based on interpretations of Q.9:29: "Fight those given scripture who do not believe in God and the last day, who do not forbid what God and His messenger have forbidden, and who do not profess the religion of truth, until they pay tribute willingly and are humbled (or humiliated)."

The status of *dhimmis* includes two qualities: protection and submission. In its most basic theoretical form, the People of the Book are protected by Muslim law as long as they submit to the hegemony of the Muslim regime and make that submission evident through certain behaviors demonstrating their secondary status: distinguishing dress, modest or deferential deportment toward Muslims, and other social restrictions. As long as they maintain their deferential position, they retain their citizenship and are protected by the state. If they do not, then they lose their protected status and may be persecuted and victimized without protection.

Contemporary Thinking on Relations with the People of the Book

Contemporary Muslim thinking about the People of the Book is highly influenced by contemporary history, politics, and religious trends. Western pressures on the Muslim world through international politics and economics and the military is interpreted by some contemporary Muslim politicians and religious leaders as forms of attack against Islam. In the last quarter of the 20th century until now, Jews and Christians (but especially Jews) have often been depicted in Muslim areas as the cause of much wrong in the world, from endemic economic and health problems even to the malfunction of machinery or bad plumbing. This victimization has often been carried out in the media and through inaccurate and even racist depictions in educational materials taught in some religious and public school systems in the Muslim world. Militant Islamists who are on the march against the West clearly identify the People of the Book with the most negative depictions found in the Qur'an and the tradition literature.

On the other hand, Sufis whose religious practice centers on striving for unity with the divine essence often desire to share and learn with people of all religions. In his discussion on relations between Muslims and non-Muslims, the well-known and highly influential contemporary Muslim scholar, Yusuf al-Qaradawi, cites Q.60:8–9: "God does not forbid you to be kind and charitable to those who do not fight you on account of religion and do not drive you from your homes, for God loves the just. God only forbids you to be friends with those who fight you on account of religion, drive you from your homes and aid in driving you out. Those who befriend them are themselves wrongdoers."[2] According to Qaradawi, this verse refers not only to non-Muslims who are the People of the Book, but ". . . even if they are idolators [*sic*] and polytheists."[3] The operative issue in his opinion is whether or not the non-Muslims fight Muslims or drive them out of their homes for religious reasons.

CHAPTER 19

The Five Pillars of Islam

The Five Pillars of Islam represent an outline or résumé of Islamic faith and practice. They are the basic elements, the minimum and certainly not the entirety of religion. The first of the five is a creedal statement that reflects the core of faith. The remaining four treat practice. All are understood as first principles, the pillars or foundations upon which the house of Islam stands firm.

1. Witnessing (Shahāda or Shahādatayn)[1]

This first principle is a statement of testimony made up of two parts: that there is but one divinity that created and powers the universe, and that Muhammad is a prophet or messenger of that great God. The first part of this testimony was considered in Part 2 when the Five Pillars of Faith were considered: "There is no god but God." The second phrase of the *shahāda* declares that Muhammad is God's messenger. Together, the phrase reads in Arabic, *lā ilāha illāllah umuḥammadun rasūlullāh.*[2] This is the foundational creedal statement of Islam, something equivalent in power and meaning to the Jewish testimony that is recited at least twice every day in the daily prayer service: "Pay attention, Israelites: The Lord our God is One!" (*shema' yisra'el adonay eloheinu adonai eḥad*—Deut. 6:4). In addition to its centrality as the quintessential article of faith, the *shahāda* is also a formula for conversion. Stating the *shahāda* freely and without compulsion before witnesses is all that is required to become a Muslim.

One peculiar aspect of Arabic (that finds an exact parallel in Hebrew) is that the construct phrase, *rasūlullāh*, can mean either "*a* prophet of God" or "*the* prophet of God." Because Islam accepts the prophethood of all the biblical characters who communicated with God as well as some extrabiblical characters found in the Qur'an such as the prophets Hūd and Ṣāliḥ, the former meaning is most accurate.

2. *Prayer (Ṣalāt)*

All four of the following pillars are designated by Arabic names that have direct Hebrew or Aramaic equivalents. The Aramaic equivalent of *ṣalāt* is *tzlota*, which simply means prayer.[3] In the Islamic system, there is a difference between the required daily prayers called *ṣalāt* and the private petitionary prayers or invocations that are called *du'ā'*. *Ṣalāt* are highly regulated, formal prayers that must be recited at fixed times with a regulated liturgy and formal body postures that include bowing, kneeling, and full prostration. *Du'ā'* are "superogatory" prayers, meaning additional personal prayers that are not required but of course always encouraged. There is no formal prayer book for the required prayers, since they are relatively short, include many repeated phrases, and are generally quite easy to remember.

As in Judaism, it is not necessary for ordained clergy to lead the prayer service. The prayer leader must be, simply, a respected and pious member of the community who knows the rules in order to lead the congregation properly. There is also no singing or music in official prayers. Muslims may pray in any clean space without undo distraction, under a roof or in the open and with any number of people or alone, although it is preferable to pray in a mosque if one is available. A prayer rug is used simply in order to ensure that the prostrations that are the core body movement of Islamic prayer are done in a clean place. The Arabic word for the rug, *sajjāda*, means "a thing for prostrating."

Islamic prayer is expected to be conducted in the Arabic language. Only the Hanafi school is open to the possibility of some prayer being conducted in another language. Additionally, communal prayer is always preferable to individual prayer. According to a respected *hadith* found in the most respected collection of Bukhari, "The prayer that a man performs in congregation is worth 25 of his prayers in his home or in the market."[4] Prayer must be oral and recited outwardly but neither too loudly nor too softly: "Do not be too loud in your prayer and not too quiet, but seek a way between them" (Q.17:110). And prayer must be engaged soberly and calmly, with concentration and intention, paying attention to the rhythm of the prayer as it unfolds.

The Mosque

The term for a prayer space in Arabic is constructed from the same root found in the word for a prayer rug (*sajjāda*). Mosque is *masjid* in Arabic, which means "place of prostration." It need not be a building. Any clean space dedicated to Muslim prayer is a *masjid*. The first mosque of the Prophet in Medina, for example, was simply an open courtyard in front of Muhammad's house. Mosque architecture may vary considerably, and while there are recognized architectural styles that emerged in the Muslim world, they are a matter of aesthetic only. There are certain requirements for a mosque, however. No images of any kind are allowed in or on a mosque. One will find no representation of God, people, or animals, and no scenes from Muslim sacred history. Decoration is typically calligraphic, often with the use of artistic and intricate scripts citing verses of the Qur'an, or complex geometric patterns of decoration. Ceramic tiles are a common medium for these artistic expressions, but one might also see exquisite wood carvings and wood inlay built into walls and beautiful crystal chandeliers.

Outside the actual prayer space is a washing area where people may engage in a ritual washing before beginning prayer. This is typically located in a courtyard one must pass before entering the building. In modern buildings and in cooler climates, the washing areas may be found within the building itself, but in a space that is separated from the prayer area.

The first thing one notices when entering the actual place of prostration is that shoes are removed and one enters into a fully carpeted room devoid of furniture. Furniture gets in the way of the prostrations that are central to the act of prayer among almost all Muslims, although chairs may be set up for older people who have difficulty engaging in the full range of body movements. There are also typically small wooden book holders for copies of the Qur'an during study or recitation. There is no altar or *bimah* in a mosque. The only two special features are the *miḥrāb* and the *minbar*. The *miḥrāb* is a marking, often a decorated niche in one wall, that designates the direction to Mecca, called *qibla*. The *miḥrāb* points to the proper direction to face in prayer (Q.2:142,150), and has a similar function to the Jewish *mizraḥ* that guides the Jewish worshiper to direct prayers eastward toward Jerusalem. While it is a Jewish *custom* to pray in the direction of Jerusalem, it is a qur'anic *requirement* for Muslims to face Mecca: "From wherever you go forth, turn your face in the direction of the Sacred Mosque, and wherever you are, turn your faces in its direction" (Q.2:150). Near the *miḥrāb* is the *minbar*, which is a pulpit from where the sermon is preached on Fridays.

When people are engaged in communal prayer they stand close together in rows, almost touching shoulders so that they may engage in a kind of community choreography of group prayer. Men and women are separated in prayer, and, as in the traditional Jewish system, that separation may take various forms. In some, there is no space for women in the actual prayer room. There may be a separate women's section in an adjoining room or in some cases women simply do not join in prayer with men in that particular mosque. In other mosques, women pray behind men in the same room, and in some women are separated to one side, sometimes with a cloth partition. Women may be prayer leaders for women's prayer groups, but men are expected to serve that function in mixed groups.

Prayer Times

Muslims are expected to engage in prayer five times daily. They begin with the Dawn (*fajr*) prayer that is recited after dawn and before sunrise, and continue with the Noon (*dhuhr*) prayer that is observed just when the sun begins to decline from its zenith, the Afternoon (*`aṣr*) prayer when the sun is about midway between high noon and setting, the Sunset (*maghrib)* prayer engaged immediately after sunset, and the Evening (*`ishā'*) prayer that may be observed between the time when the red glow of sunset disappears and midnight.

The Shi`a also require five daily prayers, but they may pray them in three distinct times rather than five. That is, they are allowed to pray the Noon and Afternoon prayers one after the other, and the Sunset and Evening prayers one after the other. The prayers are each separate and discreet but are simply joined together in time, though it is generally considered preferable to pray them at the five separate times when possible. It should be noted that three of the four Sunni schools (all but the Ḥanafi) also accept the combining of separate prayer sequences in case of rain, travel, and danger, but unlike the Shi`a, do not allow combining them for convenience. We find a parallel in Judaism, where although prayed as distinct prayers, the Afternoon (*minḥah*) and Evening (*`aravit*, also called *ma`ariv*, which is the same word as the Arabic evening prayer called *maghrib*) prayers are often prayed one after the other for convenience. In all cases, both Islamic and Jewish, when two prayers are joined, they are to be engaged at an appropriate point between the two expected times.

In pre-Islamic Arabia, it was customary for Christians to call their faithful to prayer with a wooden clapper that made a sharp sound as its parts were struck together. According to the Muslim sources, the Jews of Arabia called their faithful to prayer by blowing a shofar (ram's horn). Muhammad ordered that the Believers be gathered by the oral call of his companion, Bilāl, a former Ethiopian slave who was freed by Muhammad's close friend, Abū Bakr. The Qur'an refers to a call to prayer specifically in reference to the special

Friday prayer (Q.62:9). Each prayer time is announced by the call of a *mu'adhdhin* (sometimes spelled *mu'azzin*), who sings out a melodious, formulaic invitation or call to prayer:

> God is greatest. God is greatest. God is Greatest. God is Greatest.
> I witness that there is no god but God; I witness that there is no god but God.
> I witness that Muhammad is His messenger. I witness that Muhammad is his messenger.
> Hurry to prayer! Hurry to prayer!
> Hurry to success! Hurry to success!
> [In the early morning call, the following is also included: "Prayer is better than sleep! Prayer is better than sleep!" The Shi`a do not include this phrase. They have in its place, "Hurry to the best activity! Hurry to the best activity!" and include it in this part of every call to prayer.]
> God is greatest. God is greatest.
> There is no god but God.

Before the invention of electricity, the *mu'azzin* would climb up the minaret of the mosque and call to prayer over the rooftops of the city, town, or village. In the Muslim world today, microphones and amplifiers raise the decibel level much higher. In any case, the prayer times are announced personally, and recordings are not considered adequate. There is special merit in conducting prayer closest to the time of the call to prayer, though one fulfills one's obligation any time within the period designated for the particular prayer.

Engaging in the Ṣalāt Prayer

Prayer is a very personal act in Islam, but whether one is engaged in prayer alone or with a group, the physical movements integral to the praying process demonstrate the worshiper's absolute submission to God. This includes not only standing, bowing, and kneeling, but also full prostration in which the forehead touches the ground.[5] The prayer service is made up of cycles of these movements carried out while reciting the words of prayer.

Before engaging in prayer, Muslims must be in a state of ritual purity. Many forms of ritual pollution are removed simply through ablutions (more on the issue of ritual pollution and purity follow below). The basic ablution process is laid out in the Qur'an (5:6).

> O Believers! When you get up to pray, wash your faces and your hands and arms to the elbows, wipe your heads and your feet to the

> ankles. If you are unclean, then purify yourselves. But if you are sick or on a journey, or if one of you comes from a call of nature or if you have been intimate with women and you cannot find water, then get yourselves some fine earth or sand and wipe your faces and hands with it. God does not want to make it hard for you but wants you to be clean and to complete His favor upon you so you may be grateful. (Q.5:6)

There are slight differences in the details of the ablutions between the law schools, but the process is quite consistent across the Muslim world and is based on the *sunna* of Muhammad. Short prayers or statements meant to raise one's spiritual consciousness before prayer are recommended during the ablutions. When washing the feet, for example, some might say, "O God! Make my feet firm on the path [of justice] when feet easily slip away from the path!"

After the call to prayer and just before actually engaging in the prayer service itself, one hears the *iqāma*, which is almost identical to the call but is recited in a lower tone and quite rapidly, without pause between the sections. People line up for prayer in rows with no deference to economic or social rank, shoulder to shoulder with strangers. Even if only two people pray together, one takes the role of imam to lead the prayer. In the mosque, the leader stands with his back to the worshipers and faces the niche (*miḥrāb*), thereby indicating the proper direction of prayer.

The actual *ṣalāt* prayer begins with each participant declaring his intention to engage in prayer. This is the *niyya*, which finds a close parallel in the Jewish *kavanah*. *Niyya* is required before any ritual act. It ensures proper mental and spiritual focusing and is intended to eliminate rote and unthinking acts of prayer. But unlike most cases of *kavanah*, the *niyya* specifically articulates and commits for the practitioner exactly what he intends to do. For example, if one is about to engage in three cycles of prostration, the practitioner will state that in the *niyya* and is then required to engage in exactly what was articulated.[6]

The number of prostration cycles varies with each daily *ṣalāt* prayer, and additional prostration cycles may be added on a voluntary basis. The actual position of the hands varies slightly between groups, as do some of the finer details of the blessings and prayers, but the basic liturgy and prostration cycle are the same throughout the Muslim world. The basic prostration cycle follows. After the statement of intention,

1. The worshiper stands erect and faces Mecca with the hands usually at either side of the head and with thumbs nearly touching the earlobes. In that position, the statement called the *takbīr* is recited: "God is great" (*Allāhu akbar*). This marks the entry into the sacred

moment of prayer, and from this moment onward, the worshiper concentrates fully on the act of worship.

2. Still standing, but now with the hands either dropped and hanging loosely on either side of the body or folded gently beneath the chest, the opening chapter of the Qur'an is recited silently or in a whisper. Then another section of the Qur'an chosen by the worshiper is recited silently.
3. This is followed by a second *takbīr:* "God is Great," after which the worshiper bows, saying, "Glory be to God" (sometimes repeatedly). Then the standing position is resumed.
4. After another *takbīr,* the worshiper fluidly descends to a prostrate position without delay. The toes of both feet, both hands, both knees, and the forehead all touch the floor with palms flat on either side of the head. At that moment the worshiper utters another *takbīr* and then assumes a very specific half-kneeling half-sitting position with hands resting on the thighs. Then a second prostration is performed like the first, ending with *takbīr.*
5. After a short pause, the standing position is resumed. This then marks the end of a single prostration cycle, which is repeated according to the number of cycles required for the specific *ṣalāt.*
6. After the last prostration of the last cycle, rather than standing, the worshiper resumes the sitting position of no. 4 and recites a testimony to the unity of God and the prophethood of Muhammad that is virtually the same as the *shahāda*, followed by a prayer that God give blessings to Muhammad and his family just as God gave blessings to Abraham and his family. This may be followed by a personal prayer if the worshiper wishes.
7. Worship is ended with a short blessing called *taslīm*, the "wishing of peace": "Peace and divine blessings and mercy to you all." This is uttered twice by turning the head to the right and the left. Traditions explain this as a blessing to all fellow Muslims and by extension, to all humankind, or as a blessing to the two angels that are poised on either shoulder of the worshiper, especially at the time of prayer.[7]

Friday Prayer

The one required community prayer is the Friday Noon Prayer, which begins with a sermon that includes a teaching from the Qur'an and often a teaching also from the *Hadith.*[8] During the regular daily prayers, the minimum number required to constitute a "congregation" (for which an imam leads the prayer service) is only two. The Friday prayer requires more participants, depending on the prevailing law school, ranging from four (Hanafi) to 12 (Maliki) to 40 worshipers (Shafi`i and Hanbali). Women are not required to attend and are not counted in the minimum required number (the conceptual equivalent of the Jewish minyan).

Friday is the day of gathering, but it is not a day of rest. Islam does not have the concept of cessation from all manner of labor. Nevertheless, Muslims often take the day off and Muslim businesses usually close at least during midday on Friday to allow workers (and encourage customers) to go to the mosque. Only males are required to attend the Friday mosque. It is expected for worshipers to bathe well and to apply sweet oil if possible for this occasion, and people congregate early.

Reciting the Qur'an

Reciting the Qur'an is an act of piety in Islam. According to Islamic tradition, the Qur'an is the actual speech of God, relayed to Muhammad through the agency of the angel Gabriel and then recited verbatim by the Prophet to the people. The written Qur'an that we have in an official Arabic text is the literal record of the divine speech, so any articulation of the Qur'an is an articulation of God's word.

As mentioned above, reciting the first chapter of the Qur'an is a required component of the *ṣalāt,* as is the recitation of an additional part of the Qur'an that is up to the worshiper to choose. Particularly popular verses for these additional sections are the "Throne Verse" (Q.2:255), the "Light Verse" (Q.24:35), and some of the short, exhortatory chapters toward the end of the Qur'an in rhymed prose that are often memorized.

We have noted that many Muslims recite the "beautiful names" mentioned in Q.17:110: "Say: Call upon Allah or call upon al-Raḥmān; however you call upon Him, to Him belong the most beautiful names." Some of those many names appear in Q.59:22–24, and all are associated with the Qur'an, though not every single one appears in the actual text. In any case, reciting the beautiful names is considered an act of pious scriptural recitation. In fact, reciting the names of God with the help of the set of beads called the *misbaḥa* ("a device for praising") is a very common spiritual practice and also a means of calming one's nerves. An authoritative *Hadith* found repeated in the sources and reported on the authority of Abū Hurayra has Muhammad declaring: "God has ninety-nine names, one hundred minus one. Whoever enumerates them enters the Garden."[9]

Ritual Purity

Purity (*ṭahāra* // Hebrew *taharah*) references both a spiritual and a physical state. Although one may feel as if one is moving toward a higher spiritual state through ritual compunction in combination with personal kindness, gratitude, dedication, openness to God, and awareness of one's mortality and position as God's creature, one must also mind one's physical state. A Muslim is forbidden to perform *ṣalāt*, handle the Qur'an, or engage in rituals of the Pilgrimage, unless in a state of ritual purity. This is not unlike the parallel in Judaism, though with the destruction of the Jerusalem Temple the rules of ritual purity have been relaxed and substantially changed.

In Islam, there are two types of ritual impurity. One is external and attaches to the person by coming into contact with certain things such as blood, pus, urine, or feces of either humans or animals (human sweat, saliva, tears, and milk are considered to be clean). This contact with external sources is called *najāsa*. Wine and other alcoholic beverages are also *najāsa*, and the discharges from pigs and dogs are considered particularly impure. In the case of contact with *najāsa*, a thorough washing of the area that was in contact (or the clothing or rug or other object) is usually sufficient, though in the case of pigs and dogs, some require repeated washings, up to seven times.

The second type of ritual impurity is caused by engaging in or experiencing certain activities. This is called *ḥadath*. There are two levels of *ḥadath*: minor and major. Minor *ḥadath* is caused by intoxication, breaking wind, urination and defecation, touching human genitals with the palm of the hand, skin contact between mutually marriageable persons (especially if arousing), and sleeping or fainting. The latter renders one in a state of *ḥadath* because one is not aware whether one might have broken wind or otherwise come into contact with an object of impurity.

Minor *ḥadath* is removed by doing ablutions as described above prior to engaging in prayer. Worshipers must always do ablutions prior to the early morning (*fajr*) prayer because that regularly begins after rising from sleep, but if worshipers know that they have not incurred *ḥadath* since an earlier ablution, they need not repeat it before prayer.

Major *ḥadath* is contracted by sexual intercourse, menstruation and postpartum bleeding, and any seminal emission (kissing and fondling even while naked but without penetration incurs only minor *ḥadath*). A special term is used to denote the major pollution that derives from human sexuality, *janāba*. We need to stress that, just as in Judaism, being in a state of ritual purity or impurity in Islam is not a value judgment about one's personal value. It is, rather, related to a sense of recognition that one has entered a state in which instinctual and natural bodily drives and functions take precedence over absolute rational control. Before engaging in conscious acts of worship, one must simply transition back into a state of fuller personal volition represented by the act of ritual purification. Just as one would clean oneself up before a meeting with an important person, entering a state of ritual purity is a consciousness-raising act that helps the individual prepare for entering into a relationship with the One who created the universe.

3. Required Giving (Zakāt)

The Arabic term *"zakāt"* like many Islamic ritual terms, has a direct parallel with a Hebrew term. The Hebrew, *zekhut*, denotes merit and is associated with a sense of righteousness. In both Arabic and Hebrew, the meaning of the root is associated with purity. Qur'an 2:43 explicitly requires the giving of an alms tax. "Worship regularly, bring the *zakāt*, and bow your heads with those who bow [in prayer]." Qur'an 2:215 is more specific: "They ask you what they should spend. Say: 'Whatever good you spend is for parents, relatives, orphans, the needy and the wayfarer. God knows whatever good you do.'"

It may be of interest to Jews that the more common qur'anic term for this kind of religious act is *ṣadaqa*. "*Ṣadaqāt* are for the poor and the needy, the workers who administer them and those whose hearts are to be won over, for [ransom of] slaves, [relief of] debtors, for the path of God and the wayfarer; a duty imposed by God, for God is knowing, wise" (Q.9:60). This is exactly equivalent to the Hebrew *"tzedakah"*; there is no difference between the letter *ṣ* (*ṣād*) in the Arabic and the *tz* (*tzadi* or *tzadik*) in the Hebrew.

As may be observed from the verses cited at the beginning of this section, *ṣalāt* and *zakāt* are very closely associated in the Qur'an (see also Q.2:83,177,277, 4:77,162, etc.). Their close association reflects the view that the religious person must strive to engage in a deep and moral relationship with both God and fellow humans. One is not fulfilling one's obligation by neglecting either. This dual nature of responsibility finds a parallel in Judaism. It is generally characterized in Islam by the terms "acts of worship" (*'ibādāt*), which deal with the relationship between humans and God, and "relational behaviors" (*mu'āmalāt*), which deal with the relationship between humans. *Zakāt*, however, is considered in Islam to fit technically in the category of worship. Required contribution to the needy is an act of worshiping God.

As in Judaism, required giving is necessary to sustain the community. On a theological level, the assumption is that God is the owner of the world and all that is in it. Believers are sojourners in God's world, and it is the responsibility of Believers as sojourners to contribute to its maintenance. All wealth and all property are God's. We only handle it for a time, and we are responsible to ensure that it benefits God's creatures. As in other acts of worship, a *niyya* is made immediately prior to the giving of *zakāt*, and the Qur'an promises reward for generosity at any level. "Pray regularly and give *zakāt*, and lend unto God a good loan [understood by the tradition to mean: lend without interest]. Whatever good you put forth for the sake of your own souls you will find with God, who is good and greatest in reward. Seek forgiveness in God, for God is the most forgiving, gracious" (Q.73:20).

4. *Fasting (Ṣawm)*

The word for fasting in Arabic (*ṣiyām* or *ṣawm*) is exactly equivalent to the Hebrew *tzom*. We noted in chapter 5 how early on during Muhammad's period in Medina, the Believers engaged in a required fast called *`ashūra* on the 10th day of the month of Muharram. This is exactly equivalent to the Jewish fast on the 10th day of the 7th month *`asara betishre*: Yom Kippur. A respected *hadith* relates directly to this interesting parallel: "Yaḥya b. Yaḥya related a tradition on the authority of ibn `Abbās: The Messenger of God came to Medina and found the Jews fasting on the day of *`ashūra*. They were asked about that and said: 'This is the day that God granted Moses and the Children of Israel victory over Pharaoh, so we fast on it to glorify Him.' The Prophet said: 'We are closer to Moses than you!' So he commanded the [*`ashūra*] fast."[10]

The *`ashūra* fast dropped out of the required rituals of Islam when the verses commanding the Ramadan fast were revealed, but Muhammad was said to have continued to observe the *`ashūra* fast too. As we will observe below, the 10th of Muharram became an important day of mourning among Muslims for another reason in later history, but we return now to the topic of the great fasting month of Ramadan.

The Ramadan fast is perhaps the best-known religious act of Islam. It is a daylight fast that lasts the entire month of Ramadan. From dawn to sunset, Muslims are forbidden from eating, drinking, smoking, and marital relations. Chewing gum and the taking of medicines, aside from injection, are also prohibited during the fasting hours. Unintentional eating or drinking is forgiven, but intentional disruption of the fast is considered a serious violation. Penance for the breach (called *kaffāra* // Hebrew *kapparah*) varies from adding one more day after the end of the month to adding 60 fast days and feeding or paying the equivalent to provide 60 meals for the hungry.

On the other hand, pregnant women are forbidden from fasting, as are menstruating women or those who have recently given birth, the sick, old and feeble persons, minor children, and the clinically insane or those unable to understand the reason for fasting. Those on journey are also temporarily exempt. Travelers are expected to make up the missed days at another time during the year, minor children are encouraged to fast for part of the day in order to become accustomed to the practice, and the elderly who are able are encouraged to give the equivalent value to feed one person for each day that they miss. The Qur'an is quite explicit about fasting and about the fast of Ramadan:

> O Believers! Fasting is required of you as it was commanded to those before you, that you will be conscientious. A certain number of days, but if any of you are sick or on a journey, then the requirement is for other days. And an equivalent payment [lit. "ransom"] is required of those who are able: food for the needy. It is even better for those who volunteer greater good, though it is best for you to fast, if you only knew. The month of Ramadan is the one in which the Qur'an was revealed as guidance for humanity, clear guidance and redemption. So whoever among you is present that month should fast. But if one is sick or on a journey, then the prescribed number is from other days. God wishes ease for you, not hardship, that you complete the prescribed number and extol God for guiding you, and that you be grateful. (Q.2:183–185)

Muslims understand this verse to teach that the Ramadan fast should be personally taxing and an opportunity for one to stretch and engage in a kind of discipline that is not easy to self-impose, but that fasting should not be a negative hardship. Ramadan is also a period during which family and friends come together immediately after sunset to enjoy a large meal. It is a heightened family time with lots of food and simple entertainments. Sweets are distributed and many special foods are cooked and baked for the period. Special television series tend to be aired at this time because after the large fast-breaking meal, families typically gather and watch together. Traditional shadow-plays are given especially during this month in places such as Indonesia as well as many other entertainments throughout the Muslim world. There are book fairs and Sufi-sponsored open house programs, and much Qur'an recitation long into the night.

The Qur'an is supposed to be recited in its entirety during the month of Ramadan. Whereas Jews complete a reading of the entire Torah collectively during the course of a year by reciting a portion of it during each weekly *Shabbat* synagogue service, Muslims complete the entire Qur'an individually during the course of a month by reciting one portion every day during Ramadan. Standard Qur'ans are therefore divided not only by chapter and verse, but also by section. Each section is one thirtieth of the entire book, designed exactly for this purpose. In the Muslim world one can find reading groups and programs for covering the requisite readings during Ramadan, and one will often observe people engrossed in their reading during work breaks (and also not during work breaks) during that month.

Business and industry tend to slow down considerably during Ramadan, especially when it occurs during the long hot summer months when daylight hours are long (the particularities of the Islamic calendar will be examined below). It is not forbidden to sleep during daylight hours during Ramadan, so one may observe a significant increase in long afternoon naps and very late nights when families and friends stay up together.

Mosques often host special programs as well. One in particular is the practice of *i`tikāf*, where some vow to engage in retreat in the mosque. People who practice this custom voluntarily vow to remain in the mosque for a specified number of days (the choice of the individual) and stay inside the entire period for fasting, prayer, and Qur'an recitation. This is usually done during the last 10 days of the month, which are considered particularly sacred. One of these days is the "Night of Power," the day in which, according to tradition, the entirety of the Qur'an was brought down to the lowest level of heaven where it would subsequently be passed to Muhammad through the aegis of the angel Gabriel. One of the short and powerful qur'anic suras is devoted entirely to the "Night of Power."

The Ramadan ritual combines spiritual discipline with personal introspection. The intensive recitation of the Qur'an heightens the Believer's sense of connection with God and with community, and fasting raises one's consciousness of the plight of the poor and hungry. Note the special emphasis on one's responsibility to feed the hungry during this time of divinely authorized, self-imposed hunger. God requires the fast, but the individual must work out a system for carrying it out over a 30-day period when one may be tempted with lots of opportunities for cheating. The Ramadan fast is another ritual act that combines a number of spiritual and social benefits. It helps build a sense of community through the communal act of fasting, it helps provide for the needy, and it builds a sense of individual spirituality and deep introspection during this month of fast and attendant customs and rituals. The official Ramadan

NIGHT OF POWER

We have brought it down on the Night of Power.
What will convey to you what is the Night of Power?
The Night of Power is better than a thousand months.
The angels and the spirit descend during it, by permission of their Lord, on every matter.
It is peace, through the rising of the dawn. (Q.97:1–5)

fast ends with the Little Festival or Festival of Breaking the Fast, which is three days of feasting and heightened visits to relatives and friends.

5. *Pilgrimage (Ḥajj)*

The final pillar of Islam is the *Ḥajj*, meaning the official Islamic pilgrimage to Mecca and the required ritual activities associated with it. Linguistically, the word *"ḥajj"* is equivalent to the Hebrew, *ḥag*. In modern Hebrew, the word *ḥag* denotes any kind of festival, but in the ancient Hebrew of the Bible, it relates most specifically to the pilgrimage festivals. "Three times a year you shall hold a pilgrimage feast for Me. The feast of unleavened bread (*ḥag ha-matzot*) . . . and the feast of the harvest (*ḥag ha-katzir*) . . . and the feast of the ingathering (*ḥag ha-'asif*) . . . Three times a year every male must appear before the Sovereign, the Lord" (Exod. 23:14–17). One meaning of the Hebrew root *ḥ-w-g* is to make a circle (Job 22:14), and it seems likely that the pilgrimage in ancient Israelite religion included some act of circling. One of the hallmark rituals of the Islamic *Hajj* is exactly that: the circling of the Ka`ba in Mecca.[11]

There is in Islam both the Greater Pilgrimage and the Lesser Pilgrimage that is referred to also as *'Umra*. The *'Umra* has many features of the *Hajj*, but it is not equal to the required Pilgrimage referenced by this final pillar of Islam. What follows will be restricted to the Greater Pilgrimage, usually referred to simply as Pilgrimage or *Hajj*. Unlike the other four pillars, pilgrimage is a requirement only once in the lifetime of a Muslim, and it is required only if the individual is able physically and financially to carry it out. Money may not be borrowed for going on pilgrimage, and the pilgrim is not only required to pay for the journey and related expenses entirely, but also to continue to care for dependents and carry out all other financial responsibilities. Until recently, the journey to and from engaging in the pilgrimage was a dangerous endeavor because of the hazards of long-distance travel. Pilgrims would prepare years in advance to save the funds, and the journey itself could take months. Even today there are dangers. Recently a ship ferrying pilgrims sank with many hundreds lost, and occasionally the huge and sometimes crushing crowds of participants in the actual pilgrimage ritual has caused individuals to be injured and even killed. Anyone who dies going to or returning from the pilgrimage, or who dies while engaged in any aspect of it, is considered a martyr and is expected to enter paradise. Despite the difficulties and dangers, Muslims often note how extraordinary it is to experience the pilgrimage. To many it is perhaps the most spiritual and meaningful act of their lives. One who completes the *Hajj* is given the honorific title, *al-ḥajj*—"the Pilgrim."

Most of the actual pilgrimage ritual predates Islam. As noted, Mecca was long a religious center of pre-Islamic indigenous religion, and Arabs in the region regularly traveled to Mecca to engage in the pre-Islamic *Hajj*. The Qur'an commands engaging in the same basic ritual after Muhammad cleared out the images and most of the vestiges of polytheism from the area.

Qur'anic references to pilgrimage ritual do not always appear to be directly in line with current practice and certainly do not provide support for many of the specifics of the ritual. Much additional material is drawn from the *Hadith* to authorize current practice, and an extensive scholarly commentary literature developed to make sense of the many details of the actual procedures.

Abraham and Mecca

According to the biblical narrative, Abraham is told by God to make the journey to a land to which God would direct him (Gen. 12:1). Abraham arrives in the Land of Canaan (Gen. 12:6) and travels there for many years. He is portrayed often as building altars there that are associated with acts of divine communication (Gen. 12:7,8, 13:4,18, 22:9). When he experienced famine in the land, he went south to Egypt. Typical of the biblical narrative, many details of Abraham's travels are simply not provided, because the narrative thrust of the Torah concentrates on different issues. The Torah does not mention additional

PILGRIMAGE

"Pilgrimage to the House is a duty to humankind for whoever is able to find a way to it" (Q.3:97). "*Ṣafā* and *marwa* are among the signs of God. To whomever makes Pilgrimage to the House or the *`umra,* no wrong is associated by encircling the two of them . . ." (Q.2:158). "Announce the Pilgrimage to the people. They will come to you on foot and on every lean camel, coming from every deep ravine to witness the goodness that they have and recite the name God . . ." (Q.22:27). "Fulfill the Pilgrimage and the *`umra* to God, but if you are prevented, then substitute a sacrifice, but do not shave your heads until the sacrifice reaches the designated spot . . . The Pilgrimage is during designated months. . . . When you pour out from *`arafāt,* recite remembrance of God at *al-mash`ar al-ḥarām*. . . . Then pour out from where the people pour out and ask forgiveness of God . . . (Q.2:196–199).

travels outside the Land of Canaan. Neither does it mention that these did not occur. The Qur'an, however, extends Abraham's journeys to Mecca. Typical of his practice of building altars, Abraham is depicted in the Qur'an as building the temple in Mecca known as the House or the Ka`ba.

"Say, 'God is truthful, so follow the religion of Abraham, the monotheist who was no idolater.' Indeed, the first House set up for humankind was the one at Mecca, a blessing and guidance to humankind in which are clear signs—the Station of Abraham. Whoever enters it is secure. Pilgrimage to the House is a duty to humankind for whoever is able to find a way to it" (Q.3:95–97).

The Hajj Ritual Outline

The Pilgrimage is likened to prayer, and pilgrims enter a state of heightened ritual purity in which shaving, cutting or plucking hair, clipping the nails, washing or anointing, and wearing jewelry or perfume is forbidden. Men change into a very simple garment consisting of two white seamless cloths that are tied around the body. This garment places everyone on a single level by reducing the distinctions that dress so often make between class, educational attainment, and ethnicity or nationality. Female pilgrims may wear clothes native to their home regions, but they may also wear a simple, white garment like the men that covers them more fully. Women are obligated to keep their heads covered, and men are obligated to keep them uncovered.

Each ritual part of the Hajj must be completed at specific times from the 8th through 12th days of the month of *dhū al-ḥijja* (the Hajj month). Pilgrims first enter into the sacred area around Mecca that is called the *ḥaram*, which conveys the sense of sanctity, taboo, and purity (the English word "harem" comes from this word because it denotes a place where men are not allowed). A number of prayers and blessings are recited at various points of the ritual that space does not allow us to reproduce here.[12]

- **Before the 8th of Dhū al-ḥijja**

  The first ritual is walking around the Ka`ba seven times counterclockwise. The Ka`ba is located in the inner courtyard of the Sacred Mosque. Special prayers are recited during the encircling after which some sacred water is drunk from the Zam-zam well. Afterward, pilgrims head to the "Place of Running" where they move between two low hills called *ṣafā* and *marwa*. This is considered to be an act of solidarity and association with Hagar in her search for water for her dying son after they were left in the desert (cf. Gen. 21). According to Islamic tradition, Abraham brought Hagar and Ishmael to Mecca, where Hagar ran desperately between the two hills seven times looking for water before God provided the Zam-zam spring for Ishmael. A haircut is required at this point, but it may be fulfilled by cutting a small lock of hair. Finally, the pilgrim listens to an address at the Ka`ba in which all the rituals are rehearsed. Special guides accompany the crowds to assist them in the specifics of the ritual.

- **8th Dhū al-ḥijja**

Pilgrims leave Mecca and travel to a small town about five miles away, after which they proceed to `Arafa, about nine miles farther to the east and outside the actual sacred precinct (*al-ḥaram*) around Mecca. A huge tent-city is set up and waiting for them there, where somewhere between one million and two million people spend the night.

- **9th Dhū al-ḥijja**

The pilgrims must stand at `Arafa from the moment the sun hits its zenith at noon until sunset. This is the standing ritual (*al-wuqūf*) and it is considered by tradition to be the essence of the Hajj. A sermon is usually preached at that time by an honored religious scholar perched on a nearby hill called the Hill of Mercy. Well over one million individuals stand together on this afternoon, chanting, "I am here, O God, I am here."

When sunset approaches, the tents are struck. After sunset, a signal is given and the "pouring forth from `Arafa" is begun, quickly and with a great deal of confusion. The pilgrims make their way to a place called *al-muzdalifa* in this overwhelming confusion, pray, and then collect a number of pebbles for the stoning ritual the following day. They are not to sleep that night.

- **10th Dhū al-ḥijja**

In the morning is another standing ritual, after which there is another "pouring forth" to where the pebbles are thrown at one of three stone pillars that represents the devil. This is reminiscent of a non-qur'anic story about Abraham on his way to sacrifice Ishmael. On the journey to the sacrifice, Abraham was confronted by Satan who whispered to him and also to Ishmael not to go through with the act. A number of versions of this story exist, but in some Ishmael picked up stones and threw them at Satan. This ritual not only honors the steadfastness of both father and son, but also acts out each person's struggle with temptation and evil that is represented by Satan (*al-shayṭān*).

The stoning marks the end of the official Hajj, but there are more activities that must be carried out, the most immediate being the sacrifice of a goat, sheep, cow, or camel. This day is called the "day of sacrifice," in commemoration of the near sacrifice of Abraham's son (Q.37:107).

Following the sacrifice, the male pilgrim's head is shaved, and women have a symbolic haircut. After this the pilgrim garments may be removed, baths taken, and most of the pilgrim restrictions ended aside from sexual relations. Another visit to the Ka`ba is taken for another series of encirclements among huge crowds.

- **11–13 Dhū al-ḥijja**

  The next three days are called "Days of Stripped Meat" (*ayyām al-tashrīq*) for the strips of meat from the sacrifice that in earlier days would be dried in the sun in preparation for the journey home. These days the problem of hygiene with the tens of thousands of animal sacrifices is a huge one for the Saudi government. Fleets of equipment including refrigerator trucks are brought in to take away the uneaten meat and distribute it to the poor around the Muslim world. There are additional stonings of the symbolic devil and a final "farewell encircling" of the Ka`ba.

Many pilgrims then go to Medina to visit the tomb of the Prophet, though it is not required. During the last three days, Muslims throughout the world celebrate a festival called the Great Festival or Feast of Sacrifice. Many animal sacrifices are made and the meat eaten, new clothes are worn, and people exchange gifts. There is also a tradition of visiting cemeteries during these days, and some people spend the night among them camping in tents.

COMMON MUSLIM EXPRESSIONS

Many prayers or devotional statements pepper the daily speech of Muslims. A few of the most common are listed below. Readers may be familiar with some Jewish equivalents.

- ***Al-ḥamdu lillāh*** (often shortened to ***ḥamdillah***)—"Praise is to God." These are the opening words of the Qur'an and serve as an expression of gratitude for God's favors (Hebrew equivalent: ***baruch ha-Shem***). When asked how one is feeling, the answer is usually followed by this phrase.
- ***Bismillāhirraḥmānurraḥīm*** (this is called the ***basmalah***)—"In the name of God the merciful and the compassionate." This is a general "blessing" in Islam and serves as the general acknowledgment of God-consciousness before engaging in any kind of activity, from eating to driving a car.
- ***Allāhu akbar***—"God is most great." This, called the ***takbīr***, is part of the regular ***ṣalāt*** and is often used as an exclamation of God's awesome power and transcendence.
- ***In sha'allāh***—"God willing." This is said when speaking about the future (Hebrew equivalents: ***be`ezrat ha-Shem*** [Sephardic], ***im yirtzey hashem*** [Ashkenazic]). One might say, "See you after work, ***in sha'allāh***."
- ***Allāh ya`tīk al-`āfiya***—"May God give you healthy vigor." This is a way of thanking someone for working for you or simply acknowledging hard work.
- ***Allāh yekhallīlak yāhu(m)***—"May God preserve him (them) for you." Said often when speaking to a person about the person's children.
- ***Subḥān allāh***—"God be praised!" Said often when experiencing something wondrous or magnificent.
- ***Masha'allāh***—"As God wishes." Often said when speaking about something positive, acknowledging that the goodness is due to God's will.
- ***A`ūdhu billāh***—"I seek refuge in God." This is often said when faced with danger or if one observes errant behavior.
- ***Al-ḥamdu lillāh `assalāma***—"Praise to God for [your] well-being!" Said to someone who is returning from a journey or feeling better after not feeling well.

CHAPTER 20

A Sixth Pillar? Jihād

Although not an official pillar of Islam, some religious authorities have included jihād as virtually a sixth pillar. When they do this, they typically understand the overall meaning of the term rather than the one specific meaning that resonates so problematically with Westerners. First of all, it must be clarified that jihad does not mean fighting or warring. The root meaning of "jihad" is "to strive," "exert oneself," or "take extraordinary pains." The Arabic grammarians define it as "exerting one's utmost power, efforts, endeavors, or ability in contending with an object of condemnation."

The evil that must be opposed may come from a human enemy, the devil, or aspects of one's own self. There are a number of kinds of jihad, therefore, and most have nothing to do with fighting or war. "Jihad of the tongue," for example, means exerting one's utmost efforts to speak on behalf of the good and forbidding evil, and "jihad of the heart" denotes struggle against one's own sinful inclinations. According to a respected *hadith*, Muhammad outlined the types of jihad that a Muslim may engage in to defend Islam from corruption:

> Every prophet sent by God to a nation before me has had disciples and followers who followed in his ways and obeyed his commands. But after them came successors who preached what they did not practice and practiced what they were not commanded. Whoever strives against them with one's hand is a believer, whoever strives against them with one's tongue is a believer, whoever strives against them with one's heart

> is a believer. There is nothing greater than [the size of] a mustard seed beyond that in the way of faith. (*Muslim, Imān* #80 [1:69–70])

In addition to jihad of the tongue, the hand, and the heart, however, is "jihad of the sword," and this is the term that most commonly denotes religiously authorized warring. Jihad is often divided into two types, the "greater jihad" and the "lesser jihad." According to a famous but late legend attributed to Muhammad (and not in any of the canonical collections of *Hadith*), Muhammad or some of his warriors return from battle one day, and Muhammad immediately remarks, "We (or you) have returned from the lesser jihad to the greater jihad." When asked what he meant by that, he is said to have replied, "The greater jihad is the struggle against the enemy in your own breast." In later texts, this inward jihad may be called *mujāhada*, a different noun form that conveys the same meaning—struggle against wickedness.

Jihad, then, may be done simply by striving to behave ethically and by speaking without causing harm to others, but it is generally understood as engaging actively to defend or propagate Islam. Within the broad range of meanings associated with defending Islam, it can denote war against dissenting Muslims who denounce legitimate Muslim leadership, highway robbers and other violent people, deviant or "un-Islamic" leadership, or those defined as apostates who rebel against proper Islamic authority.

Jihad is popularly understood, however, as being directed outward against non-Muslim groups that are perceived as threatening to the well-being of the Muslim community. This form of jihad, which is authorized by God and directed against non Muslims, corresponds most closely to the Western concept of "holy war," and it is to this concept of jihad that we now turn.

In the Qur'an

Although the term appears mostly in the Qur'an in contexts that are not associated definitively with war, jihad also occurs in some qur'anic passages that treat warring. One classic example is the following passage, which is part of a larger section treating war and violence directed against the enemies of the early community of Believers:

> O you believers! When you strike out in the path of God, be discriminating, and do not say to one who greets you with peace, 'You are not a believer,' desiring the goods of the life of this world. Great spoils are with God. This is the way you were beforehand, when God bestowed favor upon you. So be discriminating, for God is aware of what

you do. Not equal are those believers who sit [at home], except for those who are hurt, from those who engage in jihad [literally, "those who are strivers" = *al-mujāhidūn*] in the path of God with their property and their persons. God prefers/favors those who engage in jihad with their property and their persons a step above those who sit at home. God promised goodness to all, but God favors those who engage in jihad over those who sit at home with a big reward. (Q.4:94–95)

The far more common term for fighting or making war in the Qur'an and elsewhere is the word "*qitāl*," and "fighting in the path of God" (*al-qitāl fī sabīl allāh*) is the operative technical term for most discussions on divinely authorized warring. We have observed previously that the Qur'an does not appear consistent in its position on war. It includes a number of verses that would seem to call for a quietist or at least nonmilitant approach to resolving conflict with non-Muslims. "Follow what has been revealed to you from your Lord; there is no God but He, and turn away from the idolaters" (Q.6:106). Even in the face of strong opposition or even betrayal, some verses teach forgiveness and reconciliation. In relation to the People of the Book, "Because of their breaking their covenant, We cursed them and hardened their hearts. . . . You will continue to uncover treachery from all but a few of them, but be forgiving and pardon, for God loves the kindly" (Q.5:13). And when there is a serious quarrel, Q.29:46 teaches, "Only argue nicely with the People of the Book, except with the oppressors among them. Say: We believe in what has been revealed to us and revealed to you. Our God and your God is one, and it is Him to whom we surrender."

Other verses, however, express a militant approach to conflict. Some, such as Q.2:190, call for fighting only in defense and with extreme caution not to exceed moral limits: "Fight (*waqātilū*) in the path of God against those who fight against you, but do not transgress limits, for God does not love transgressors." But the following verses (191–193) give a far more agressive message: "Kill them wherever you find them, and drive them out of the places from which they drove you out, for temptation [most early commentators define temptation here as engaging in idolatry] is worse than killing. . . . And fight them until there is no more temptation and religion is entirely God's. But if they cease, let there be no hostility except to the oppressors."

In the Legal Literature

"Jihad" is the term that is often used to convey divinely authorized warring in the traditional and juridical literature, and "jihad in God's cause" can (but does not necessarily) mean "divinely ordained war." Because it is sanctioned by God, it is often translated as "holy war" in the West, but unlike some Western notions, jihad is not to be invoked for the purpose of forcing non-Muslims to convert to Islam through force of arms. Opinions differ in the juridical literature over what circumstances allow or require "jihad in God's cause." There is disagreement among both traditional jurists and modern thinkers over whether the requirement to engage in jihad is eternally in force in order to spread the political hegemony of Islam, under what conditions it may be legally invoked, whether it can be waged without an official call to war on the authority of the caliph, and so forth.

Muslim jurists developed a highly sophisticated legal doctrine of warring in the path of God. One of the greatest and most well-known even in the West was Averroes (Muhammad ibn Rushd, d.1198), who makes the following points. It is a collective legal obligation for healthy adult free men who have the means at their disposal to go to war. All polytheists must be fought (Jews and Christians are not included in this group). The aim of warfare when engaged against Peoples of the Book is domination, indicated either through conversion to Islam or payment of the *jizya* tax signaling subjugation to Islam. Damage inflicted on the enemy may consist of damage to his property, injury to his person, or violation of his personal liberty (slavery). Certain individuals among the enemy may receive the status of safe conduct in order to conduct political or economic activities. In time of war all adult able-bodied unbelieving males may be slain, but noncombatants may not. There is much additional discussion on "rules of engagement" in war that include principles of proportionality, the use of weapons of mass destruction (usually forbidden), how much damage may be inflicted on the property of the enemy, truces, etc.

Jihad and Realpolitik

Islamic doctrines of jihad were formulated during the classical period of Islam when Islam was the dominant religiopolitical civilization, and it seemed that God was ensuring its unstoppable development and expansion. Perpetual war against the non-Muslim world seemed natural until victory, but the juggernaut did not continue forever. It slowed, continued in fits and starts, halted, and even reversed in some areas such as Spain and southern and eastern Europe. Yet there was little reevaluation of the previous expectations of ultimate and total victory. Reversals were considered temporary, so until the modern period little new thought was given by Muslim scholars to Islamic military doctrines, whether legal or ethical. Political diplomacy was always a tool of the caliphs and sultans, of course, but until the last century there was little interest in reexamining basic assumptions underlying doctrines of jihad.

Serious new thinking began with the impact of European colonization, but only in the past few years has there emerged much interest in other forms of conflict resolution. The attacks of September 11, 2001, and the response of the United States in attempting to destroy what is often called "Islamic terrorism" have shocked the Muslim world and encouraged some reevaluation of the doctrines of jihad. What will emerge from this will only become evident in the next decades and beyond, but at the time of this writing, there is virtually universal agreement that jihad is required in cases of defense of the *umma*. Jihad is a necessary community responsibility in order to defend Islam and Muslims.

It is at this point that that controversy can get heated, because there is a wide range of honest opinion over what constitutes defense of Islam and Muslims. Invasion of a Muslim country by a non-Muslim enemy is considered by virtually every Muslim to be an offense that requires jihad, and this is based on many Qur'an passages, including Q.22:39: "Those who have been fought against are given license because they have been done injustice, and God is well able to help them—those unjustly expelled from their homes simply because they say, 'Our Lord is God.' If God had not warded off some people by means of others, then monasteries and churches and synagogues and mosques in which the name of God is often cited would have been destroyed. God will surely deliver those who support Him, for God is powerful, mighty."

But despite agreement over defense of Muslims against an enemy invader, not all Muslims would agree about the definition of "enemy" and even the definition of "Muslim." What about invasion of a Muslim country by a coalition of forces that includes many Muslims? The invasion of a sovereign Muslim country by another Muslim country? Damaging political and economic exploitation of a Muslim community (or nation) through non-military means? Public ridicule of Islam or the Qur'an in such a way that it publicly denigrates the word of God or the Prophet of Islam? What about the killings of Muslims by a non-Muslim nation or government by military incursion or shooting over the border? The killing or massacre of Muslims residing in a nation-state that is situated outside of the Muslim world? An indigenous secular government of a Muslim country that prevents full Islamic religious expression or intimidates and persecutes Muslim religious leaders?

Since the last quarter of the 20th century these scenarios have not been hypothetical. Each is complex, and different ways of considering them often lead to different responses among Muslims. There is much ongoing debate both within the Muslim world and in the West over these questions as they are applied in real time to contemporary wars and aggression. The discussion has been complicated by the growth in globalism during this period, along with the resilience of local dictators and what is overwhelmingly considered to be unfair and unsympathetic Western interference in local affairs. The frustration and resentment have grown to such an extent that certain violent behaviors that have been previously unknown in Muslim history have become commonplace. The most striking example is suicide bombing.

"Suicide Bombing"/"Martyrdom Operations"

The Qur'an does not really address the issue of suicide. Later jurists considered a number of verses and suggested that they might treat the topic,[1] but the authoritative source clearly forbidding suicide in Islam is the *Hadith*. Traditions are repeated frequently that condemn it outright. Even a great warrior who fights valiantly but becomes mortally wounded and then falls on his sword is condemned to hell for taking his own life (cf. 2 Samuel 31, 1 Chronicles 10).[2] " . . . 'Whoever commits suicide with an iron [implement] will be punished with the same iron [eternally] in the Fire.' . . . The Prophet said, 'A man was inflicted with wounds and he killed himself, so God said: My slave has caused death on himself hurriedly, so I forbid Paradise for him.' The Prophet said, 'Whoever kills himself by strangling will strangle himself [eternally] in the Fire and whoever [kills himself] by stabbing will stab himself [eternally] in the Fire."[3]

Suicide, therefore, is clearly forbidden in Islam. Martyrdom, on the other hand, is praised in both the Qur'an and the *Hadith*. "And if you be killed or die in the path of God, forgiveness and mercy from God are better than all that others amass. If you die or are killed, you are gathered to God" (Q.3:157–158). "Do not consider those killed in the path of God as dead. On the contrary, they are living with their Lord, who gives them sustenance" (Q.3:169).[4]

The *Hadith* promises great reward for engaging in fighting in God's cause, and it is likely that the emphasis on rewards for engaging in jihad was at least partially a reaction to the inclination among many in the early Muslim community to hold back from going out on military campaigns.[5] The traditional literature claims that fighters will gain deserved material spoils and rewards when successful in the campaigns, and if they are killed or even wounded while warring in the path of God, they will be admitted to paradise.[6] "Any slave [of God] whose feet get covered with dust in the path of God, the Fire will not touch him."[7] The reward for martyrdom is emphasized, even if the victim dies while not actually engaged on the battlefield,[8] and as many as 70 members of one's family who would have been doomed to hellfire will be ensured entry into paradise because of the intercession of the martyr in the path of God.[9] "The Prophet said: No slave [of God] who dies and has goodness with God wants to return to the world, even if he would have the world and all that is in it, except the martyr, for when he sees the greatness of martyrdom, he will want to return to the world and be killed again."[10]

Death in combat thus became a noble way to depart this life. Some medieval Sunni sources depict mothers expressing gratitude rather than mourning at the news of their sons' death through battlefield martyrdom. However, after the decrease in the number of battlefield martyrs following the early Conquest, the definition of a martyr was broadened to such an extent that the meaning of martyrdom itself was diminished. Those who performed their religious duties as Muslims were considered martyrs,[11] and so were those killed innocently by disease, fire, accident, or in childbirth as a way of ensuring their entry into the Garden.[12] Among Sufis, adepts could be living martyrs who are engaged in the "greater jihad" of fighting their own evil inclinations. According to this view, the battlefield martyr is only a martyr externally, while the true martyr is one who has successfully slain his own ego in his quest to live a life of holiness.

Thus far we have learned that suicide is forbidden but that martyrdom is highly meritorious, and that the emphasis on military martyrdom declined in relation to the general decline in militarism after the Conquest. We need to add that the killing of noncombatants is forbidden, according to most authorities, and some sources say that includes even noncombatant idolaters.[13] Where does that lead us in the issue of "suicide bombing"?

That depends upon how one defines "suicide" and "martyrdom." In the past quarter century, the earlier distinction between martyrdom and suicide has been blurred. What Westerners view as suicide and the killing of innocent noncombatants has become increasingly viewed by many Muslims as martyrdom and the killing of combatants. The popular Egyptian Muslim legal scholar, Yusuf Qaradawi, who is said to take a "moderate traditional" position on Islamic issues, has repeatedly condoned and even encouraged "martyrdom operations" by Muslims against Israelis and against U.S. and coalition forces in Iraq. He does not extend his ruling to the killings of Spanish and English citizens in the famous subway bombings in Madrid on March 11, 2004, and in London on July 7, 2005. Qaradawi and others who take this position have caused a significant amount of turmoil in both the Western and Muslim worlds because it seems to go against the earlier trend in Islam to define martyrdom in ways that remove it from militant actions. There are other Muslim voices that condemn these kinds of operations, such as the Egyptian professor of Islamic law, Dr. Muhammad Rafat 'Othman: "[A] person who blows himself up is committing suicide. This opinion is based on sources that categorically forbid self-killing. The Koran says: 'Do not kill yourself, surely Allah is ever merciful to you.' There are also such sources in the *Sunna* and in the general consensus of scholars. No text in Islamic religious law permits a person to kill himself. Even in the case of jihad, which is the pinnacle of religious duties, Islam does not permit a person to kill himself. What Islamic religious law does permit is for a person to wage jihad, facing one of two options—victory or martyrdom. He may risk being killed by someone else, but may not kill himself."[14]

The tendency in recent decades to condone suicide bombings is indicative of how religious interpretation (among Jews and Christians as well as Muslims) is so profoundly influenced by historical context. But suicide bombing is truly an innovation that lacks support in the authoritative sources of Qur'an and *Hadith*. While it currently seems to be the loudest voice, it is unlikely that it can be sustained for long because it is ultimately untenable.

The practice has been extended to the mass killings of Shi`ites by Sunnis and vice versa, especially in Iraq during the period after Saddam Hussein was forcibly removed from power in 2003. This is indicative of the mixing of cultural motivations for blood vengeance and for protecting family and tribal honor with religious ideals of justice and martyrdom. The result is that justification for this kind of random violence has become extremely subjective, and the blurring of religious with cultural rationalization has increased the rage and brutality, making immediate resolution of the problem difficult, but a long-term solution essential. Attempts to resolve the problem continue from within the Muslim community, but it is unlikely that a swift resolution will be possible with the current destabilization that is so endemic in much of the Muslim world, and especially the Arab Muslim world today.

Not only is it overly simplistic to ignore the range of voices and the subtleties and complexities that make up these scenarios in our contemporary world, it is also counterproductive to draw quick conclusions without careful analysis. Doing so may also cause negative consequences because it is liable to lead to poor political, economic and military decision-making. The result can be terrible and unnecessary damage and destruction to whole populations of people, including our own. Intuitive perceptions across cultural and religious boundaries are often wrong. What applies in one context does not necessarily apply in another. If the Jewish community wants to be responsible about its own future and the future of the world we live in, then it must make careful policy decisions without jumping to quick conclusions.

CHAPTER 21

The Range of Practice among Muslims

In the scholarly discussion of Christianity, it is becoming increasingly common to speak of "Christianities," since there is so much variety among Christian practices, theologies, ritual, and behaviors. In Judaism, as well, there is a great spread of practices, rituals, and ideologies or theologies among Jewish communities throughout the world. Yet despite the many differences between these two related "families" of religion, they have much in common. Both are monotheistic, revere the Hebrew Bible/Old Testament, include a great emphasis on ethics, have messianic ideas and views, and both accept the notion of judgment and a world to come. What, then, actually distinguishes the two? There are of course many important aspects that differentiate between Judaism and Christianity, ranging from organizing principles to views of scripture, theologies, rituals, and religious expectations and behaviors. Despite the many disputes and arguments between the various movements or denominations *within* each religious system, there remains a tacit assumption of certain, generally accepted, even if largely unarticulated, boundaries beyond which a believer cannot go and remain within the system.

The same is true of Islam, which, while sharing a great deal with Judaism and Christianity, represents a unique form of monotheism that contains within it a variety of movements, trends, and denominations. And as with Christianity and Judaism, there have always been attempts by individuals, communities, or rulers to define and enforce what they believe is true Islam. There have been inquisitions enforced by ruling authorities, excommunications, and executions of people accused of apostasy. Some Muslims have engaged in public acquiescence to so-called orthodox religion while practicing their own rituals and practices in private.

For most Muslims, true Islam consists of one or another form of religious practice and ideals that are followed by Sunni Muslims, based on the Qur'an and the Sunni collections of *Hadith*, the teachings and interpretations of the early religious scholars, and the four surviving Sunni schools of law. Although some have referred to this Islam as orthodox, the people who count themselves within this world nevertheless embody a variety of practices and range of attitudes and beliefs. Attempts to unify theology and practice from the earliest generations to the present have not succeeded. In fact, a famous *Hadith* found in the collection of Abū Dāwud (among others)[1] has Abū Hurayra quoting Muhammad as having said, "The Jews are split into seventy-one or seventy-two sects; and the Christians into seventy-one or seventy-two sects; and my community will be split up into seventy-three sects." The *hadith* that follows cites Muhammad as having said, "The People of the Book before were split up into seventy-two sects, and this [Muslim] community will be split up into seventy-three. Seventy-two of them will go to Hell and one of them will go to Paradise. . . ."

It has thus been recognized by Muslims from early times that unifying the *umma* would be a difficult if not impossible task. Islam has never developed any ecclesiastical hierarchy as in Christianity under the one universal Church ("One, Holy, Catholic and Apostolic"), but functions more like the diffused hierarchy of Jewish communities. Nevertheless, and despite lack of overall institutional structure, actual worship practices in the required daily prayers are quite uniform across the Muslim world and between groups such as Sunnis, Shi`is, Sufis, and others. They are certainly more uniform than the worship practices among Christian or Jewish denominations. There is also a general consensus on major issues such as Islamic articulations of monotheism, scripture, prophethood, and prayer. Yet, many local customs and observances distinguish between geographic, ethnic, and religious ideological divides. And while the obligation to engage in prayer five times per day is the universally accepted requirement in Islam, a number of my Muslim academic colleagues have questioned whether half the world population of Muslims pray even one time per day, let alone five.[2]

There is a general desire among Muslims for unity, as there is among most religious communities. The concept of the Muslim *umma* is an expression of this natural aspiration, and many Muslims choose to ignore or deny the fact that Islamic practice can vary widely in the Muslim world. As within each of the three great families of monotheism that we call Judaism, Christianity, and Islam, certain basic assumptions, acknowledgments, beliefs, and practices are shared by nearly all who count themselves within the system. It is these that serve as the thread binding together the tens or hundreds of millions of people who consider themselves Jews, or Christians, or Muslims. Yet despite these general commonalities, not all Jews, for example, would agree upon exactly which common beliefs, practices, and assumptions would be necessary in order to be counted "in." The specifics vary between communities and denominations. This reality makes it impossible, therefore, to list any but the absolutely most basic commonalities of any system. Most religionists would agree on the minimal basics, but would also require others for which there would not be universal agreement. They would also inevitably hold differences in their understanding of the deep or full meaning of even some of the minimal basics.

The Five Pillars of Islam serve as the unifying minimum for Islam: profession that there is no deity aside from God and that Muhammad is God's prophet, prayer, required giving, fasting during Ramadan, and engaging in pilgrimage. Yet plenty of differences exist among the conceptions and meaning of God's uniqueness and in the meaning and role of Muhammad as God's prophet. Similarly, despite the overall commonality in the practice of the required prayers, distinctions exist between individuals and communities, and significant disagreements are common over other kinds of prayer and worship rituals. Not only are there differences in ritual practices based on interpretations of religious tradition and law, significant disparity in practice results from the intrusion of local custom.

"Law" vs. "Custom" (Circumcision and Family Honor)

We discussed earlier how the raw material out of which Islamic law developed is scripture (the Qur'an), tradition (the *Hadith*), and custom. Custom was not accepted as one of the official sources of Islamic law for both positive and negative reasons. The negative was that it was not a part of the divine will as established through the Qur'an and the *Hadith*. The positive was that it represented customary pre-Islamic practices that were considered to have been abrogated by the revelation of the Qur'an. Nevertheless, custom was intuitively drawn on as a source of law throughout the history of Islam, and it continues to influence practice in the Muslim world to this day.

When a distinction is drawn between custom and religious law, it is recognized in Arabic as a distinction between *'urf* (custom) and *sharī'a*. The issue of what constitutes human custom and divinely ordained religious law is probably as old as religion itself, and Judaism also knows of the tension between *minhag* (custom) and *halakhah* (religious law). It is of course the hope of religious leaders that divine law becomes thoroughly infused in daily life such that it becomes second nature—custom. But the opposite also occurs. Social customs sometimes become enshrined as religious law. The two specific topics reflecting the tension between custom and religious law that most concern Westerners (as well as very many Muslims) are female circumcision (increasingly called female genital mutilation) and violence against women in the name of family honor.

Circumcision

Circumcision (*khitān*) is a very basic part of Islamic practice, though it is not referenced in the Qur'an. The *Hadith* mentions the circumcision of Abraham and some traditions mention that Muhammad was born circumcised (birth without a foreskin occurs naturally on occasion). All the schools of Islamic law consider male circumcision to be obligatory or highly recommended. In practice, all Muslim males are circumcised. At what age the child may or must be circumcised, however, varies considerably throughout the Muslim world. Accordingly, boys may be circumcised at different ages but must be circumcised by the time they reach adulthood. Customs vary from the age of seven days to the age of 15, and the rites and traditions vary as to how the incision is made and what kinds of religious or cultural occasions are made of the act. There is no official ceremonial rite for circumcision. The practice seems to be thoroughly based on custom that became a part of religious law.

Islam also knows of female circumcision, more properly defined as female genital cutting or female genital mutilation. This too emerged out of custom. Of the four schools of Islamic law, only the Shafi`i school requires a minor incision. Al-Nawawī, in his commentary on the *Hadith* collection of Muslim ibn al-Ḥajjāj, mentions that "it is obligatory to cut off a small part of the skin in the highest part of the genitals," which seems to refer to a slight trimming of the hood of the clitoris.[3] In some areas of the Muslim world such as Somalia, Sudan, Ethiopia, and Mali, the custom is extremely widespread and the procedure much more invasive than described by Al-Nawawī. In other areas it is virtually unknown.

The problem with eliminating the practice is that the custom has become deeply ingrained, including among those women who both suffer and perform the procedure. According to many, it is presumed to be divinely authorized, and at least one well-respected *hadith* depicts Muhammad as referring to a circumcised woman positively.[4] Al-Azhar University in Cairo, the oldest and most prestigious institution of Islamic learning, endorsed female genital cutting in the 1940s, '50s, and even the '80s. Religious scholars are still not entirely in agreement about the practice and today there is a trend that opposes it. There is currently public discussion, debate, television programming, blogging, and educational programming that collectively argue for ending female circumcision.

"Honor" Violence Against Women

In general, among communities where customary law is highly influential, public authority tends to be relatively weak (or vice versa). This applies particularly to the category of family law and customs. That is, public authority may be strong in relation to some civic concerns and less so in relation to others. We have noted that the one area in which civil government traditionally has had less influence in the Muslim world is in the area of family custom.

In traditional communities in the Middle East, North Africa, and Central Asia, whether Muslim or not, a woman's ties with her male blood relatives remain very strong even after she is married. The male relatives (father, uncles, brothers) often continue to play a role as guardian of the woman, and that guardianship includes both the honor of the woman and the honor of the family. A sexual offense associated with a woman is generally viewed as an offense against the honor of her male relatives. Sexual offense can be broadly defined, so that even flirtatious conversation or conversation with possible sexual overtones can offend family honor.

Adultery or elopement is understood as an offense against the honor or reputation of the guardians of the woman in traditional settings, because it makes them appear unable to defend their honor or control their women. The penalty for such behaviors can be harsh. In some places an unchaste woman is in real danger of being killed by her male relatives. It must be kept in mind, however, that this is in no way universal, and it is not sanctioned by Islam.

The Islamic position on adultery is that it is an obscenity based on Qur'an 17:22: "Do not draw near to adultery, for it is an obscenity, an evil path." In Qur'an 25:68–69, adultery in addition to idolatry and murder are three of the worst crimes for which divine punishment is doubled. This parallels the Jewish categorization of the same three behaviors as particularly abhorrent (B. Pes. 25a, Yoma 82a, Sanh. 74a).

According to the Qur'an, convicting a woman accused of a sexual crime requires four witnesses. "As for those women who are engaged in obscenity, call four of you to witness against them, and if they give [confirming] evidence, then keep them in houses until death takes them or God makes a way for them" (Q.4:15). Stoning has become the traditional punishment for adultery in Islam, though it cannot be justified directly from the Qur'an. It is a form of capital punishment in the Torah, however, usually for certain acts of idolatry (Lev. 20:2,27, Deut. 13:7–11). Adultery or fornication is also a capital crime in the Torah, though not punishable by stoning (Lev. 20:10, Deut. 22:22), except for one case (in Deut. 23:7–21). The *Hadith*, however, stipulates stoning as a punishment, and the Islamic tradition literature contains a number of versions of an interesting story concerning the punishment for adultery that also treats Jewish sources. The following version is found in the authoritative *Hadith* of Bukhari (*Ḥudūd* 24, 37).

> [Muhammad b. `Uthmān . . . ibn `Umar:] A Jewish man and woman who had committed a sin together [euphemism for illegal sex] were brought to the messenger of God. He said to them: What is found in your scripture? They said: Our sages innovated [the punishment of] blackening the faces and *tajbiyya* [parading the two partners through town on a donkey with their faces in opposite directions as a public humiliation]. `Abdallah b. Salām[5] said: "O Messenger of God, call them to bring the Torah," so they brought the Torah. One of [their sages] put his hand over the verse of stoning and proceeded to read what came before it and what came after it. ibn Salām said: "Lift up your hand!" And there was the verse of stoning under his hand. So the Apostle of God commanded that they be stoned.

This story seems to reflect a level of uneasiness among early Muslims about the proper punishment for sexual transgression. Whereas in the Jewish system the harsh capital punishment of the Torah is reduced in later Jewish tradition literature, the more lenient punishment stipulated in the Qur'an became more severe in later Islamic tradition literature. Of course, the issue is far more complex than can be presented here. As one might expect, the schools of law differed on a number of issues associated with adultery. In any case, there is absolutely no stipulation in the *Sharī`a* for family members to take on the responsibility to judge and punish their own family member who might be accused of the crime. Such an act is extrajudicial and finds no support in either the Qur'an or the *Hadith*.

"Official" Islam and "Popular" Islam

Who determines what is official in religion? From the standpoint of the academic study of religion, the answer to this question tends to be complex, and it varies from one religious system to another. Issues such as authority, power, and influence have a tremendous impact, and these vary with the nature of society, culture, government, and history. The discerning observer will note various powers or factions vying for positions that will influence or determine the nature of what is deemed official in many religious movements and systems. This is quite clear among world Catholics and Anglicans in the first years of the 21st century, among factions of Orthodox Jews in Israel and the Diaspora, and among many groups in the Muslim world: various so-called Islamist groups, traditionalists, progressives, modernizers, and so forth.

Popular religion refers to actual beliefs, practices, and behaviors practiced by the common folk, even when not sanctioned by religious authorities. Culture determines popular religion, so that it is often impossible to separate aspects of religion from culture, and vice versa. A classic example of this phenomenon is celebration of the Christmas tree. The custom of decorating coniferous trees at the winter solstice celebrating the rebirth of the sun-god (around December 21) originated in northern Europe in pre-Christian times, when the trees were seen as phallic symbols representing the fertility of nature gods. When Christianity came to the region and December 25th was proclaimed as the day of the birth of Christ, the popular custom of tree decoration was easily brought into a Christian context. There was nothing official about the custom, but its popularity helped it to become so. Today a massive Christmas tree is decorated every year in St. Peter's Square in the Vatican, the most sacred spot of official religion in Catholicism.

There is a wide variety of popular religious practices among Muslims. The Badawiya order of Sufi practice in Egypt, for example, includes fertility rituals associated with holy places in Tanta, especially during the *mawlid* or birthday festival associated with its founder, Sīdī Aḥmad al-Badawī. The origin of these rituals almost certainly predates the coming of Islam to Egypt, but it has become integrated into Badawiya practice (and vigorously opposed by those who are influenced by the sober expressions of Islam supported and promoted by prominent Saudis and others).

Another Sufi group known as the Mawlawis, named for the Sufi founder, Mawlana Jalāl al-Dīn al-Rūmī, is known for the popular meditative dancing known by the names of the dancers, "whirling dervishes." Other Sufi groups engage in a variety of popular meditative worship practices known collectively as *dhikr* (or *zikr*), meaning "remembering" God (Hebrew linguistic parallel, *zakhor*). These can be silent or audible, associated with the required prayers or done independently of the prayers, and engaged in individually or within a group. All forms of *dhikr* are unofficial, "popular" practice.

CHAPTER 22

Sufism

Islamic mysticism organizes its practices and doctrines around seeking out a form of unity with God, and Sufism is the name applied to its many different schools and expressions. The term is derived from the Arabic word to describe a person who is engaged in the mystic path: *ṣufī*. There is some uncertainty about the root meaning of the word, but most accept that it derives from the word for wool, *ṣūf*, and refers to the coarse, woolen garments that were worn by early Muslim ascetics. Some also believe that this term for mysticism comes from *ṣafā'*, meaning "purity."

Sources of Sufi Spirituality

Muhammad was a mystic, and his very role of prophet confirms the mystical sense of communication with the ultimate, with a transcendent relationship with God. On the other hand, he was a worldly leader who also engaged in the mundane issues of human life as a social, political, religious, and military, as well as prophetic leader. He is considered to be exceptional by Muslims because of his unique ability to transcend what are usually separate and conflicting aspects of human leadership. Different Muslims, then, relate to Muhammad differently: some in terms of social or political leadership, some in terms of military leadership, and some in terms of his mystical qualities as the recipient of divine revelation and what is generally considered to have been his intimate relationship with God.

In the early years under Muhammad's leadership, God seemed extremely immanent. As Muhammad articulated the divine word in the Qur'an, "We created humanity and We know what the soul whispers inside, for We are closer to humanity than the jugular vein" (Q.50:16). New religious movements invariably exude an excitement and immediacy that tend to subside when they become successful, grow in numbers and strength, and build the necessary institutions to manage a large community. Normalization brings formalization, hierarchies, and bureaucracies. Much of the initial spontaneity inevitably becomes institutionalized through the routine of ritual, even though a major goal of ritual is to re-create and "democratize" the original spirituality of a few by bringing it to a larger mass of participants. But as the devotional life of Muslims became more formalized and dominated by a religious leadership associated with institutional mosques, many yearned for the warmer and more immediate spirituality that was associated with Muhammad and the original, intimate community of Believers.

The entire career of the Prophet took place before there was an empire. The revelations of the Qur'an, the *Sunna* of the Prophet, and all the stories of the righteous companions in the deserts of Arabia took place in a simpler time before the corrupting influence of wealth and power. Soon after, Islam became a major justification for empire within the caliphates, and it naturally became associated by many with harsh rule, greed, and injustice. By only a few decades after the death of the Prophet, the revolutionary and progressive Arabian religious movement of Islam had become the religion of Mediterranean and Middle Eastern empires and bureaucracies, armies, and realpolitik. In reaction, many Muslims began looking for something deeper, something more closely connected to the transcendent. They longed for the experience of an ultimate reality that exists beyond the limits of power, wealth, and political influence. They aspired to retrieve the emphasis on love that epitomized for them the core of the divine relationship. In Muslim circles, those movements that strove and continue to strive to recapture the mystical intimacy and immediacy of the religious experience are called Sufism.

Sufi Qur'an Interpretation

As noted in Part 2, Qur'an interpretation evolved into two general categories (and many subcategories within them). One is called *tafsīr* and relates to the contextual or "plain" interpretation of the outward, literal, and essential meanings of the Qur'an. The other is called *ta'wīl* and relates to the investigation of internal, allegorical, and symbolic meanings. Sufis became deeply involved in the latter approach. According to those engaged in *ta'wīl*, there are, in addition to the plain or evident meanings of Qur'an verses (sometimes called the "obvious" meanings), hidden or internal meanings that get to the issues that transcend normative, mundane life.

The Qur'an has always been the most important source for inspiration and contemplation among mystically inclined Muslims. As you will note from many of the Qur'an citations provided in this book, the Qur'an can be highly esoteric. The "Light Verse" (Q.24:35), for example, presents God in the imagery of a sublime, majestic, and unfathomable light, which opened up a great amount of interpretations. The discourse of the Qur'an is such that it sometimes asks obscure questions that may seem rhetorical. Sometimes it refers to strange and wonderful aspects of God's greatness and mystery. One of these is the oft-repeated reference to God's signs (*āyāt*).

The signs of God are sometimes similar to the biblical sense of "signs and wonders" (*otot umoftim*) in Creation or extraordinary divine acts, and the Hebrew and Arabic words are related (*otot // āyāt*).[1] So, for example in Qur'an 13:2–3, "God is the one who raised up the heavens without pillars that you can see, then mounted the throne and subjected the sun and the moon, each moving according to a certain period. He arranges the order and determines the signs so that you will be certain to meet your Lord. It is God who spread out the earth and made hills and rivers on it, who made the two genders of fruits and who covers the day with the night. In this are signs for those who reflect." The Qur'an itself mentions that God's signs have the purpose of calling on humanity to give thanks and acknowledge God (Q.30:46, 45:1–11). According to mystical interpretations, reflection on these and other signs of God are a means of understanding the mysteries of Creation, of nature, and ultimately, therefore, of God.

God's immanence was noted above in Qur'an 50:16 where it likens the nearness of God with the nearness of the jugular vein. Other verses such as 2:186 and 2:115 are pointed to by mystics to demonstrate the same sentiment. The latter, especially, has been of interest to Sufi interpretation: "To God is the east and the west. Wherever you turn, there is the face of God. God is everywhere, knowing all." So too, is 55:26–27: "Everything on [earth] perishes. There remains only the face of your Lord, the sublime, the honored." The "face of God" became a metaphor in mystical interpretation, for like the rationalist theologians, the mystics did not consider God to exist in bodily form with human characteristics. But the imagery of God's face raised the question for Sufis of exactly how human beings can perceive God. Most thought that while God could not be seen visually, he could nevertheless be perceived through the human heart and through divine manifestations in the world of Creation.

The Qur'an repeatedly uses the word *"dhikr"* (or *"zikr"*—"remembering," or "mentioning"), and this term has very special meaning for Sufis. Muhammad is commanded, "Remember your Lord within your soul, humbly and with awe, not loudly, in the mornings and the evenings" (Q.7:205). In another passage (Q.4:103), it is commanded, "When you have concluded your prayers, then remember God standing, sitting, and on your sides . . ." (This is remarkably similar to the command in Deut. 6:7: "Teach [Torah and God's love] to your children and speak of them when you stay at home and when you are away, when you lie down and when you get up.") This oft-repeated usage of "remember" in the Qur'an means something like "call God to mind" or "remind yourself of God." Sufis took this command literally and very seriously by establishing methods of meditation centered around reciting God's names. Some are quiet and inward while others are ecstatic. Some are chanted in a monotone, while others have a very musical sense to them, and some evolved into meditative dance, such as that of the famous "whirling dervishes" associated with the Sufi master, Jalal al-Din al-Rumi.

Sufi Hadith

While the Qur'an is the primary source of Sufi spirituality, the Prophet represents the most perfect expression of human spirituality. The Qur'an itself proclaims, "You have a good example in the messenger of God for whoever looks to God and the Last Day and remembers God greatly" (Q.33:21). Muhammad, of course, was in intimate relationship with God for the last two decades of his life and more, but the most important event of his life from the perspective of Sufi theosophy was his Night Journey to Jerusalem and especially his subsequent Ascension from the rock through the seven heavens to arrive at the presence of God (Q.17:1). This extraordinary experience, referenced perhaps indirectly in the Qur'an but expanded greatly in the *Hadith* and in mystical writings, finds a fascinating parallel in the midrashim about Moses' ascension from Mount Sinai through the various levels of heaven to reach the presence of God (cf. Exod. 24:15–18). Another, earlier Jewish parallel may be found in the activities of the "*Merkavah* Mystics" of the Land of Israel in the first few centuries of the Common Era, who attempted to engage in mystic ascensions to transcend the mundane world in order to reach the godhead.

As one might logically and correctly assume, just as Qur'an and *Hadith* are the primary authoritative sources for deriving Islamic law and theology, so are they the primary sources for Islamic spirituality and mysticism. And just as in the other disciplines, while there is universal agreement about the canon of the Qur'an, there is plenty of disagreement among mystics and especially between mystics and nonmystics over the reliability and accuracy of the *hadith*s cited by various authorities.

One unique *genre* of *Hadith* that is particularly important to Sufis finds a place in the hierarchy of literatures somewhere between the divine revelation of the Qur'an and the divinely guided human acts and discourse of the Prophet. This is a small collection called the "Divine [lit. sacred] Sayings" (*Ḥadīth Qudsī*). These are snippets of God's revelation that do not appear in the Qur'an, but that are associated by some to have originated with God, though conveyed in the words of Muhammad. The difference between the *Hadith* Qudsi and Prophetic *Hadith* is that in the former Muhammad says that God was the actual source of the message. Whereas the meanings of the *hadith*s were purported to have been revealed to Muhammad, he put them into his own words. This differs from the Qur'an, which is considered to be the actual word of God that was conveyed to the public by Muhammad exactly as it was revealed to him.

> From the *Hadith* Qudsi:[2]
>
> #1. "When God decreed the Creation, He pledged Himself by writing in His book which is laid down with Him: My mercy prevails over my wrath."
>
> #4. "The sons of Adam inveigh against time, but I am time, and My hand is the night and the day."
>
> #19. "Pride is My cloak and greatness My robe, and whoever competes with Me in respect to either of them I shall cast into the Fire."
>
> #23. "Where are they who love one another through My glory? Today I will give them shade in My shade, that being the day when there is no shade but My shade."
>
> #31. "A man once said, 'By God, God will not forgive so-and-so!' whereupon the Almighty said, 'Who is it who says in My name that I will not forgive so-and-so? I have most certainly forgiven so-and-so, but I have nullified your own [good] deeds!'"

It is easy to see the "soft" nature of these short *Hadith Qudsi*, their tendency toward obscure images and language, and their concern with ethical behaviors. Among Sufi collections of Prophetic *Hadith* may be found many of the same *hadith*s found in the canonical *Hadith* collections accepted as sound by mainstream jurists, but many other traditions are also included as well that are not found in the canonical collections. This raised a certain suspicion among legalists as to the legitimacy of Sufism in general, since so much of Muslim religious and legal behaviors are authorized by the *Hadith*.

Types of Sufism

There has always been a tension within Islam, as within Judaism and Christianity, between different modes of understanding, interpreting, and living out the divine imperative. Some tend toward the theological, some toward the theosophical; some tend toward the strict observance of law, while others toward a free spirit response and inspiration in relation to God. These different approaches have often raised tensions within religious communities, and sometimes these have resulted in persecution and violence.

A wide variety of ideas and practices were developed among Sufis that resulted in the development of many schools, known as paths (*tarīqa*s), and orders. The schools tend to follow a particular method or approach, while the orders are organized around the teachings of specific teachers. One of the best-known Sufi orders is the *Mawlawiyya,* named for its founder, *mawlānā* ("our master") Jalal al-Din al-Rumi (d.1273). Rumi founded the order in Konya in today's Turkey, though he himself was ethnically Persian. In Turkey today the order is popular and known as the Mevlevi order. This is the order out of which developed the meditative dance known in the West as the "whirling dervishes," which is truly a beautiful and moving sight to behold. Like many other Sufi masters, Rumi was an exceptional and somewhat eccentric individual. He is known especially for his exquisite poetry written in Persian, composed in rhymed couplets and called *mathnawī*s (or *mathnavi*s). His collected work is usually called *al-Mathnawī*.[3]

The following are a few excerpts from among the thousands found in the Mathnavi. Unfortunately, the translation cannot reach the beauty of the original Persian, but the content is nevertheless of interest.[4]

- Think it not strange if the spirit veils the Beloved: Engage in ascetic discipline and leave aside the tumultuous ego! (173)
- "I" and "we" are a stopper of mud and straw—remove the stopper, behold that you yourself are a vat of wine! (173)
- Behold a world apparently nonexistent but existent in essence; and this other world, apparently existent, but without permanence! (175)
- What is love? Perfect thirst. So let me explain the Water of Life. (195)
- Love is the kernel, the world the shell; Love is the sweetmeat, the world the cauldron. (198)
- All the hopes, desires, loves, and affections that people have for different things—father, mothers, friends, heavens, the earth, gardens, palaces, sciences, works, food, drink—the saint knows that these are desires for God and all those things are veils. When men leave this world and see the King without these veils, then they will know that all were veils and coverings, that the object of their desire was in reality that One Thing. . . . They will see all things face to face. (201)

- Let me wash my heart of all knowledge, let me make myself heedless of self: One must not go before the auspicious Beloved as a master of all sorts of sciences. The spirits of madmen know that this spirit is the shell of the spirit: For the sake of this knowledge, you must pass beyond knowledge into madness. (227)

Sufi orders may be found in virtually all parts of the Muslim world. The Suhrawardīya order is influential in India and Bangladesh, the Shādhilīya in many parts of the Arabic-speaking world, the Bektāshīya officially banned by the secular state of Mustafa Kemal Ataturk in 1925 but still existing in one form or another in Turkey, the Badawīya in Egypt, Nakshbandīya in Uzbekistan and neighboring areas in Central Asia, and so forth. In many countries there are a number of different orders and, in fact, Sufism has influenced the general practice of mainstream Islam.

Sufi Practices

The most common Sufi practice is *dhikr*, which is, literally, "remembrance" of God. It is a devotional, meditative act that includes the repetition of the divine names, and especially *Allah, Ḥayy* ("the Living One"), *Qayyūm* ("the Eternal"), or, simply, *Huw* ("He"). Sometimes *dhikr* will include other material from the Qur'an or *Hadith*, such as recitation of "there is no deity but God." The type of *dhikr* called *dhikr al-awqāt* is performed daily, under the direction of one's master and after at least two of the obligatory prayers. The *dhikr al-khafī* is personal, associated with breath control, and can be quite complex, requiring inhalation on certain words or syllables, exhalation at others, and much practice ensuring that other organs involved in the process are trained in order to engage and channel a kind of energy through the body. *Dhikr*s are often ritualized ceremonies that may include meditative recitation, singing, instrumental music, dance, and engaging in trances, sometimes with the help of incense, candles, costumes, and other accoutrements that contribute to a meditative mood.

The *ḥaḍra* (or *dhikr al-ḥaḍra*) is a term that may often be interchanged with *dhikr* and used mostly in the Arabic-speaking world. It refers to a variety of supererogatory Sufi rituals (chanting, dance, meditative recitation with or without music, etc.) practiced as a group. They are sometimes regularly scheduled, such as on Thursday evenings after the night prayer or after the *jum'a* prayer on Friday at noon. *Ḥaḍra* features various practices of *dhikr*, but also sermons, study, Qur'an recitation, reciting poetry, and so forth.

Samā' (Hebrew // *shemi'ah*) is a complex form of *ḥaḍra*, a group *dhikr* with music and dance. It can be ecstatic, which raised the ire of traditionalists who felt that such practices would simply degenerate into forbidden sensuality.

Qawwāli is a form of Sufi music common in India, Pakistan, Afghanistan, Iran, and Turkey. It is popular enough to have become associated also with some secular music from these countries as well. One interesting example of how a *qawwāli* entered Jewish religious circles is in a particular melodic setting for Psalm 150, "*Hallelu hallelu hallelu,*" which originates with a song written by the recently deceased Sufi musician, Nusrat Fateh Ali Khan, in which the words are *Allah hu Allah hu Allah hu.*[5]

Much more could be included here about Sufism, but many books are available that have been written on the subject. Suffice it to say that the tensions between mystical and "orthodox" modes of religiosity in Islam have never been eliminated. With the coming of Western influence along with European colonialism, especially in the 19th and 20th centuries, attempts at "modernizing" Islam among reformers included a heavy negativity toward Sufi practices and ideologies. Today, however, one can observe that many of the "children of Westernization" in the Muslim world who grew up in communities that were estranged from the mosque are now seeking a form of Islamic religious commitment that is neither mainstream orthodox nor radical Islamist. Many are attracted to Sufism, which has enjoyed a surge in some sectors of the Muslim world. One such surge is taking place in Turkey at a variety of levels and among a number of groups or *tarīqa*s, from the Alevi-Bektahsi community to the Nurcu movement founded by Said Nursi (d.1960) to the followers of the contemporary leader, Fethullah Gülen. Each has a different way of relating to tradition and modernity, the secular state and the world.[6] Some scholars of contemporary Islam point out how aspects of Sufism today have moved past what was once considered stable boundaries to penetrate and infuse the practice and worldview of many Muslims who would not define themselves specifically as Sufi. Some of these aspects include relating to the teachings and piety of Sufi masters as a source of faith, and drawing understanding of ethics and identity from Sufi poetry and narrative.

CHAPTER 23

The Shī`a

Shi`a Islam emerged out of major differences among the followers of Muhammad over who should lead the community. The majority sided with the system that developed into the caliphate. These became known as Sunni Muslims. A significant minority, however, believed that the direct descendants of Muhammad were the best source of knowledge about the Qur'an and Muslim practice. Some believe that a special spiritual essence—some have called it a divine spark—exists among Muhammad's family, the "people of the Prophet's house" (*ahl al-bayt*). Some base the authority for such a special consideration for the family line of Muhammad on Qur'an 33:33, a verse that follows a section treating women and then the wives of Muhammad in particular: "And settle in your homes, and do not dress up with ornaments as was done during the earlier *jāhiliyya* [pre-Islamic "period of ignorance"]. Be steadfast in prayer, give the *zakāt*, and obey God and His messenger, for God wishes to remove defilement from you, *ahl al-bayt*, and to purify you thoroughly."

According to tradition, Muhammad's cousin, `Alī ibn Abī Ṭālib, was the first person to become a Believer after Muhammad's wife, Khadīja. The Shi`a believe that Muhammad appointed Ali to be his successor, but Sunnis do not agree that Muhammad appointed anyone to succeed him. Ali married Muhammad's daughter Fāṭima, and together they gave birth to a line of leaders known as *imāms* who, according to Ali's followers, should have been accepted as the rightful leaders of the *umma*. Those who took this position were known as the "Party of Ali." In Arabic, this is *shī`at `alī*, which was shortened in popular discourse to "the Shi`a."

According to the Shi`a, the only legitimate and divinely sanctioned leaders of the *umma* could be men from the bloodline of Ali and Fāṭima. These are the *imāmate*, the "leadership" that derives from the *ahl al-bayt*. It is worth noting the terminology, since it is somewhat confusing: the expression of Islam that reflects the position of the Shi`a is called Shi`a Islam, and a member of that community is called a Shi`i Muslim or a member of the Shi`a (*shī`i*, plural: *shī`iyyūn*).

Shi`a Practice and Doctrine

We have already outlined one small difference between Sunni and Shi`a customs in prayer. Other minor differences would be noticed by Muslims themselves but would be lost by most outsiders because the differences are so slight. They include slight variations in the practice of purification before prayer, the position of the hands at various points in the prostration cycle, and so forth.

The Shi`a community known as Ja`faris pays, in addition to the *zakāt*, a tax called *khums*, meaning "one fifth." It applies to one fifth of the extra income from earnings at the end of the year. They also recognize a form of temporary marriage called "marriage for pleasure" (*mut`a*). It is a formal relationship that may include lawful sexual intercourse but expires at a certain specified time. This is derived from Qur'an 4:24, the same source as Sunni law on marriage. The previous verses outline forbidden marriages, including "married women except those whose safety you control. This is God's requirement for you. But beyond these it is permissible for you, provided you court them with your property positively and without prostituting them. And for your enjoyment with them, give them their due as prescribed. There is nothing bad about coming to terms of mutual agreement in this regard after it is determined, for God is all-knowing, wise." The Arabic of this verse is indeed open to a wide range of interpretation, and English translations vary significantly on its meaning.[1]

*Mut`ah* marriage, as it is called, is used among the Shi`a to satisfy sexual needs in a variety of contexts. It is not considered prostitution. In some contexts today such as when two people of the opposite sex share housing, it is used without sexual consequences simply to formalize the relationship so that the woman can remove her head covering in the male's company. Young unmarried couples may decide to use it as a means to engage in something very similar to Western relations before permanent marriage, since it is always possible to make the temporary *mut`ah* relationship into a permanent one. Some men and women become disillusioned with permanent marriage and prefer to only commit for a few years at a time. But some women purportedly earn money by engaging in temporary marriage with pilgrims and even religious scholars in places of pilgrimage in what would appear to be a form of legalized prostitution. As one can imagine, the issue of *mut'ah* marriage remains highly controversial between Sunnis and Shi'is.

There tends to be little significant doctrinal differences between Sunni and Shi'a Islam aside from the major difference of sanctioned governance. All Muslims revere the family of the Prophet, but Shi'is take the reverence to a higher level of pious expectation. And as noted, Sunnis relate to the command to engage in jihad at a variety of levels, from the "lesser" to the "greater" jihad, while some within the Shi'a tend to elevate the requirement to a level virtually on par with that of the Five Pillars.

In the area of religious law, I have already mentioned that Shi'a Islam has its own major Ja'fari school associated with the 6th Imam, as well as other schools associated with other groups within the Shi'a. As would be expected, the Shi'a also view authoritative *Hadith* differently than Sunni schools of law. For example, the first three caliphs, Abū Bakr, 'Umar, and 'Uthmān, are not considered authoritative or reliable by many within the Shi'a. The *Hadith* of the Shi'a are authorized by Muhammad and his descendants through Fāṭima and 'Alī, who are considered to have known the Prophet best and who were particularly reliable in their transmission of traditions. Closely related to this is the doctrinal assumption of the infallibility of the imams as well as the Prophet. According to some within the Shi'a, 14 individuals were protected from error by God through *'iṣma*, which is understood in this context to mean divinely established infallibility. Thus Muhammad, his daughter Fāṭima, and the 12 imams are all *ma'ṣūm*, meaning infallible or sinless. It is all the more upsetting to Shi'is, therefore, that the imams and their families were often persecuted and even killed by Sunni rulers.

Because the Shi'a revere so many holy figures, they also emphasize pilgrimage to the tombs of the imams and other sainted individuals. These are called "visits" as opposed to pilgrimage. Many Shi'a visitation sites are located in today's Iraq, including Kufa, where Ali was killed by an assassin; Najaf, where Ali's tomb is located; Karbala, where the third imam Ḥussein was killed; Qum, in Iran, where the righteous Fāṭima (the wife of Imam 'Alī al-Riḍā') is buried; Mashhad, in Iran, where the 8th imam is buried; and so forth. As noted above, the practice of visits to the tombs and mausoleums of holy individuals is particularly offensive to traditionalist Sunnis such as the Wahhabis, who excoriate such activities as a form of idolatry.

CHAPTER 24

Mosque and Clergy

The Mosque

As noted above, any clean prayer space where Muslims prostrate themselves as part of the worship ritual is a mosque, a "place of prostration." It should be empty of paintings, pictures, and images, but it need not be dedicated only to the act of Muslim prayer.

The Friday mosque (*jāmi'*) is a multipurpose communal building as well as prayer space. Important community announcements are made there, particularly during the Friday prayer when more people gather together for prayer than at any other time during the week. Crowds will gather at the Friday mosque on any day during times of crisis. The Friday sermon will often treat contemporary issues, including political as well as religious and social issues, but this has always been complicated by the close but not always amicable relationship between governments and religious leadership in the Muslim world. In some times and places, the Friday sermons are expected to toe the line, while in others they are forums for raising issues of concern even if they might challenge governmental policies or structures.

Friday mosques may also serve as educational centers. Famous religious scholars are sometimes associated with great mosques, and many mosques also include additional buildings for Qur'an studies, recitations, and the study of religious tradition and *Sharī'a*. They are not only centers for study, but also refuges for students who wish to take their schoolwork to a quiet place. In busy urban areas, the mosque is a tranquil and calm place where one may get away from the crowds and noise to find a spot to meditate, rest, or even lie down and take a nap. This applies mostly to men, as the mosque remains a bastion of male camaraderie. Men may plan to meet at the mosque and socialize or even find a quiet corner in which to eat. In the Muslim world, the closest shops or stalls sell candles, prayer beads, incense and perfumes, and, of course, Qur'ans and other religious books. When large numbers of travelers descend upon a town or city, it has been a normal procedure for those without accommodation to sleep in the mosque.

In the Muslim world, mosques are usually built and maintained by individual benefactors, trusts set up by families, or government. In the West, individual benefactors or family trusts continue to build mosques for public use, but governmental support is not an option in most Western nations. Some Muslim benefactors from the Arab world have given large sums to support the growing Muslim communities in the West, but this support has often included significant influence in religious practice and expectations, accomplished frequently by procuring imams supported by outside benefactors with particular religious perspectives to serve those communities. Different models are now being explored by Muslim communities in the West in order to sustain the large costs necessary to build or purchase and then maintain a mosque, and one of them is the congregational model that has become standard for other religious communities in the United States. It is quite likely that the style and expectation for governance in such communities will change along with the changes and development in their modes of financial support.

Clergy

As mentioned earlier, worship services need not be led by clergy and there developed no official rank of clergy in Islam. There are no rites that are restricted to a priestly class and no official document that permits a person to lead prayer. To this day, any pious male individual who is respected in the community and knows the prayers is entitled to lead a community in prayer. Females may lead an entirely female community.[1] The person who delivers the Friday sermon is often a scholar, but may even be a government official who is assigned to preach in the mosque. In the United States, different traditions mix. In some places, a resident imam who functions much like a congregational minister or rabbi in American Christian or Jewish congregations might deliver the Friday sermon, or the honor might be given to various qualified people at various occasions.

Muslim scholars traditionally proved themselves by their knowledge and their piety. Traditionally, a scholar might give a sign of approval to a student, which communicated that the student had learned all the traditional lore that he could from the scholar. In some cases, that would be simply a notation by the scholar on the notebook of the student, who would then move on to another scholar to learn more traditions and law or a different methodology.

Traditionally, great scholars might teach from their homes or from a room attached to a Friday mosque. However, universities have been functioning in the Muslim world from long before an equivalent existed in Europe. Al-Azhar University in Cairo is one such institution, founded originally in the 10th century under the Shi`a Fatimid caliphate. Al-Azhar is one of the largest Muslim universities in the world and attracts tens of thousands of students from around the world every year to its courses and programs. Students may major in Islamic religious sciences and receive a diploma from Al-Azhar or dozens of universities throughout the Muslim world from Morocco to Malaysia. These universities vary in their doctrinal and political approach to religious practice, leadership, and relations with other Muslims and other religions. A very new phenomenon in the Western world is the incipient development of training centers for Western Muslim religious leaders. They may be found in various stages of development and growth in Great Britain, France, Belgium, and the United States.

CHAPTER 25

The Calendar

Calendars not only mark time and seasons, they also convey messages that extend beyond what one usually associates with the marking of the years. Take "year one" of a calendar, for example. The event that marks the point from which one counts time often conveys a message about authority and power. In the current Western Gregorian Calendar, the counting of years begins from the traditional birth of Jesus. It is almost as if time (or significant time) only begins from that momentous occasion. And so, the notation of years following Jesus's birth is A.D., meaning in the Latin, *anno Domini*—"the year of our Lord." This is the reason, by the way, that Jews, Muslims, and many other non-Christians prefer to use C.E.—"the common era," meaning "according to the common system of counting years." Because of the tremendous influence of the Western world during the past two centuries, the Gregorian calendar has become the most common system for naming periods of time in the entire world. Using C.E. and B.C.E. removes a narrow and particularist theological reference point from what has become a virtually universal system.

Most calendars, including many references in the Bible, count "year one" as the first year of the reign of a king, such as "in the twenty-sixth year of Asa, king of Judah . . ." (1 Kings 17:8), "In the 12th year of Yoram son of Ahab king of Israel . . ." (2 Kings 8:25). The Rabbinic calendar places "year one" at the first day of Creation, thereby placing God (as referenced by Jews) as the focal point for all time.

Calendars have historically been one way in which contending or competing communities establish their authority. In Jewish history, for example, arguments between Babylonian and Palestinian geonim (religious leader-scholars) over subtle issues relating to the calendar reflected battles for power and influence over the larger Jewish world. And for the same reason there remain differences to this day between Christian denominations over the date of Christmas and Easter. It should not be surprising that three different but related monotheistic religious systems should have three separate systems for calculating the passing of the years and seasons.

The Islamic calendar begins with the year that Muhammad made his Hijra (emigration) from Mecca to Medina. The real success of Islam only became apparent after the move from Mecca to Medina in 622, so 17 years later, in 638, the second caliph, `Umar, designated that important event to be the marker from which time in the Muslim world would be counted. The Islamic calendar is therefore referred to often as the Hijri calendar. The standard notation for this among Westerners is A.H., from the Latin *anno hegirae*—"the year of the Hijra," and dates in Islamic history are sometimes given according to both calendars (i.e., 1347 A.H./1929 C.E.). Today, this notation is usually thought of in English as "after the Hijra." The first year of the Islamic calendar, however, does not begin on the day that Muhammad entered Medina. It begins, rather, in the first month of the year in which he made the Hijra. The Hijra is celebrated in the Muslim world annually on the eighth day of the month of Rabī`a, about 66 days after the first day of that calendar year.

The Islamic Lunar Calendar

The Qur'an stipulates that the year has 12 months (Q.9:36) and designates the moon to be the source for measuring time: "It is God who has made the sun shine and the moon glow, and has determined for it phases so you might know the numbering of the years and the computation" (Q.10:5). This is the basis for Islam's lunar calendar, which is very much like the Jewish lunar calendar. Each system marks the beginning of the month with the new moon, so the months of the Jewish and Islamic calendars usually begin on the same day. A slight variation sometimes occurs when the actual instant of the least visible moon occurs close to the moment that is designated to distinguish between two days. Each system deals with the problem in a slightly different way, which results occasionally in a divergence that is then corrected the following month. Unlike the Jewish calendar, however, the Islamic calendar does not correct for the difference between the lunar "year" and the solar year.

Twelve lunar months come out to 354 days, so the 12-month lunar cycle is approximately 11 days shorter than the solar cycle. That is corrected in the Jewish calendar by adding an extra month every second or third year, for a total of seven times in a cycle of 19 years. No correction is made in the Islamic calendar. The Muslim year thus falls back by 11 days each solar year, causing the Islamic calendar to "lose" one solar year every 32 Hijri years. As a result, the Islamic holidays and festivals range through all the seasons.

The calendar in pre-Islamic Arabia was also lunar, but it included a system of intercalation through which the lunar calendar was adjusted to fit with the solar year, as in the Jewish calendar. Some scholars of Islam believe that removing the system of intercalation was a purposeful act. It forced the old seasonal festivals tied to the changes in weather, agriculture, and fertility to be removed from these markers that were associated with nature deities. This change weakened the old ties with polytheism and therefore "Islamized" an important way for people to relate to nature.

The months of the Islamic calendar thus cycle through the seasons of the year. The most important impact that has on Muslims is through the revolving cycle of festivals, and especially the observance of Ramadan; and somewhat less so in the observance of the *Hajj*. The Ramadan fast is a daylight fast, so when it occurs in the winter it is shorter and the days are cooler. When it occurs in the summer the days are long and hot in much of the Muslim world, and refraining from eating and drinking becomes much more of a challenge. Muslims therefore regard the variability of the calendar to be a mercy from God, because it distributes the hardships and succors evenly throughout the seasons in the long 32-year cycle of observance. The *Hajj* also moves through the seasons, and since Mecca is an extraordinarily hot place in the summer, making the pilgrimage during that season is a more difficult experience, though many consider the added difficulty of the weather to add to its reward.

Friday and Shabbat

As we noted above in the section treating prayer, Friday is the day of congregation in Islam, as opposed to Saturday for Jews and Sunday for Christians. The Qur'an commands that Believers come together on the "day of congregation," which in Arabic is also the word for Friday (*yawm al-jumu'a*): "O Believers! When the call to pray is given on the day of congregation, hurry to remember God, leaving business aside . . ." (Q.62:9). There is some question among historians how Friday became the day of congregation for Muslims. Some have suggested that Friday was a day of gathering among the Jews of Medina to purchase provision for the following day, *Shabbat,* in which no manner of work or buying was allowed. Those at the market tended to end their business on Friday at about noon, which would have been a logical time for the Believers to institute a time of congregational prayer.

The canonical *Hadith* offers traditions that authorize Friday as the best day for prayer based on a traditional mode of interpretation that has interesting parallels with Judaism. "Harmala b. Yaḥyā reported through a chain of transmitters originating with Abū Hurayra that the Prophet said, 'The best day on which the sun has risen is Friday. Adam was created on it, he was brought into the Garden on it, and on it he was expelled from it.'"[1] Judaism has a tradition from the Talmud given in the name of Yohanan bar Hanina: "[Friday] was of twelve hours. In the first hour, [Adam's] dust was gathered; the second, it was shaped into a mass; the third, his limbs were extended; the fourth, a soul was inserted into him; the fifth, he stood on his feet; the sixth, he gave [the creatures their] names; the seventh, Eve became his mate; the eighth, they ascended to bed as two and descended as four [i.e., their children were born]; the ninth, he was commanded not to eat of the tree; the tenth, he sinned; the eleventh, he was tried; and the twelfth, he was expelled and departed."[2]

In another tradition from the same canonical collection, Muhammad is reported to have said, "We [Muslims] who are the last are the first on the Day of Resurrection. Although they were given the Book before us and we were given it after them, this is their day that was obligatory for them. But they disagreed about it, so God guided us to it and they came afterward. Therefore, the Jews [observe it] the following day, and the Christians the day after that."[3]

Major Holidays

The following chart places the festivals in relation to the 12 months of the Islamic year cycle. Not all festivals have deep religious significance (such as "new year's day" on 1 Muḥarram), some are not observed by all Muslims, and some, such as Muhammad's birthday, are forbidden to be celebrated by the more austere denominations. The common canonical festivals and observances are marked in italics and bold.

1. **Muḥarram**
    - **1st** Muḥarram: Hijrah New Year: A holiday in many countries to commemorate the Hijrah of the Prophet Muhammad from Mecca to Medinah in 622 C.E.
    - **10th** Muḥarram: \`Ashūra: The old 24-hour *\`ashūra* fast, now optional. Shi'a observance of the martyrdom of Imam Ḥussayn.
2. **Safar**
3. **Rabī\`u al-Awwal (Rabī\` I)**
    - **12th** Rabī\` I: *Milād al-Nabī* (or *mawlid al-nabī*): The birthday of Muhammad.
4. **Rabī\` al-Ākhir (Rabī\` II)**
5. **Jumāda al-\`ūlā (Jumāda I)**

6. Jumāda al-Ukhrā (Jumāda II)

7. Rajab

- **27th** Rajab: *Laylat al-mi`raj*: The Ascent of the Prophet to heaven from the rock in Jerusalem.

8. Sha`bān

9. Ramaḍān

- ***Ramadan monthlong daylight fast.***
- **23rd** Ramadan: *Laylat al-Qadr* (Night of destiny): The night when the Qur'an was brought down from the throne of God to be revealed to Muhammad. Many Muslims engage in special prayers throughout the night.

10. Shawwāl

- **1st** Shawwāl: ***`īd al-fiṭr***: Marks the end of Ramadan and beginning of three days of feasting. Known as *Seker Bayram* in Turkish, *Hari Raya Puasa* in Southeast Asia.

11. Dhū al-Qa`da

12. Dhū al-Ḥijja. Month for the Hajj.

- **10th** Dhu al-Hijja: ***`īd al-aḍḥā***: at conclusion of Hajj, commemorates Abraham's near-sacrifice of his son. Begins three days of *ayām al-tashrīk*. Known as *Kurban Bayram* in Turkish, *Hari Raya Hajj* in Southeast Asia and *Tabaski* in parts of Africa.

CHAPTER 26

The Muslim Life-Cycle

Muslims throughout the world practice a number of rites and ceremonies that recognize the stages of life. These rituals developed from the native cultures upon which Islam took root as well as formal religious requirements of Islam, so they differ quite markedly from one area to the next. In fact, many life-cycle rituals that are recognized popularly as Islamic are actually cultural rather than religious. The three common life-stages that are shared throughout the Muslim world are circumcision, marriage, and death, but we shall examine some other practices that have absorbed religious overtones despite their being cultural in origin.

Birth, Naming, and Circumcision

The Qur'an does not require any particular ritual associated with birth or the first period of life, but there are some prophetic traditions and customs that suggest certain activities. Muhammad is purported to have articulated the call to prayer in the right ear of his newborn grandson, Ḥasan, and the similar call that is made in the mosque just before the prayer service in his left. It became customary, therefore, for a male relative or pious individual to do the same for a newborn after it has been washed and swaddled. The opening chapter of the Qur'an is then recited for the protection and health of the baby, and people often bring gifts.

A special ceremony and sacrifice called *'aqīqa* occurs on the 7th day after birth (or later for some). The purpose is to give thanks to God, to express joy at the birth of a child, and to announce the birth publicly. The word is associated with the sacrifice or with the child's hair that is often shaved off on this occasion. The root meaning in Arabic comes from the verb "to split" or "to rip" and means roughly, "being irreverent or disobedient" (*ʿuqūq* means "disobedience" or "recalcitrance"). It is possible that the custom emerged from a cultural wish to demonstrate the religious obedience of the parents or to forestall lack of obedience of the child. In any case, the ritual sacrifice is the responsibility of the parents or grandparents and is considered "recommended" by most jurists but not mandatory. In most places, two sheep are sacrificed for a boy and one for a girl, but an egalitarian trend recommends only one for a girl or a boy, based on a tradition that Muhammad sacrificed one lamb for each of his grandsons, Hasan and Husayn. The meat of the animal is divided like the sacrifice at the end of the *Hajj* period, one third for the poor, one third for friends, and one third for the family. But one may also give all the meat to the needy. For those who shave the infant's hair there is a custom to give charity of equal value to the

MUSLIM NAMES

According to both the Bible and the Qur'an, one of the first human acts was that of naming (Gen. 2:18–20, Q.2:30–33). While the actual story is told somewhat differently in each scripture, they agree on the significance of names—knowing names and giving names. Naming is important in most cultures—perhaps in every culture—because the giving of a name provides grounding for a newborn child in family, history, culture, values, and religion. Just as Jewish names have special meaning in relation to Jewish tradition, family tradition, and ritual practice, so do Muslim names provide a special grounding for belonging and for meaning within the religious context of Islam.

Most Muslim names are Arabic in origin because of the Arabic linguistic environment out of which Islam and the Qur'an first emerged. Persian became another medium for naming because of the influence of its culture on developing Islam, and Turkish became a third medium for Muslim names. Jews and Christians who lived in Arabic-speaking lands often took on Arabic names too, though they rarely took on religious names known from Islamic religious history. The exception to that is the vernacular use among Jews and Christians of biblical names that occur in the Qur'an in Arabic. Perhaps the most common are Mūsā for Moshe, Yūsuf for Yosef, and Yaʿqūb for Yakov.

weight in silver of their baby's hair. Another custom is to circumcise the baby boy at seven days, although this specific timing for the circumcision is only a custom.

It is common to name the baby on the occasion of the *ʿaqīqa*, though it is not required, and some name the baby at birth or shortly thereafter. There are some common customs regarding names. It is conventional and fully accepted to name children after living or deceased relatives or after famous or pious individuals. Muhammad is said to have recommended for boys the name Abdallah (servant of God) or Abd al-Raḥmān (servant of the Merciful), and perhaps the most common name for boys is Muhammad, Aḥmad, or Maḥmūd (all from the same root as the name Muhammad). Girls may be named after wives of the Prophet or other saintly persons in Muslim history.

As in Judaism and in the Hindu traditions, the birth mother is rendered ritually impure as a result of childbirth. According to Islamic custom, she is excused from ritual duties for 40 days. In the Bible (Lev. 12:1–8), the birth mother remains in a state of ritual impurity of 33 days for a male and 66 days for a female, after which she must bring a lamb as a sacrifice. In some Muslim circles, the 40th day after birth, which marks the end of the period of ritual impurity, is an occasion for celebration.

As the child gets older and begins to speak, it is taught religious formulas and phrases like the *basmalah* and other phrases and devotional statements. The Qur'an is the basis around which most religious learning revolves, so children are encouraged to learn and memorize sections of the Qur'an. If the child has a gifted memory it will be taught to know the entire Qur'an by heart. If the child attends a religious day school it will learn the Islamic religious sciences, and if the child attends a nonreligious school, it will usually learn Islam in afternoon programs and Friday schools. In the United States, a growing network of Islamic day schools is growing, and there are also afternoon Islamic schools and "Sunday schools" for children attending public school.

As mentioned above ("Law versus Custom"), male circumcision is a universal expectation of Islam even though it is not mentioned in the Qur'an. The circumcision is often performed by a person whose job is to conduct such procedures, though today it is often performed in a hospital or clinic. The Arabic name for circumcisor is *khātin* or *muṭahhir*, who functions as a barber-surgeon, somewhat parallel to the Jewish *mohel*, though in the Jewish profession the person must also be learned in the intricacies of Jewish law and ritual associated with the procedure, whereas there is less need to know legal religious technicalities in the Islamic equivalent.

Marriage and Sexuality

Asceticism is frowned upon in Islam, and that includes celibacy. In the first *hadith* of the section on marriage in the most authoritative *Hadith* collection of Al-Bukhari, Muhammad is confronted by three men who ask how the Prophet worshiped. When they heard Muhammad's message they felt that they had to change their ways in order for their sins to be forgiven, so after leaving his presense, each one undertook to engage in some ascetic act that they hoped would merit forgiveness. One said, "I will forever pray through the night." Another said, "I will fast forever and never break it."[1] The last one said, "I will refrain from women and never marry." When Muhammad heard what they had said, he sought them out and said to them, "Are you the ones who said that? By God, I have more fear and consciousness of God than you, yet I fast and break my fast, I pray and then go to sleep, and I marry. Whoever disapproves of my practice is not a follower."[2] Another authoritative *hadith* from the same collection is often cited in relation to marriage. One day a group of young men with few resources available to them that would enable marriage were sitting with the Prophet. "The Messenger of God said to us, 'O young people! Whoever has the means to marry should do so for it will lower one's gaze and strengthen his control, and whoever is unable to marry should fast, for it is exhausting."[3]

Sexual pleasure, per se, is neither prohibited nor frowned upon in Islam. Sheikh Yusuf al-Qaradawi, whom I have cited previously and takes a moderately traditional position, writes the following.

> Sex is a strong driving force in the human being which demands satisfaction and fulfillment. Human beings have responded to the demands of the sexual appetite in three different ways: (1) One way is to satisfy one's sexual need freely with whomever is available and whenever one pleases . . . (2) The second approach is to suppress, and try to annihilate, the sexual drive . . . (3) The third approach is to regulate the satisfaction of this urge, allowing it to operate within certain limits, neither suppressing nor giving it free rein. This is the stand of the revealed religions, which have instituted marriage and have prohibited fornication and adultery. In particular, Islam duly recognizes the role of the sexual drive, facilitates its satisfaction through lawful marriage, and just as it strictly prohibits sex outside of marriage . . . , it also prohibits celibacy and the shunning of women. This is the just and intermediate position. If marriage were not permitted, the sexual instinct would not play its role in the continuation of the human species; while if fornication and adultery were not prohibited, the foundation of the family would be eroded. Unquestionably, it is only in the shade of a

> stable family that mercy, love, affection, and the capacity to sacrifice for others develop in a human being, emotions without which a cohesive society cannot come into being. Thus, if there had been no family system, there would have been no society through which mankind would be able to progress toward perfection.[4]

Some Muslim modernists would note that Qaradawi is writing more about men than about women, and would bemoan the tendency of Muslim religious scholars to express more concern about the sexual rights of the male gender than the female. Nevertheless, both the Qur'an and the tradition make clear that the purpose of sexual relations is not restricted to procreation but includes the right to satisfy one's sexual desire and to channel it in a positive direction.

It should be noted here that Islam forbids homosexual relations, though this is challenged currently by some gay and lesbian Muslim activists who are calling for a review of the issues. The Qur'an refers to male homosexuality five times in references to the behavior of Lot's people (Q.7:80–84, 11:78–81, 26:162–168, 27:55–57, and 29:28–30), and perhaps another time in Qur'an 4:15–16. The term in 4:15 is abomination (*fāḥisha*), which most interpreters understand as heterosexual adultery or fornication (*zinā*). A minority opinion understands the references to indicate female and male homosexual relations. All these references are negative.

In the qur'anic descriptions of paradise there is reference to "immortal boys" in Qur'an 56:17 and 76:19, or perhaps "immortal children," and "young men" as cupbearers to those who merit entrance. The exegetical tradition does not suggest that these have a homosexual function, but some literary works do, sometimes with humor. In later legal discussions, an analogy is sometimes made with the use of wine in paradise that is permitted while forbidden in the life of this world.

Marriage

Islam directs all physical sexual engagement to the institution of marriage. The Qur'an is often cited in support of this. "Wed those among you who are unmarried, and the righteous among your male and female slaves. If they are poor, God will provide for them from His bounty. God is infinite, all knowing. Those who cannot find [the means for] marriage should be chaste until God provides for them from His bounty" (Q.24:32–33).

The Qur'an has much to say about marriage and gender relations, and these have been interpreted to convey a range of meaning. On the one hand, a famous verse seems to require only the satisfaction of the male: "Your wives are a cultivable field for you, so enter your field as you wish . . ." (Q.2:223). Other verses such as Qur'an 2:187 are cited to support sexual mutuality: "It is permitted to you to have sex with your wives on the night of a fast. They are a garment for you and you are a garment for them . . . so lie with them and seek out what God has decreed for you" (Q.2:187). In one Qur'an verse that seems to be rarely cited (possibly because it seems to critique Muhammad who was later assumed to be immune from error), God actually appears to condemn the Prophet for failing to satisfy the sexual desires of his wives: "O Prophet! Why do you prohibit what God has permitted for you, striving for the satisfaction of your wives? God is forgiving, merciful!" (Q.66:1).

These and many other verses have been interpreted in a variety of ways by traditional and modern Qur'an scholars and jurists to support diverse views. Cultural sensibilities and traditions are often deeply interwoven with religious values, and it is often impossible to separate the two. Moreover, the various schools of law differ over many of the details associated with the institution of marriage. For the purposes of this introduction to Islam, I can only treat the most basic consensus positions, though I hope to make it clear that as with so many other subjects, Islam is not monolithic on matters of marriage, sexuality, and women's issues.[5]

Most marriages in the Muslim world, including in the West, are arranged by the parents of the bride, and often the groom as well. The male, however, tends to be much more active than the female in seeking a mate. Unlike the woman, he may engage in the process on his own. A woman who has not been married previously is usually represented by a guardian who may be her father or other close male relative. If none are available, a male adult may be appointed for the purpose. It is the male guardian who will sign the wedding contract for the wife, who essentially assigns him power of attorney.[6] Potential marriage partners may visit with each other before the wedding, but never without chaperons. Islam prohibits a man and woman who are not related in such a way that they may not marry to be alone together. It is becoming increasingly common to see young couples sitting together and talking in very public, sometimes crowded places in the Muslim world in order to meet and get to know each other. Dating and courtship as known in the West is not generally acceptable.

Arranged marriages are expected in Islam, but no marriage is possible without the consent of both partners. An authoritative *hadith* states, "The Prophet said, 'A widow may not be given away in marriage unless she consent and a virgin may not be given away in marriage unless she agrees.' They asked, 'O messenger of God! How can we know her permission?' He answered, 'Her silence [indicates her permission].'" That is followed by another *hadith:* "Khansā' bint Khidām al-Anṣāriyya said that her father gave her in marriage when she was a widow, but she did not like that, so she went to the

Messenger of God and he declared the father's arrangement invalid."[7] Despite such protection, the fact is that traditional Islamic marriages are family affairs that carry the stresses and influences of more individuals than only the two parties who will become husband and wife. Sometimes this works out for the best, as the high divorce rate in the West might attest. But sometimes the pressures can force people to marry against their will, or at least against the will of the woman.

The Marriage Contract

Marriage is not a sacrament in the Christian sense, but carries more the sense of a revocable legal agreement as in the Jewish sense of marriage. As in Judaism, it is a relationship based on a formal contract. The term referenced in passing in the Qur'an is *"mithāq ghalīẓ,"* which should be translated as "a powerful contract" (Q.4:21). The contract in essence legalizes sexual relations between the partners and includes a number of stipulations for each. The most basic is mutual good treatment, which is not legally defined. Each partner has rights and duties, which are differentiated by gender but are interrelated. If one partner fails his or her responsibility, that partner may jeopardize his or her claim to a particular right.

The husband's first duty is to pay a sum of wealth, often in gold jewelry, to his wife. This is called the *mahr* and has a parallel in the Bible (*mohar:* Gen. 34:12, Exod. 22:16). There is no set amount, but whatever is pledged becomes legally hers and she may save, spend, or invest it however she chooses. In exchange for the *mahr,* the husband receives power or authority over the marriage or over the contract. This is often understood as control over the relationship, including the sexual rights of the relationship, which therefore grants the husband the right to end the marriage by pronouncing repudiation of the contract. If the wife wishes to end the marriage, she must essentially buy out the contract by paying legal compensation. There are also grounds for divorce that vary between the schools of law, through which the wife may seek a judicial decision.

The wife also has the right to lodging, clothing, and support (compare Exod. 21:10). If her husband has other wives, she also has the right to an equal share of her husband's time. In exchange for the husband's support of his wife, jurists hold that a husband has the right to restrict her movements and to expect that she be available for sexual intimacy. A wife who does not comply may legally loose her right to support as well as any claim to a portion of her husband's time.

Some jurists accept added stipulations in the contract designed to secure more rights and privileges for the wife. The most common are that the husband will not take any additional wives or relocate from the wife's home town. The Hanbali school holds that if the husband violates such added stipulations, the wife has the right to dissolve her marriage, but the other schools do not accept the validity of these two clauses. They may be included in the marriage contract but are not enforceable unless the husband had delegated to her a right to divorce on grounds that one of the stipulations was breached. Another way to validate them is for the husband to pronounce a suspended divorce, which would take effect automatically if he violated one of them. The effect of this is to protect the binding power of the husband while providing more protection for the personal needs of the wife.

The complex issues associated with the rights and duties of husband and wife through a legal contract find a close parallel in the traditional Jewish system. For many Jews as well as Muslims, the traditional system is an acceptable way of establishing and guaranteeing rights and responsibilities for both partners. For those who would work toward equalizing the rights and independence of the wife, some wish to work within the parameters established by the legal basis of the traditional marriage contract. Others object to the overall framework of differentiated rights and duties or to unequal male prerogatives, and for these, modifications to the traditional marriage contract cannot resolve the problems. They call for a fundamental rethinking of the legal presumptions in the marriage contract and the particular style of relationship that such a contract tends to promote.

Wedding ceremonies vary significantly throughout the Muslim world. Even between upper and lower Egypt or between the Atlas Mountains and the coastal cities of Morocco, regional customs make the actual wedding ceremonies quite diverse. They vary even more between the many different regions and ethnic groups among Muslims living in Arab lands, Indonesia and Malaysia, India and Pakistan, Central Asia, Sub-Saharan Africa, and China. Public celebrations with bright and colorful decorations, contracts, henna ceremonies, deal-making, and other preparations join families as well as individuals; and the music, wedding banquets, and parties may easily last for more than a week after the official wedding contract is signed. I have witnessed many kinds of wedding bands, dancing horses, huge fireworks displays, celebratory gunfire of automatic weapons, and even modest parades of the groom or the groom and his bride to their new home together.

Polygamy

Unlike the Bible, which has no limit to the number of wives a man may take, the Qur'an limits the number to four at the same time. In reference to the treatment of orphans the Qur'an says, "If you fear that you will not deal fairly with orphans, then marry those women who seem good to you—two, three or four. But if you fear that you will not be just, then one, or [a woman] whom your right hands possess.[8] That is the best to avoid being unjust" (Q.4:3). Later in the same chapter and using the same language, the Qur'an conveys the message, "You will never be able to be just with wives even if you try" (Q.4:129).

Muhammad had special dispensation to take more than four wives (Q.33:50–51). The tradition literature mentions that he took wives to save them from destitution and that women came to him with the hopes that he would take them into his entourage. The Qur'an, however, eventually forbade him in Q.33:52 from taking additional wives: "No more wives are permitted to you. . . ."

The traditional commentaries claim that polygamy was a common practice in the pre-Islamic period and that the Qur'an provided limits and special protection for multiple wives that were not available prior to this revelation, but some modern scholars believe that polygamy was actually a qur'anic innovation that was responding to the unfair treatment of female dependents who were neglected by their guardians in Medina.[9] In any case, Qur'an 4:129 would seem to suggest a preference for monogamy in the Qur'an.

Contraception

Because Islam forbids sexual relations outside of marriage, the classic discussions about birth control focus on contraception between husband and wife. The Qur'an does not treat contraception directly, but Muslims who oppose contraception often cite the following verses treating infanticide for support: "Do not kill your children out of fear of poverty. We will provide for them and for you" (Q.6:151, 17:31). Others cite Qur'an 42:49–50: "To God belongs the dominion of the heavens and the earth. He creates whatever He wills, giving to whomever He wills a female [child] and giving to whomever He wills a male [child]; or He combines them male and female, and He makes barren whomever he wills, for He is omniscient, powerful."

Most of the law schools allow contraception under certain conditions. Coitus interruptus (*'azl*) was practiced by pre-Islamic Arabs and continued to be used during time of the Prophet with his knowledge. In one authoritative *hadith*, Muhammad is asked whether in the case of legally acquired female captives the contraceptive technique of *'azl* is permitted. He responded, "You are not required to refrain from it. There is no soul that God determines should be born that will not be born."[10] The practice of withdrawal may diminish the sexual gratification of the female partner, and it is also entirely the prerogative of the male partner who must be sensitive to his impending ejaculation. Some authorities, therefore, such as Ahmad ibn Hanbal (d.855, the originator of the Hanbali legal school) required the consent of the wife for contraception because she has the right of sexual enjoyment and to be a part of the decision of having a child. The form of contraception mentioned in the *Hadith* is *`azl*, but some modern jurists accept other forms as well.

Abortion

Abortion is *ijhāḍ* in Arabic, but as in other systems, it is related to miscarriage, which in Arabic means "losing [lit. "the falling of"] the fetus or "having been slipped out". The Qur'an does not include these terms, so the jurists extrapolated from the two central verses forbidding infanticide mentioned above (Q.6:151, 17:31). The *Hadith* rarely mentions *ijhāḍ*, but occasionally references miscarriage caused by violence to a woman rather than intentional abortion. In the *Hadith* references, the question is what damages must be paid to the woman, and the answer is the payment of a male or female slave.[11]

From this the jurists derived the general consensus that the killing of a fetus is not permissible as soon as one can speak of it as a formed person. The payment of blood money is required if the baby is aborted alive and then dies, while a fine of lesser amount is to be paid if it is aborted dead. There is no agreement among legal scholars as to when the fetus would be considered a fully formed person. In fact, there are substantial differences between the four legal schools, not only over at what point in the pregnancy abortion would be forbidden, but also over the conditions that would allow interfering with the natural processes of pregnancy and birth. All agree that abortion is permissible up to 40 days, while the Hanafi and Shafi`i schools allow up to 120 days. The schools apply certain conditions in some cases, such as that both parents agree to the procedure or that the mother fears she may run out of milk under the physical stress of a new pregnancy.

Exceptions to these limits are made by some authorities if the life of the mother is endangered, based on Qur'an 2:233: "No mother should be harmed on account of a child of hers." According to Qaradawi's reading of the jurists, "If . . . after the baby is completely formed, it is reliably established that the continuation of the pregnancy would necessarily result in the death of the mother, then, in accordance with the general principle of the Shari`ah, that of choosing the lesser of two evils, abortion must be performed."[12]

Divorce

Divorce (*ṭalāq*) is of course not a necessary part of the Islamic lifecycle. In fact, although fully legal, it is not common. This is due partly to the fact that marriage ties families as well as individuals together, and family pressures tend to foil the possible desire of the partners themselves to divorce. Nevertheless, sometimes the relationship between husband and wife becomes extremely strained, as is recognized in the Qur'an. In a discussion about difficulties in relationship between a married couple, the Qur'an teaches the following: "And if you fear dissention between them, then send an arbitrator from his family and from hers. If they wish to reconcile, then God will bring agreement between them, for God is knowing, aware" (Q.4:35). Arbitration is not always successful in bringing understanding to a marriage relationship. The Qur'an has a lot to say about divorce, and it reflects the patriarchal society out of which Islam emerged in 7th century Arabia. Divorce is accepted, but it is the prerogative of the husband; he initiates the proceedings. A divorced woman must wait for three menstrual cycles before remarrying (Q.2:228) in order to maintain that she is not pregnant, because the father of the child is entitled to paternity and to raise the child. The Qur'an is explicit that the husband is a rank above the wife in this regard (Q.2:227–232), but it also provides certain protections for the woman. At issue here is the difficult problem of paternal responsibility and privilege over the children as well as the same over the wife.

After the husband declares a divorce, there is a required waiting period called *`idda* (from the root meaning "to count") of four months (Q.2:226) during which the wife may not remarry and actually must remain in the home of the husband. They are nevertheless officially divorced by the husband's declaration. During the *`idda* period they may be reconciled without the requirement of remarriage, but after the period has passed they are officially divorced. Based on Qur'an 2:229, the husband may reconcile with his wife twice, but if he declares the woman divorced a third time it is a permanent enactment that cannot be undone without the writing up of a new marriage contract. The wife's expenses during the waiting period are the responsibility of the husband. She cannot be expelled from her place of residence and any harassment on the part of the husband may constitute a criminal as well as a moral offense. In case of divorce, the young children remain in the custody of their divorced mother but the father is responsible for their maintenance.

The wife can also divorce her husband if that is stipulated in the marriage contract, say, for taking another wife. This type of divorce is called "delegated divorce." Marriage can also be dissolved through mutual consent, though it is actually the husband's prerogative to make it official. The problem for women is that it is almost impossible by traditional procedures for a woman to initiate a successful divorce. This, by the way, is a problem that is found also in the traditional Jewish community, and various attempts by secular courts to enable the rights of women in this regard have not been satisfactory. There is also a form of divorce mentioned above among the protections of the wife called *khul`* ("removal" or "repudiation"), through which the wife essentially buys out her wedding contract, but this is usually accepted only with the husband's permission and can elicit the husband making extortionate demands. There are other forms of divorce as well, such as *li'ān* (mutual cursing) or a kind of annulment called *faskh* or *tafrīq*. All tend to favor the husband over the wife.

A recent Egyptian law, approved by the chief jurist of the most respected institution of Islamic jurisprudence in Egypt and perhaps the entire Sunni Muslim world, Al-Azhar, provides an alternate approach. Beginning in March 2000, Egypt has granted the wife the right to obtain a *khul'* divorce without the husband's consent if she returns the full dowry that she received at marriage. By the middle of the first year after the law was passed, some 3,000 petitions seeking divorce under these provisions had been filed in Cairo, a city of some 18 million residents.

Inheritance

The Muslim law of inheritance is quite complex and cannot be explored here in any detail. It is based on Qur'an 4:11–12: "God directs you concerning your children: the male gets the equivalent of the portion of two females, but if they are more than two daughters, they get two thirds of what one leaves. If there is only one, she gets half. . . ." The verses continue to outline a complex set of relations and percentages of inheritance, which is made much more complicated in the juridical literature. A person may make a will, but that can affect only up to one third of the estate, the remainder regulated by the legal formulas. The net result, if one compares the system with that of the Hebrew Bible, is significantly better for women because they are fully entitled to inherit, though at a reduced rate of men (cf. Num. 27:8–11). The system seems to have been developed in an environment that was not agrarian because it is impossible for any single inheritor to retain an unequally large portion of land. Land becomes divided equally along with other forms of wealth. The result has often been to divide viable land-holdings into increasingly smaller shares among survivors in each generation until it becomes difficult or even impossible for sustainable farming through inheritance. Lands must then be purchased outside of the family plot, which then makes the farming all that much more difficult. The same problem applies to businesses that often become unviable after one or two generations.

One way to get around the problem is through the institution of the charitable trust or foundation (*waqf*). This avoids some of the problems of inheritance division, but it also dissolves the business that generated the income in the first place. The *waqf* was designed to fund public institutions such as mosques, schools, hospitals, market buildings, and libraries. The advantage for the family is that relatives may be employed to administer the institution that is funded, thereby creating and maintaining jobs for generations of family members. *Waqf*s remain private and not open to government interference. This very independence sometimes causes difficulties, because if the funds dry up, the property may end up abandoned and taken out of circulation without the ability of government to possess it for refurbishing.

Death, Burial, and Mourning

As with many other Islamic rituals, death practices tend to vary from place to place and reflect the cultures over which Islam became dominant. It is customary to turn the dying person's face in the direction of the *qibla* (toward Mecca) if possible, and to recite the *shahāda*. This is equivalent to the Jewish custom of reciting *Shema* at the moment before death.

It is also customary to recite chapter 36 of the Qur'an, called *yā sīn*, which treats resurrection of the dead and final judgment in comforting terms. "It is We who will revive the dead and record what they have sent before and what they have left. We have made an accounting for everything in a clear book" (Q.36:12). Of particular consolation are verses 51–58: "The trumpet will sound and they will rush out of their graves to their Lord, crying out, 'woe is us! Who roused us from our bed? This is what the Merciful One promised. The messengers spoke the truth!' In only one shout they are present before Us. So on that day no soul will be wronged in the least, nor shall you be rewarded except for what you have done. Those destined for the Garden are joyful today for their activity, they and their spouses reclining on couches, joyful there, having all they desire. 'Peace,' spoken from a merciful Lord."

As soon as possible after death, the body is washed and prepared for burial. As in Judaism, embalming is not permitted. The washing is the final ablution for the deceased. It is particularly meritorious to be engaged in this act, men performing it for men and women for women except for children or spouses, who may be washed by their mates or parents regardless of gender. Usually, the body is washed three times, the hair combed and, if long, braided. The body is then dried and perfumed, and then wrapped in a simple white cotton shroud. A coffin is not necessary but is permitted. The point is that it be simple and no costly materials be used. If the deceased is a martyr, the body is not washed. It is assumed that the martyr's death purifies, and the martyr is immediately entered into heaven.

The body may be carried to the mosque, taken to any clean place, or remain at the home for the funeral service (*janāza*). The body in a coffin or on a bier is placed in front of the worshipers, and the service is led by a close male relative or a professional or appointed imam. The funeral service is performed standing and there are no prostrations. It includes four *takbīrs*, the opening chapter of the Qur'an, and any number of variants of supplications for Muhammad, on behalf of the deceased, and for all Muslims. An example might be something like "O God! Grant forgiveness to our living and to our dead, and to those who are present and to those who are absent, and to our young and our old folk, and to our males and females. O God! Whomever you grant to live from among us, help him to live in God; and whom of us you cause to die, help him to die in faith. O God! Do not deprive us of the reward for patience on his loss, and do not make us subject to travail after him." Prayers are recited for the forgiveness of the deceased's sins (unless it is a child who is assumed to be pure of sin). The prayer service ends with the normal conclusion of *taslīm* facing right and then left.

The body should be buried on the day of death, if at all possible. If the death occurs in the afternoon or evening, it may be buried the following day, if necessary. After completing the *jināza* prayers, the body is taken to the cemetery. Mourners walk in front or beside the bier; those who are riding or driving follow it. The funeral procession proceeds in silence, if possible.

The grave should be deep and the body should face Mecca. When lowering the body, a prayer-statement may be recited: "In the name of God and with God, and according to the *sunna* of the messenger of God upon whom be the blessings and peace of God." Other prayers may be offered as well, and it is common to recite Qur'an 20:55 which follows a reference to God having created the earth as a bed or couch to lie on: "We created you from it and We shall return you to it, and We shall bring you forth from it another time." A stone, brick, or amount of soil is placed under the head of the deceased to raise it up. After placing the body in the grave, the attendees fill the pit with soil and raise the level to about a foot above the level of the surrounding earth. This may be followed by another recitation of the *Fātiḥa*. There are, of course, any number of variations in the ritual, depending on custom, denomination, and location.

The official period of intense mourning is three days, during which loved ones and close relatives receive visitors and condolences and avoid decorative clothing and jewelry. A lesser level of mourning continues until the end of 40 days after burial. During this period, there may be special meals, prayers, and Qur'an recitations to honor and remember the dead. Widows observe an extended mourning period, four months and 10 days long, based on Qur'an 2:234. During this time, a widow is not to remarry, move from her home, or wear decorative clothing, jewelry, or perfume.

The grave itself may or may not be marked or decorated. As noted above in the discussion of "Wahhabi" and similar expressions of Islam, any embellishment of graves is highly disapproved of by some groups. Nevertheless, it is common to have grave markers, and anyone who has visited Cairo and seen the City of the Dead must be impressed by the many necropolises and mausoleums that are customary in Egypt. It is considered meritorious to visit cemeteries and meditate on the meaning of life and death.

Before ending this section on the life-cycle, it is fitting to revisit the Islamic notion of final judgment. We have observed how resurrection of the dead is a basic creed of Islam. That resurrection will occur at the end of days, when all souls will be subject to a final divine judgment and then eternity in heaven or hell. The period between death and resurrection is called *barzakh*, which means "interval" or "gap" and derives from Qur'an 23:99–100: "Until death comes to one of them, he will say, 'My Lord, send me back that I may do right by what I have neglected.' No way! That is only talk. Before them is a gap until the day they will be resurrected." In the tradition and folk literatures, this is a period during which the angel of death or his assistants will separate the soul from the body, either painlessly or harshly depending on how righteous the person was while living. Three events are said to make up this period: the separation of the soul from the body, an interrogation of faith for the soul by the angels Nakīr and Munkar, and then possible torment or horror of the grave. As strange as these events may seem to Jews unfamiliar with Islamic eschatology, an interesting *hadith* appears in a number of authoritative sources that suggests that the Jews of Medina had a very similar notion.

> Muhammad's youngest wife `Ā'isha said: The Messenger of God came to me [once] when a Jewish woman was with me, and she said: 'Did you know that you will be tested in the grave?' `Ā'isha continued: The Messenger of God was frightened [in response] and said: 'It is the Jews who will be tested!' `Ā'isha said: We stayed together some nights, and then the Messenger of God said: Did you know that I was given a revelation that you will be tested in the grave? `Ā'isha said: Thereafter I heard the Apostle of God seeking refuge from the torment of the grave.[13]

CHAPTER 27

Personal Observance

Dietary Laws and Customs

Islam observes a system of permitted and forbidden foods that has a number of parallels with Judaism, but as we noted previously, Judaism is stricter with regard to its dietary laws than Islam. This is duly noted in the Qur'an, which criticizes what it considers to be the overly restrictive attitudes of Jews toward permitted foods. As always, the anonymous qur'anic voice is the word of God. "We have forbidden to the Jews everything with claws, and of the oxen and the flocks we have forbidden the fat except what they carry on their backs or intestines or what is mixed with the bone. This we repaid them for their iniquity, for We are truthful" (Q.6:146). This is contrasted with what is articulated as a more generous system. "Say: 'I do not find in what was revealed to me any restrictions about eating except what is [already] dead, or blood poured out, or pig flesh—for that is an abomination—or what is sinfully offered to other than God.' But if one is compelled without desiring it and without backsliding, God is forgiving, compassionate" (Q.6:145).

The frame for the qur'anic articulation of dietary rules is beneficence rather than restriction. "Believers, eat of the good things that We have provided you, and give thanks to God if it is He whom you worship. He has only forbidden you dead animals (*al-mayta*), the blood (*al-damm*), and the flesh of pigs (*laḥm al-khinzīr*), and what has been offered up to other than God. But if one is compelled without desiring it or backsliding, then no sin accrues to him, for God is forgiving, compassionate" (Q.2:172–173). As has been noted above, it is not unusual for the Qur'an to repeat phrases and themes, so like the Torah (cf. Leviticus 11, Deuteronomy 14), the rules are spelled out more than once. The Qur'an associates eating with God's generosity. As in reference to other aspects of God's creations, food is made available to humanity through God's mercy and compassion, but that does not permit humanity to be ungrateful or careless. "It is God who originated gardens, trellised and un-trellised, and the date-palm, and various seeded foods, the olive and the pomegranate, the like and the unlike. Eat of the fruit that they bear, and pay what is due on the day of harvest. But do not be wasteful, for God does not love the wasteful" (Q.6:141).

The term for permitted foods is *ḥalāl*, and for forbidden foods, *ḥarām*. These terms are used also for other activities or items that are permitted or forbidden in Islam. As we have noted above, however, the juridical traditions include moderating terms such as *makrūh*, which refers to behaviors or objects disapproved but not forbidden. This applies to certain foods as well. As may be gathered from some of the earlier references, the Qur'an forbids outright many of the same categories that are forbidden also by the Torah. "Forbidden to you is dead animals, the blood, the flesh of pigs and what has been offered to other than God, that which has been strangled, beaten to death or has fallen, has been gored or has been eaten by [other] wild animals except what you have slaughtered yourselves,[1] and what has been sacrificed on a stone pillar, and what you have divined by means of divining arrows. This is an abomination . . . but if anyone is compelled by hunger and not disinclination, God is forgiving, merciful" (Q.5:3).[2] This clearly restricts the choice of permitted foods, but as in the earlier citation it is framed as beneficence and generosity. The following two verses continue, "They ask what is permitted to them. Say: good things are permitted to you, and what you have taught hunting animals to catch by teaching them what God has taught you. So eat what they catch for you, but pronounce the name of God over it and be God-fearers, for God is swift in accounting. Today good things are permitted to you, and the food of those who have been given the Book is permitted to you, and your food is permitted to them . . ." (Q.5:4–5).

While there are many parallels between qur'anic and tora'itic rules regarding forbidden animals, they are not equal. It is true that both agree on certain conditions that forbid the consumption of normally permitted animals (such as having died before being slaughtered) or the consumption of certain parts (such as blood), but the Qur'an is less restrictive even in its articulation of the system. Whereas the Torah approaches the topic by delineating certain categories of permitted animals, and then restricting all others that fall outside of those categories, the Qur'an lists certain specific forbidden animals and then assumes that all others are permitted.

The restriction against "boiling a kid in the milk of its mother" (Exod. 23:19, 34:26, Deut. 14:21) does not appear in the Qur'an, and all the dietary laws of Rabbinic Judaism that derive from these verses have no meaning in Islam. The more lenient Islamic position has generally allowed Muslims to eat foods that are kosher by Jewish standards, but has not allowed Jews to eat foods that are *ḥalāl* by Muslim standards.

Proper slaughtering is called *dhabīḥat ḥalāl*, related linguistically to the Hebrew word for sacrifice, *zevah*. The process is quite similar to that of kosher *sheḥitah* (Hebrew for slaughtering). In both, a very sharp nonserrated blade is pulled across the neck of the animal in one swipe, severing the main vessels. The blood of the animal is then immediately drained. It is also expected in both that a mentally competent adult member of the religion do the slaughtering, though some Muslim authorities allow meat slaughtered competently by Jews and Christians. And finally, God's name must be pronounced before slaughter. The common Islamic utterance is "In the name of God, God is most great" (*bismillāhi, allāhu akbar*). In Judaism, it is given in the form of a blessing (*berachah*) that acknowledges God's requirement to slaughter the animal properly. In both Islam and Judaism, the slaughtered animal is then examined to determine whether it is fit for consumption. There are some minor differences between Islamic *dhabīḥa* and Jewish *sheḥitah*. In the Jewish act, the trachea, the esophagus, the carotid arteries, and jugular veins must all be severed, whereas in Islamic slaughtering it is not as specific as to exactly which vessels are required to be severed. Certain parts of the animal that must be removed in Jewish slaughtering need not be removed according to Islam.

Observant Muslims, like observant Jews, will read the ingredients of processed foods to look for forbidden ingredients (for Muslims, pork products, alcohol and gelatin, animal shortening, hydrolyzed animal protein, and a host of other items). In the United States, there is *ḥalāl* certification sponsored by the Islamic Food and Nutrition Council of America (ISFANCA) and the Islamic Society of North America (ISNA). With the growth in the institutionalization of the American Muslim community, new certification will certainly develop as well. One interesting general rule of thumb suggested by the ISNA is an abecedarium of Islamic dietary rules: "In Islam, every thing is permitted except 'ABCD IS' prohibited.

A: Alcohol and drugs
B: Blood (flowing or congealed)
C: Carnivorous animals and birds of prey
D: Dead animal/bird (animal/bird that died of itself)
I: Immolated food
S: Swine and its by-products."[3]

No expression of Islam requires vegetarianism, but neither is it forbidden. The cultural traditions out of which Islam emerged were pastoral and the main food item was therefore meat.[4] In a purely pastoral economy, vegetarianism was virtually impossible, so it is less common to see vegetarians in traditional Muslim societies than in the West. Nevertheless, there is a small vegetarian movement among Muslims today.

Intoxicants (Alcohol, Coffee, Smoking, Drugs)

Although Islam forbids the consumption of alcohol, the Qur'an is not entirely consistent about it. In a section that treats the consumption of acceptable foods, Qur'an 16:67 places alcohol in the same category of wholesome food: "From the fruits of the date palm and the grape you make intoxicating beverage and wholesome food. This is certainly a sign for those who understand." Qur'an 4:43 restricts only the consumption of alcohol just prior to prayer: "O Believers! Do not approach prayer while you are intoxicated until you know what you are saying . . ." (compare this with Lev. 10:9). Qur'an 2:219 does not forbid alcohol entirely either, though it is clearly more critical: "They ask you about fermented beverage and gambling. Say, 'There is great sin and [also] utility in them for people, but the sin is greater than the utility.'" Finally, Qur'an 5:90–91 is unambiguous: "O Believers! Fermented beverage and gambling and idolatry and divination are an abomination and the work of Satan, so keep away from them so that you may thrive. Satan only desires to instill hostility and hatred among you through fermented beverage and gambling, and to hinder you from remembering God and from prayer. So will you stop?"

As observed in Part 2 (see chapter 14, "The Interpretive Tradition"), the problem of apparent inconsistency in the Qur'an was resolved through attempts to contextualize the revelations and thereby determine which of two seemingly contrary verses may have been abrogated. In the case of alcohol, it was decided by Qur'an interpreters that the revelations treating alcohol were received in the order listed here, thereby gradually forbidding its consumption. Consuming alcohol is therefore absolutely prohibited in Islam. This is not only restricted to the act of drinking, according to most authorities, but also excludes the use of alcohol in medicines and cooking with wine. Others, however, argue that medicinal advantage overrides the use of small amounts of alcohol, and that the cooking process causes the evaporation of alcohol, thereby allowing the use of wine in cooking. Negativity toward the consumption of alcohol is visceral to many Muslims, just as the eating of pork is to many Jews (and Muslims). Many Muslim jurists prohibit the trading in alcoholic beverages or engaging in any kind of activity that might promote its use. This has raised some interesting cultural dissonances in the West. One example is the case in the United States where Muslim taxi drivers have refused to accept passengers who have obviously been drinking, which has caused some consternation as the American public has increasingly encouraged the use of taxis to avoid driving while under the influence of alcohol.

Narcotics are included in the category of alcohol as intoxicants and are therefore forbidden, based on Qur'an 5:90–91. In general, consumption of tea, coffee, and tobacco is acceptable for Muslims, although some Muslims prohibit these substances. In some regions where *khat* is a traditional recreational drug that is ingested by chewing, especially by men, it is acceptable, largely because it is considered ineradicable.[5] Smoking hashish is also a traditional recreational use of drugs in parts of the Muslim world (in fact, the word is the Arabic word for "grass"), but this has been more fully condemned, including bans enacted against its use in Egypt in the 11th and 12th centuries. Coffee, too, was banned in Arabia soon after it was first introduced from Ethiopia, but it eventually came to be accepted. Antismoking campaigns have not been successful in the Muslim world, and the rate of smoking is particularly high. Some modern thinkers and religious scholars have argued that it is forbidden based on Qur'an and *Hadith* that prohibits self-harm (Q.2:195, 4:29, 7:157) or wasteful use of resources (Q.17:26–27).

It is difficult to study the problem of alcohol and drug abuse in the Muslim world. This is due partly to the sensitive nature of the topic, since consumption at any level is religiously forbidden in these regions where religion is a very powerful social force, and shame on individuals and their family are issues of major concern. Additionally, virtually all the nations of the Muslim world are run by dictatorial governments. In such environments, negative statistics tend to be suppressed because they reflect badly on the rulers. Whatever the reality of alcoholism and drug abuse, both of which definitely occur at some level in Muslim countries, it is much less public than in the West.

Modesty and Clothing

Nakedness, and especially the exposure of genitalia, has been an issue of some importance to most human cultures for almost as long as we have a written record of human society. The first narrative treating humanity in the book of Genesis explores the issue of nakedness, sexuality, and awareness, and the scene ends with God making the first couple garments with which they were to be covered (Gen. 3:21, Q.7:26).

The Qur'an has a great deal to say about modest dress, boundaries between men and women, and modesty in general. Qur'an 25:63 has "The servants of the most Merciful are those who walk on earth humbly, and when ignorant people address them, they say 'peace.'"[6] In another section, the Qur'an begins the discussion of modest dress with exactly the same words for both men and women:

> Tell the male Believers to lower their eyes and guard their private parts. That is most innocent for them. God is fully aware of what you do. And tell the female Believers to lower their eyes and guard their private parts, and to show only their outward ornaments, and to draw their coverings over their breasts, and to show their ornaments only to their husbands or their fathers, or their husbands' fathers, or their sons, or their husbands' sons, or their brothers, or their brothers' sons, or their sisters' sons, or their women, or those under their ownership, or those male servants who do not have a [sexual] desire, or children who do not recognize the sexual nakedness (*'awra*) of women, and let them not stamp their feet in order to make known the ornaments they hide. Turn to God together, O Believers, so that you may be happy. (Q.24:30–31)

It is clear from these verses that more concern is expressed for the sexual attractiveness of women (or the presumed weakness of sexual control among men) than vice versa. Perhaps the best definition of *'awra*, translated above as "sexual nakedness," is "modesty zone."[7] It is this area that must always be covered. Later Islamic jurisprudence upholds the differentiation in the Qur'an verse and designates the modesty zone of the female body to be much greater than that of the male body. Most Islamic legal schools consider the entire body of a free woman to constitute her modesty zone aside from her face and palms (the Hanbali school considers the palms also included in the area of *'awra*). Most schools agree that the modesty zone of a man ranges from the navel to the knees. The discussions in the legal traditions treat the covering of the modesty zone in general and the covering of the same areas in prayer. There is generally not much difference whether one is at prayer or simply in the presence of someone whose relationship requires that all designated parts of the modesty zone be covered.

One finds a general parallel in these sentiments with Jewish tradition. In a discussion of the required twice-daily reciting of the Shema in Judaism (the personal acknowledgment of God's unity), the question is asked whether it is acceptable to do so in the presence of a person whose modesty zone is uncovered. The response is that it is permissible even if they are naked as long as they are householders, at home, and they are in their minority. After a discussion of what age constitutes one's minority, the discussion shifts to the nakedness of adult women. A leg or thigh of a woman is considered by a leading sage to be within the modesty zone. One voice considers even looking at the finger of a woman who is not one's wife to be equivalent to looking at her genitals. Another mentioned that even a woman's voice is considered sexually arousing: "the voice of a woman is within the modesty zone" (B. Ber. 24a). As might be expected, a similar sentiment about the female voice is found among some Muslim scholars (not the Qur'an), but just as among Jewish scholars, it is a minority opinion. Nevertheless, it is interesting to note that the Arabic words associating a woman's voice with sexual arousal are almost identical semantically with the words of the Talmud: "The intonation of a woman is within the modesty zone." This position seems to be a later development in Islam.

While the Qur'an requires modest covering of the modesty zone, it does not mandate any particular garment for that purpose. The word *ḥijāb* occurs in the Qur'an seven times, but its meaning there is "screen" or "curtain" that separates, usually truth from falsehood or light from darkness (Q.7:46, 17:45, 19:17, 33:53, 38:32, 41:5, 42:51). One can find much discussion in Sufi Qur'an interpretation about *ḥijāb* as a barrier between humans and God that must be transcended in order to reach ultimate unity. In common parlance, however, *ḥijāb* has come to be understood as various types of clothing that are worn by women to cover their modesty zone.

The Qur'an verse in which *ḥijāb* occurs most closely in association with women is Q.33:53: "O Believers, do not enter the houses of the Prophet unless you are given permission for food . . . and when you ask the women for something, ask from behind a *ḥijāb*. This is most pure for your hearts and for their hearts. . . ." The section continues with a list of people with whom the wives of Muhammad could interact that is similar to Q.24:31 above. "There is nothing bad for them [Muhammad's wives] among their fathers, their sons, their brothers, their brothers' sons, their sisters' sons, their women, or those under their ownership as long as they are conscious of God, for God is witness to all things" (Q.33:55). Three verses later, the thread continues: "O Prophet, tell your wives, your daughters and the women of the Believers to draw their cloaks (or "their mantles") closely over themselves. This is best so that they be recognized but not annoyed. God is forgiving, most merciful" (Q.33:59).

The first verse in this sequence (Q.33:53) is known popularly as the "*ḥijāb* verse," and the last as the "mantle verse." The proximity of these two verses characterizes the close relationship between the two distinct but related notions: space that secludes, and clothing that conceals. Muslim thinkers noticed another distinction, that being between the wives and women in the household of the Prophet, and Muslim women in general. Most of the qur'anic material seems to single out the wives of the Prophet because of their (and his) special status, but the last verse (Q.33:59) clearly extends the injunction to all female Believers. Some scholars have understood the separate references to the women in the household of Muhammad to mean that special restrictions are directed only to them, arguing that their status required a special level of seclusion from the eyes of the public. Other scholars consider the injunctions to be a kind of democratizing program that places all Muslim women in a like category with the ruling elite.

There is certainly historical support for the latter position, since it had been a custom among Persian and other cultures for women of the elite classes to be secluded and veiled from the public eye, while leaving others without such special consideration. In other words, veiling had been an indicator of social class. The wealthy and the powerful were veiled, while the peasants were not. This distinction was not eliminated entirely by Islam, since the women in villages and among poor families in the Muslim world have been much more likely to appear unveiled in public or with a far less complete covering.

There is a tradition of veiling in Judaism as well that hearkens back to the earliest reference in Genesis 24:63–65, the scene in which Rebecca and Isaac first meet. "Isaac went out walking in the field toward evening. He looked up and saw camels approaching. Rebecca lifted her eyes and saw Isaac, so she alighted from the camel. She said to the servant, 'Who is that man walking in the field toward us?' The servant answered, 'That is my master.' So she took the shawl and covered herself."

The word used for the shawl or veil in this scene is *tza'if*, which occurs only one other time in the entire Hebrew Bible. In the second occurence, it is a covering that Tamar uses to cover her face when she acts as a prostitute in order to entice Judah to have sexual relations with her (Gen. 38:14–19). In the first scene, Rebecca covers herself because she is making contact with a person who is not (yet) in a kinship relationship that would allow her to be with him without it (it is not specified in the text exactly what she covered). In the second scene, it is quite clear that Tamar covered her face and that this act is associated with prostitutes, though prostitutes may have been a subset among all women who must cover their faces in public so as not to be viewed by strangers.

The Mishnah (M. Ket. 7:6) mentions that married Jewish women were not to go out in public with their hair loose, though this was allowed before marriage (M. Ket. 2:1,10). The Talmud (M. Ket. 72a-b) considers going into public with loosened hair to be sexually enticing based on the test of a woman accused of adultery in Numbers 5:18, so required that the hair of married women be covered. The same discussion notes that married women were expected to have their arms covered in public as well.

In a discussion in the Mishnah on the kinds of clothing that Jewish women are allowed to wear in public on the Sabbath (M. Shab. 6:6), it is mentioned that Jewish women living in Arabia during the 2nd century would be covered and Jewish women living in Persia (Median women) would also be covered, though the words to describe "covering" in each case are different and the concise meanings of the terms are not explained.[8] It is clear, therefore, that Jews engaged in the same kinds of covering as was the general custom in various regions, and that covering was a custom among the Persians and the Arabs centuries before the emergence of Islam. Genizah documents many centuries later show that Jewish women living in Egypt veiled at about the same rate as their Muslim counterparts. On the other hand, if Muslim families had the means, they built their houses with separate areas for women that kept them apart from nonfamily members who might visit, something that was not common among Jews and Christians. This spacial separation reflects the meaning of the qur'anic term *ḥijāb*, but the meaning of the word has shifted from a spacial boundary to a personal boundary reflected by certain types of modest clothing, particularly a covering for the head. Other terms are used as well, such as *khimār, burqa', jilbāb, niqāb,* and *chador.* These reflect cultural and linguistic as well as religious differences between communities. Although the word "veil" in English tends to connote a covering specifically for the face, the word in Islamic discourse does not. Veiling may refer to covering the hair and neck, leaving the face entirely revealed. Veiling often refers to modest clothing in general, including loose-fitting clothing that does not exentuate the shape of the body. It is sometimes ironic, therefore, to observe some young Muslim women covering their hair, ears, and neck while wearing tight-fitting clothes that reveal a great deal of the figure.

In the modern period, the issue of female veiling has become very closely tied in with contemporary cultural and political as well as religious issues, and it has been complicated by the fact that veiling had always remained an indicator of social class. With the modernizing influences of the 19th and early 20th centuries, removing or wearing the *ḥijāb* became associated at various times with Westernization, modernization, colonialism, nationalism, pan-Arabism, socialism, and a return to tradition, Islam, or traditional values. When unveiling was in vogue, some in the upper classes resisted because peasants had always been unveiled. In Egypt during the British occupation in the early 20th century, the most resistant were the petite bourgeoisie, the newly middle class, who felt the need to project their newly acquired status.

Conservative thinkers have always tended to associate veiling with a traditional social and domestic role for women. Many women, however, have taken to wearing the veil as a sign of reaffirming their religious devotion in a manner that is parallel to Jewish men donning a *kippah* or Jewish women wearing more modest clothing among those who are returning to more traditional religious lifestyles. To many other women, veiling includes a political statement as a kind of liberation from fashion expectations of modern life, or from being viewed as a sexual object by men who have abandoned many of the strictures of the traditional Muslim lifestyle. As among all forms of clothing, subtle differences in the style, color, pattern, and fit of veils in Muslim communities communicate political and social as well as religious (and fashion) statements that tend to evolve over time.

It is impossible for the noninitiated to understand the subtleties of dress and the messages they are intended to convey. Very often, in fact, these culturally defined messages are misinterpreted by outside observers to convey meaning that is completely unintended. This is not uncommon in an increasingly complex and ever more culturally and religiously mixed world in which cultural cues are often misread cross-culturally, sometimes leading to shock, fear, anger, and resentment.

Epilogue

One of the pleasures of writing this book has been the challenge of researching and thinking about the myriad ways in which Islam and Judaism exemplify fascinating parallels while simultaneously maintaining distinct and profound differences. Jews and Muslims have a tendency to misread each other, sometimes precisely because of the subtle similarities and distinctions between them. We usually are not aware when we are misreading the "Other," but we tend to notice quite intensely when the other is misreading us.

As a student of both Judaism and Islam, and having lived both in the Muslim world and in Israel and major Jewish communities in the United States, I am painfully aware of such misreadings, and sometimes feel as if I am stuck in an interpretive no-man's-land between them. I often find myself trying to explain Islam sympathetically to Jews, and Judaism sympathetically to Muslims, even as both communities are inclined to be suspicious and fearful of the other. The same kind of mutual misreading occurs when Americans think about Arabs, and vice versa. Indeed, American Jews are as deeply influenced by their American cultural identity as Arab Muslims are influenced by their Arab identity.

A classic example is the observation I encountered while living in Egypt in 2006. More than once I heard people there criticize American culture for its innately violent nature and declare that Americans are an aggressive and brutal people who lack respect for human life. Some Egyptians who made the case pointed to the extraordinary level of violence in American film and television. Some cited the results of American studies published in the Arab press that establish the murder rate in the United States as one of the highest in the world, and off the charts when compared to nations with a similar standard of living and cultural level. As one Egyptian acquaintance told me, "You Americans start wars all over the world, but you never fight for your own soil or on your own land. You exploit the fears and pain of others in order to take over somebody else's natural resources or exploit their labor."

I was shocked the first time I encountered this view because, although I consider myself critical of many aspects of American culture, what I heard is simply not the perception that I have of myself and my fellow Americans. It also gave me pause about many Americans' opinions about Muslims and Arabs, because, in fact, it is common to hear virtually the same critique by Americans leveled against Arabs: "Arab culture (or Islam) is innately violent, and Arabs (Muslims) are an aggressive and brutal people who lack respect for human life."

I found that my Arab and Muslim friends feel the same hurt about the stereotype placed on them and the same personal disconnect from it as I felt when I heard it directed against me. Stereotypes may be inevitable, but the level of negativity in stereotypes tends to reflect the level of tension in the society in which the stereotypes exist. When people of different cultures, religions, or nations live in fear or resentment of one another, negative stereotypes grow apace. The emotions and stereotypes then feed off each other and the situation worsens. How to break the destructive cycle? One way is to personally experience the other, sincerely and honestly, and for the other to experience us. And one of the best ways to do this is through dialogue.

Like all religions, Islam has always engaged in dialogue and debate, both internally and in relation to other religions. This has been part of Islamic history and has shaped much of its theology and practice since the earliest days of the Prophet in Mecca, when Muhammad was challenged by his tribe to prove the authenticity of his revelation and the correctness of his message. Dialogue has never ceased in Islam; it continues to this day. Like all religions, both internal and interreligious dialogue is sometimes angry, polemical, and even violent; sometimes it is nothing less than the highest spiritual quest for meaning and relationship.

When we refer to interreligious dialogue today, we mean dialogue that is not for the purpose of scoring points or gaining converts. We expect something of far greater value. Dialogue can bring a deeper and more realistic understanding and appreciation between people of different faith traditions. Understanding and appreciation can lead to other positive outcomes as well, such as problem solving and conflict resolution.

Happily, the Qur'an acknowledges that it is natural for groups of people to differ in their religion, ethnicity, and gender: "O humankind! We have created you male and female, and have made you nations and tribes that you may know one another. The noblest of you in the sight of God is the most conscious of God. God is the Knower, the Aware" (Q.49:13).

Concerning the Peoples of the Book (Jews and Christians), the Qur'an repeatedly argues that their religious systems not only should be respected, they also represent a truth that will gain them entry into the world to come. "Believers, Jews, Christians and Sabaeans—whoever believes in God and the Last Day and who work righteousness: they have their reward with their Lord, they shall not fear nor should they grieve" (Q.2:62; see also 5:69, 22:17). One of the most interesting and complex verses relating Islam to prior scripture and religion is Qur'an 5:48:

> We have revealed the Book in truth, confirming the Book you have before you and preserving it. So judge between them by what God has revealed and do not follow their desires away from the truth that has been revealed to you. For every one We have appointed a divine law and custom. If God had wished, He would have made you all one *umma*, but [the intent is] to test you by what He has given you. So compete together in doing good works! You will all return to God, and He will then inform you of how you differ.

While there are some passages in the Qur'an that call for proselytizing (Q.14:44, 25:56–7), others clearly demonstrate respect for religious diversity. "If your Lord had wished, all people in the world would believe as a [single] body; will you then compel people until they become believers?" (Q.10:99). This and other qur'anic passages supporting pluralism serve as authentic scriptural support for Muslims to engage in open dialogue with believers of other faiths.

But dialogue with the Other can be frightening, and it often causes anxiety and a certain unease. In my research and teaching I have had occasion to ask people who are engaged in religious dialogue why they do it, and I found a wide range of answers. Most have affirmed that their engagement in interreligious dialogue has been a means of deepening their understanding of their own religion. But for those who told me that they have been involved in dialogues that have failed, they say that it is because one side or the other believed that it was their duty to "teach the faith." Inevitably, when one side comes to teach, the other side will close up. Such encounters cannot be sustained. But when each side comes to learn from the other, then the other side *must* teach (after having been invited to do so and with certain limits), so that both learning and teaching naturally occur.[1]

As we learn more about our partners in dialogue, we naturally discard the misinformation we have accumulated about them through ignorance.

That is a good thing, because it builds honest knowing, trust, and appreciation based on reality and true experience. But there is more, because when we engage in dialogue we also learn more about ourselves. As the great religious dialogist, Leonard Swidler, has taught, "Our dialogue partner likewise becomes for us something of a mirror in which we perceive our selves in ways we could not otherwise do. In the very process of responding to the questions of our partners we look into our inner selves and into our traditions in ways that we perhaps never would otherwise, and thus come to know ourselves as we could not have outside of the dialogue."[2] In response to my question about why one should engage in dialogue, one person immediately answered, "Why not? Dialoguing is life. You can die or you can dialogue," not realizing that he had made a pun that has real meaning at a variety of levels.

There is an interesting Jewish parallel to that statement. When the famous Talmudic rabbi, Honi, was not able to continue in the dialogic learning with his peers and colleagues that served as the mode of education in the house of study, he died. The rabbis of the house of study coined the following idiom in response, in their native Aramaic: *o ḥevruta o mituta*, meaning "without a social environment [for learning] one dies."[3] The dialogic nature of the learning environment for Jewish sages was one in which they were constantly challenged to think through their assumptions, often by their colleagues holding up a mirror to them.

Much in Judaism is directed inward, toward internal dialogue and the survival or benefit of the Jewish community; but much in Judaism is also directed outward, toward *tikun olam*—making the world as a whole a better place. In fact, Judaism contains within it a profound tension between concern for the community of Israel and for the world at large. This is articulated in such traditional texts as the Talmud, where it is taught that every person must first take responsibility for the behavior of his household, then the behavior of those of his town or city, and then the behavior of all of humanity (B. Shab. 54b).

Islam contains a similar tension, as we have learned from our reading of its sources and its practices. The tension between the particular and the universal in religion seems never to be fully resolved, and that tension may be part of the dynamic of religion in general. The late Muslim scholar and teacher, Fazlur Rahman, articulated something of this tension:

> The Qur'an is a teaching primarily interested in producing the right moral attitude for human action. The *correct* action, whether it be political, religious or social, it considers to be *'ibada*, or the "service of God." The Qur'an, therefore, emphasizes all those moral tensions and psychological factors that generate the right frame of mind for action. It warns against human pride and sense of self-sufficiency, i.e.

> pure humanism on the one hand, and the moral turpitude of hopelessness and defeatism, on the other. It constantly insists on . . . "fear of God" on the one hand and the "mercy of God and essential goodness of man" on the other.[4]

Rahman notes how the Qur'an, as the foundational text of Islam, serves as an authority for engaging in positive activism through what many Jews would recognize as *tikun olam*. Like Judaism, Islam provides a religious framework for ethical responsibility and actions to heal the world. Elsewhere Rahman acknowledges that certain inward-looking trends in Islam counter the positive sense of universal responsibility and activism that he considers to be at the core of his religion. Of course, both positions may be supported by citing authentic sources from the Qur'an and the *Ḥadīth,* just as similar tensions in Judaism may be supported by citing authentic sources from the Bible and Rabbinic literature.

One may easily observe how the tension between inwardness and positive universal responsibility is played out in the Muslim world today. We need to engage with Muslims as we need to engage with other Jews to encourage the kinds of positive activism that will bring both internal *tikun* and make the world a better place for all. It is my hope that this book has offered some of the tools and frameworks for doing just that. As the Qur'an states so eloquently in Qur'an 5:48,

If
God
had wished,
He would have made
you all one nation, but [the intent is]
to test you by what He has given you. So
compete together in doing good works! You will all return
to God, and He will then inform you of how you differ.

وَلَوْ شَاء اللهُ لَجَعَلَكُمْ أُمَّةً وَاحِدَةً وَلَـكِن لِّيَبْلُوَكُمْ فِي مَا آتَاكُم

فَاسْتَبِقُوا الخَيْرَاتِ إِلَى اللهِ مَرْجِعُكُمْ جَمِيعًا

فَيُنَبِّئُكُم بِمَا كُنتُمْ فِيهِ تَخْتَلِفُونَ:

صَدَقَ اللهُ العَظِيم

أمين

Endnotes

Preface

1. *Children of Abraham: An Introduction to Judaism for Muslims* (New York: Ktav, 2001) translated into Turkish, 2004: *Yahudiliği Anlamak İbrahim'in/Avraam'ın Çocukları*, translated into Arabic 2008: *Dhuriyat Ibrahim: muqaddima `an al-yahudiyya lil-muslimin.*

2. Mishnah, Pirkei Avot 2:4 אל תדין את הברך עד שתגיע למקומו.

3. Marmaduke Pickthall, *The Glorious Qur'an* Bi-lingual Edition with English translation (Istanbul: Enes Matbaasi, 1999); Muhammad Asad, *The Message of the Qur'an* (Gibraltar: Dar al-Andalus, 1980); Thomas Cleary, *The Qur'an: A New Translation* (Chicago: Starlatch Press, 2004).

4. Muhammad Muhsin Khan, *The Translation of the Meanings of Sahih Al-Bukhari* (bilingual edition), 9 Vols. (Lahore: Kazi Publications, 1983).

Chapter 2

1. The archaic term "Babylonian" fell out of general use when the Babylonian Empire was destroyed by the Persians in the 6th century BCE. But the Jews of Mesopotamia (today's Iraq) have called themselves "Babylonian" (Hebrew: *bavli*) and the region as Babylon until this day.

2. Richard Kalmin, *Sages Stories, Authors and Editors in Rabbinic Babylonia* (Atlanta: Scholars Press, 1994), 264–71.

Chapter 3

1. Robert G. Hoyland, *Arabia and the Arabs from the Bronze Age to the Coming of Islam* (London: Routledge, 2001), 147.

2. Some think this might be a reference to tefillin.

3. My translation of ibn Hishām, *Al-Sīra al-Nabawiyya* (Beirut: Dar al-Thiqafa al-Arabiya n.d.), Vol. 1, pp. 26–27. A version of this work has been translated by Alfred Guillaume as *The Life of Muhammad: A Translation of ibn Ishaq's Sirat Rasul Allah* (Oxford: Oxford University Press, 1955), and his translation for this story, which is a bit awkward, is found on p. 10. This work is an important early-9th-century reference. I will henceforth provide my own translation of the Arabic but cite the equivalent page in Guillaume's translation.

Chapter 4

1. "Believers" is capitalized here because it seems to be a term referencing a specific community, being those who followed Muhammad and his revelations. The Qur'an itself refers to that community more often as "Believers" than as "Muslims."

2. Guillaume, *The Life of Muhammad,* 232–33.

3. Ibid., 136.

4. See, for example, the anti-Jewish hostility expressed in the Gospel of Matthew, chap. 23, and the Gospel of John, chap. 8. And in the Torah, note all the violent hostility directed against Canaanites and their religions, such as is expressed in Deuteronomy, chap. 7 and elsewhere.

Chapter 5

1. The one exception to this rule is in the Church of Jesus Christ of Latter-Day Saints (Mormons), which theoretically allows for ongoing revelation. However, the possibility of revelation is narrowed extremely and restricted only to the head of the Church so that it is extremely rare when any new revelation occurs.

2. Gillaume, 197–98.

3. The Qur'an (2:142–143) makes reference to an earlier direction of prayer that was changed to the direction of the Ka`ba in Mecca. Although the earlier direction is not mentioned explicitly in the Qur'an, the exegetical literature unanimously considers it to have been Jerusalem.

4. In Aramaic, the date of Yom Kippur is *`asora de'tishre,* while the Arabic word for 10 is *`ashara.*

5. See Deuteronomy 18:15–22.

6. According to our general self-image, Jews were a powerless people trying to eke out a living in a difficult and often hostile world for most of the last 2,000 years. While this view is correct overall, there were occasional periods and places where Jews controlled militias and armies and were even renown as mighty warriors. One well-known Jewish group that involved in militant actions in the Muslim world followed a Jewish messianic leader named

Abū ʿĪsa al-Iṣfahānī in the 8th century, who engaged in a losing war against the caliphate.

7. For a study of this phenomenon and its impact on the conflict in Medina, see Firestone, "The Failure of a Jewish Program of Public Satire in the Squares of Medina," in *Judaism* (Fall 1997): 438–52.

8. This is a reference to an enigmatic qur'anic reference to the Jews having been turned into apes by God for having transgressed the Sabbath (Q.2:65, 7:163–166).

9. This and the previous citations are from Guillaume, 461–64.

10. See Genesis 34, 1 Samuel 18:7, 17–27, etc.

11. Gillaume, 501.

12. Ibid., 504.

13. Ibid., 507.

14. Ibid., 516.

15. Ibid.

16. For a more detailed portrayal of this episode, see W. Montgomery Watt, *Muhammad: Prophet and Statesman* (New York: Oxford University Press, 1961), 198–203.

17. Watt, 214.

Chapter 6

1. Gillaume, 651.

2. Ibid., 683.

3. *Man kuntu mawlāhu faʿAlī mawlāhu.* (L. Vaglieri, "Ghadīr Khumm," in the *Encyclopaedia of Islam* [New Edition: Leiden: Brill, 1983], Vol.2, p.993).

4. A common traditional Arabic idiom of giving one's word, as in the English, "By God!"

5. Traditional Arabic reports by medieval geographers and cited by Guy Le Strange, *Palestine Under the Moslems: A Description of Syria and the Holy Land from* A.D. *650 to 1500* (1890; Beirut: Khayats, 1965), 143.

6. This is formalized under the so-called Pact of ʿUmar (*ʿahd ʿumar* or *al-ʿuhda al-ʿumariyya*), which will be examined in more detail below.

Chapter 7

1. Fred M. Donner, "From Believers to Muslims: Confessional Self-Identity in the Early Islamic Community," *al-Abhath Journal of the Faculty of Arts and Sciences, American University of Beirut,* Vol. 50–51 (2002–3), p. 28.

2. "Their armies used to go in each year to distant lands and provinces, raiding and plundering from all peoples under heaven. And from every person they demanded only tribute, and each one could remain in whatever faith he chose. There were also among them Christians, not a few . . ." (Donner, 44).

3. See Majid Khadduri, *The Islamic Law of Nations: Shaybani's Siyar* (Baltimore: Johns Hopkins University Press, 1966), 10–14.

4. Richard Bulliet, *Conversion to Islam in the Medieval Period* (Cambridge: Harvard

University Press, 1979).

5. David Wasserstein, "Islamisation and the Conversion of the Jews," in *Conversions islamiques. Identités religieuses en Islam méditerranéen,* ed. Mercedes García-Arenal, European Science Foundation (Paris: Maisonneuve et Larose, 2001), 49–60.

Chapter 8

1. Mark Cohen, *Under Crescent and Cross: The Jews in the Middle Ages* (Princeton, NJ: Princeton University Press, 1994).

Chapter 9

1. Daniel Brown, *A New Introduction to Islam* (Oxford: Blackwell, 2004), 210.

Chapter 10

1. See Qur'an 5:72–73, 4:171–172.

2. Some believe that the rosary beads of the Roman Catholic Church is derived from the *misbaha,* for it became popular in western Europe during the 13th century after more than two centuries of contact between Franks and Arabs during the Crusades.

3. The Hebrew, *rabbi,* actually means "my greatness."

4. *Rabbān* is probably derived from the Aramaic for "our teacher" (or "our lord"): רַבָּן Arabic *ḥākhām* = Heb. חָכָם, learned or wise individual, Arabic *ḥabr* = Hebrew חָבֵר, which was a term used in the Talmud for a religious scholar that was probably slightly lower in rank from *rav* or rabbi.

5. The "last day" is mentioned 26 times in the Qur'an, and is also referred to as the "day of judgment" (*yawm al-dīn*) 13 times. The "day of resurrection" (*yawm al-qiyāma*) is mentioned 70 times, and it is not clear how distinct these three terms are or the phenomena they describe.

6. Note again the close linguistic affinity with the Hebrew terms, the Garden (*ha-gan*), the Fire (*ner*), or Hell, constructed in Hebrew from the Ben Hinom Valley of 2 Sam. 23:10 and elsewhere (*gey ben-hinom // jahannum*). References to paradise and hell are ubiquitous in the Qur'an and will be examined in some detail below.

7. See Romans chap. 5, 1; Corinthians 15:21–23, 44–49; F. R. Tennant, *The Sources of the Doctrines of the Fall and Original Sin* (New York: Schocken, 1968).

Chapter 11

1. This translates exactly into Hebrew: אין אל אלא האל (או האלהים).

2. This statement was occasionally forced upon Jews during times of persecution. A legend has it that in one instance, a Jewish religious authority allowed articulation of the statement (but only under threat of severe injury or death), because the first section does

not contradict the most basic theology of Judaism, and the second section can be read either as Muhammad being *the* messenger of God, or simply being *a* messenger of God, and it was assumed that the person verbalizing the statement would consider silently the additional words, "to them."

3. *Wanaḥnu lahu muslimīn.* This verse is nearly identical to Qur'an 3:84.

4. Some translate this word as "Criterion" and consider it synonymous with the Qur'an. The Arabic is derived from the Hebrew/Aramaic, *purqan/purqena'*, which carries a meaning of redemption.

5. The Qur'an does indeed have more to say about dietary laws, but it certainly does not conform with the strictures of the Torah (cf. Leviticus 11, Deuteronomy 14). For a good overview of the Qur'anic injunctions, see *Encyclopedia of the Qur'an,* 2:216–223, 3:93.

6. See also Qur'an 4:46, 5:41, 7:162, etc.

7. As noted above in chapter 5. For some examples from the Hebrew Bible, see Numbers 33:50–53, Deuteronomy 4:1–7. For some classic examples from the New Testament, see Matthew 23, John 8:37–47.

8. See also Qur'an 81: 1When the sun is folded up, 2and when the stars shoot downward, 3and when the mountains pass away, 4and when the pregnant camels are neglected, 5and when the wild beasts are herded, 6and when the oceans are swollen, 7and when the souls are matched, and 8when the infant girl buried alive is asked 9for what offense she was killed, 10and when the pages are made known, 11and when the sky is uncovered, 12and when hell is afire, 13and when the garden is drawn near, 14each soul will know what it has brought about.

9. Helmer Ringgren, *Studies in Arabian Fatalism* (Uppsala: A. B. Lundequistska, 1955), 30–31.

Chapter 13

1. The Arabic meaning of the root *f-r-q* is "to separate, divide, make a distinction," related to the Hebrew, *p-r-q.* In old Ethiopian, it is "to set free," which seems to be related to the Aramaic.

2. Farid Esack, *The Qur'an: A Short Introduction* (Oxford: Oneworld, 2002), 70.

3. Frederick Denny, *An Introduction to Islam* (New York: Macmillan, 1985), 171.

4. Firestone, *Jihad: The Origin of Holy War in Islam* (New York: Oxford University Press, 1999), 47–65.

5. Firestone, "Holy War in Modern Judaism? 'Mitzvah War' and the Problem of the 'Three Vows,'" *Journal of the American Academy of Religion* 74 (December 2006): 954–82.

6. See also Qur'an 10:38, 11:13, 17:88, 52:33–34.

Chapter 14

1. See also Qur'an 12:1, 26:2, 195, 27:1, 28:2, etc.

2. The word is found only once in the Bible, in Ecclesiastes 8:1, and is translated as "interpretation." The more common biblical term for "interpret" is the related word *patar* (Gen. 40:16, 22, etc.), while the same base-root, *p-sh-r* is more common in Jewish and Christian Aramaic. It has been suggested that the Arabic word *fassara* may derive from the Aramaic.

3. Qur'an 12:6, 21, 36, 37, 44, 45, 100, 101, and note the parallel with the repeated use of the Hebrew *patar* in the Genesis Joseph story in chaps. 41–42.

4. See Qur'an 7:75, 12:4, 19:3, 26:70, 106, 124, 142, 27:7, 37:140, 38:41, 46:21, etc.

5. Much of this information on modern Qur'an interpretation is drawn from Rotraud Wielandt, "Exegesis of the Qur'an: Early Modern and Contemporary," *Encyclopedia of the Qur'an*, 6 Vols. (Leiden: Brill, 2002), 2:124–142.

6. Bukhari, *Saḥīḥ: Virtues of the Qur'an*, 20 (Lahore: Kazi, 1983), 6:501.

Chapter 15

1. The other canonical collections are those of Abū Dāwud (d.888), Al-Nisā'ī (d.915), Al-Tirmidhī (d.892), and ibn Majā (d.896). Shi`ites have different collections of *Hadith* that will be considered below.

2. This has been translated into English by Alfred Guillaume as *The Life of Muhammad: A Translation of Ibn Ishaq's Sirat Rasul Allah* (Karachi: Oxford University Press, 1955). Most references below are from this translation.

3. *Ahl* in Arabic means "family," and it derives from the same root as the Hebrew, *ohel*, meaning "tent." In pastoral societies, a family would be represented by their tent. The term *bayt*, or "house," has the same meaning in both Hebrew and Arabic. It can mean both a structure in which a family lives and the family itself. The "house of Aaron" (*beyt aharon*) refers to the extended and dynastic family of Aaron.

4. Sunnis and Shi`a differ over the date of Muhammad's birth. Sunnis consider it to be the 12th day of the month of Rabī` al-Awwal, while the Shi`is consider it to be the 17th day of the month (calendrical differences often distinguish religious communities, such as the Armenian Christians or Coptic Christians from the Catholics on the dates of Christmas and Easter).

Chapter 16

1. The basic meaning of the Arabic root is "to begin, start, commence." In modern Arabic, the common name for "street" is *shāri`*, which communicates a sense of path. Other forms of the root refer to something being lawful or legitimate (*shar`ī*), legislation (*tashrī`*), and permissible (*mashrū`*). Interestingly, one of the names for the Jordan River is *nahr al-sharī`a*—the "river of the water source."

2. N. J. Coulson, *A History of Islamic Law* (Edinburgh: University of Edinburgh Press, 1964), 12.

3. The Hebrew equivalent is *hekesh*, which is a well-known and well-used exegetical principle in Jewish law.

4. See, for example, *Messages to the World: Statements of Osama Bin Laden*, ed. Bruce Lawrence (London: Verso, 2005). One needs to be familiar with *fiqh* to pick apart the arguments, but the (mis)application of qur'anic verses and Prophetic *Sunna* in such declarations as found on p.61 demonstrates real creativity and innovation (i.e., *bid`a*).

5. Evidence of the practice among pre-Islamic Arabs is found in the *Hadith* (Bukhari, *Ṣaḥīḥ*, Revelation (vol. 1, bk 1, no. 6). On the custom of female circumcision in pre-Islamic Arabia, see *Maghāzī*, vol. 5, bk 59, no. 399, trans. Muhsin Khan.

Chapter 17

1. Judith Romney Wagner wrote an accessible comparison of the two systems: "Halakhah and Sharī`a: Roots of Law and Norms of Conduct in Theocratic Systems," *Central Conference of American Rabbis Journal* (Fall 2000): 81–95.

2. Many Jews know him only through his support of Palestinian suicide bombings (called by him, "martyrdom operations") against Israelis and against American soldiers in Iraq. Although on this issue he takes a more radical position, his teachings have been extremely influential and it is appropriate to cite him here.

3. Yusuf Al-Qaradawi, *The Lawful and the Prohibited in Islam*, trans. Kamal El-Helbawy, M. Moinuddin Siddique, and Syed Shukry (Indianopolis: American Trust Publications, n.d.).

4. Mishnah, Pirkei Avot 1:6. According to Jewish tradition, this rabbi was a teacher of Jesus.

Chapter 18

1. Qu'ran 2:12 extends the inclusiveness even further. "Indeed, whoever surrenders himself to God and is a doer of good will have his reward with his Lord. They need have no fear nor should they grieve" (note the similar language with Q.2:62).

2. Qaradawi, 335.

3. Ibid., 336.

Chapter 19

1. *Shahāda* means "witnessing" or "testimony." Because this creedal statement is composed of two parts, it is sometimes called the "double witnessing" (*shahādatayn*).

2. The word in this phrase referring to Muhammad is the Arabic *rasūl*, meaning "messenger." He is also a prophet (*nabi*). Both words are found repeatedly in the Qur'an, and the interpreters are not in agreement about the distinction between them.

3. The Jewish Aramaic word is found in the traditional *Shabbat* prayer recited shortly after the opening of the Ark during the Torah service. The prayer begins, *berikh shmey de-*

mare' 'alma and includes the line, *ulekabel tzelotana beraḥamin*—"and accept our prayer with compassion." The prayer is known to many by the ending that is sometimes sung in the synagogue, "*bey ana raḥeytz. . . .*"

4. *Adhān* chap. 30, 31 (Kazi 1:351–352), *Ṣalāt* chap. 87 (Kazi 1:277).

5. All of these positions and acts are found in the Qur'an (2:238, 2:43, 4:102, 2:125, 3:43, 9:112, etc.). One may pray without these specific movements if unable to do so physically or because one is on a journey or fearful for one's safety (Q.2:239).

6. In most cases, the Jewish *kavanah* does not lay out the specifics of the ritual act to be performed. One exception is the statement in the Passover home ritual called the *seder*, during which participants recite a formula stating that they are about to fulfill the obligation of drinking each of the four cups of wine (*heneni mukhan umezuman lekayyem mitzvat kos rishon/sheni . . .*). While it has been suggested that the Islamic custom of the *niyya* may have been influenced by Judaism, it is likely that this *seder* custom was actually influenced by the Muslim custom.

7. My family recites a similar blessing at the end of *Shabbat* during the Jewish *Havdalah* ritual in fifteenth-century Spanish (Ladino). It expresses the hope that we will be guided and protected in the coming week, *ala derecha michael y ala siedra gabriel y ala cabeza shekhina de'el, kadhadia kadhanoche* (on the right, [by the angel] Michael, on the left, [by the angel] Gabriel, and on the head the Divine Presence all day and all night).

8. This prayer service is called *ṣalāt al-jamā'a* (sometimes called *jum'a* prayer). *Jum'a* comes from the root meaning "to gather together or unite," and Friday in Arabic is *yawm al-jum'a*—"the day of congregation." Large mosques built to accommodate large Friday crowds are often called *jāmi'* mosques.

9. Bukhari, *Ṣaḥīḥ*, "Conditions" (*Shurūṭ*) 18:894 (Kazi 3:575); "Invocations" (*da'wāt*), 70:419 (Kazi 8:280–281).

10. Muslim *ṣiyām/ṣawm* 19. The tradition literature is not consistent about the origin of the Muslim custom. Other *hadiths* in the same chapter provide a different origin of the fast. Some claim that Muhammad's tribe was accustomed to fast on that day in the pre-Islamic period. Muhammad fasted on that day and commanded his followers to do so as well until the divine command of the Ramadan fast in Qur'an 2:185.

11. Jews include circling rituals in current synagogue services as well. When the Torah scrolls are removed from the Ark and then returned to it, they are first walked entirely around the congregation of worshipers. Even more striking is the custom of the festival of Sukkot during which Torah scrolls and clusters of palm branches with parts of other vegetation are marched around to encircle the congregation. These derive from ancient customs that have remained in one form or another in a number of religions.

12. For a comprehensive history of the Pilgrimage, see F. E. Peters, *The Hajj* (Princeton, NJ: Princeton University Press, 1994).

Chapter 20

1. Qu'ran 2:54, 195, 4:29, 65, 18:6.

2. Bukhari *Jihād* #297 (Kazi 4:189–190).

3. *Janā'iz* #445–446 (Kazi 2:251–252).

4. See also Qu'ran 4:74, 9:111, 47:4–5

5. Firestone, *Jihād: The Origin of Holy War in Islam* (New York: Oxford University Press, 1999), 67–91.

6. Bukhārī, *Kitāb al-Jihād* 2:46 (Kazi 4:38), 10:39 (Kazi 4:46), *Kitāb al-Maghāzī* 16:377–378 (Kazi 5:260–261), Kitāb al-Tawḥīd 28:549 (Kazi 9:413); Abū Dāwud 2497 (vol. 3, p. 8), *Tirmidhī Kitāb Faḍā'il al-Jihād* 13:1640–1641 (vol. 4, pp. 150–151), etc. The very meaning of Tirmidhī's chapter is "The Book of the Merits of Jihād."

7. Bukhārī, *Kitāb al-Jihād* 16:66 (vol. 4, p. 51); *Tirmidhī Kitāb Faḍā'il al-Jihād* (vol. 4, p. 146).

8. Abū Dāwud, *Kitāb al-Jihād* 2499–2501 (Vol. 3: pp. 8–10) al-Nasā'i, *Kitāb al-Jihād, bāb man takaffalah Allāh liman yujhid bī sabīl allāh* 6:16–17 (Cairo: Dar al-Hadith, 1987/1407). On the other hand, other traditions state that good Muslims will enter Paradise whether or not they actually engage in *jihad* in the path of God: " . . . Abū Hurayra: The Prophet said: Whoever believes in God and in His Apostle, establishes prayer and fasts on Ramadan, it is absolute to God that He cause him to enter the Garden whether he makes *jihad* in the path of God or sits on the land upon which he was born (*jalasa fī arḍihi allatī wulida fīhā*)" (Bukhari, *Kitāb al-Jihād* 4:48 (Kazi 4:39–40).

9. Abū Dāwud 2522 (vol. 3, p. 15).

10. Bukhārī, *Kitāb al-Jihād* 6.53 (vol. 4, p. 42); Tirmidhī *Kitāb Faḍā'il al-Jihād* 13.1640 (vol. 4, p. 151), 25.1661 (vol. 4, p. 160), etc.

11. Ahmad b. Hanbal, *Musnad*, 6 vols. (Beirut: Dar al-Sadr, n.d.), 1:63, 237; 4:200.

12. "The man or woman who dies of plague is a martyr (*shahīd*)" (Bukhari, *Ṣaḥīḥ* [Lahore: Kazi 1983] 7:422), one who drowns is a martyr (Abū Dāwud, *Sunan* 4 vols. [Cairo: Dar al-Miṣriyya wal-Lubnaniyya, 1988] 3:7; "One who goes forth in the path of God and dies or is killed is a martyr . . . or [suffers] any kind of death is a martyr and has [a future life of] the Garden" (Abū Dāwud, 3:8–9). Even "The dead away from one's native country are martyrs (*mawt ghurbatin shuhadī'*)" (ibn Majā, *Sunan*, 2 vols. [Beirut: al-Maktaba al-`ilmiyya, n.d.] 1:515).

13. Peters, *Jihad in Classical and Modern Islam*, 34–35, and see also Bukhari, *Jihād* #256–158 (Kazi 4:158–160).

14. "Sheikh Al-Qaradhawi and Other Islamic Scholars Debate Suicide Operations in a Counter-Terrorism Conference Held in Sharm Al-Sheikh," *MEMRI Special Dispatch Series* No. 971, August 26, 2005.

Chapter 21

1. Abū Dāwud, *Sunan*, the first *hadith* in *Kitāb al-Sunna* # 4579, trans. of Ahmad Hasan

(New Delhi: Kitab Bhavan, 1993), 3:1290; found also in the collections of al-Tirmidhī, ibn Majah, and Aḥmad ibn Ḥanbal.

2. Similarly among Jews, it is hardly possible to believe that half the population worldwide engage in prayer three times daily, though Jews tend to be more willing to acknowledge the influence of secularizing movements on their identity.

3. *Ṭahāra* trad. 50, as found in the *Encyclopaedia of Islam*, 2nd ed., 5:20.

4. Aḥmad ibn Ḥanbal, *Musnad* (Arabic) (Beirut: Dar al-Sadr, n.d.), 5:75. The language there is "Abdallah related [the tradition according to a chain of transmitters going back to] the father of Abū Malīḥ b. `Usāma that the Prophet said: Circumcision is sanctioned by law for men (*sunna lil-rijāl*) and honorable for women (*makrama lil-nisā'*)."

5. `Abdallah b. Salām is famous in the tradition literature for being one of the few learned Jews who believed in the prophethood of Muhammad and became a Muslim.

Chapter 22

1. Linguists generally consider the word in Arabic *āyat* to have derived from the Aramaic *atha*, which is related to the Hebrew *oth* (ot).

2. *Forty Hadith Qudsi*, bilingual edition selected and translated by Ezzeddin Ibrahim and Denys Johnson-Davies (Beirut: Dar al-Qur'an al-Karim, 1980-1400).

3. Or sometimes, Masnawi or Masnavi. Many Arabic words are pronounced differently in Turkic or Persian languages, Urdu, Malay, and others that do not share all the sounds of the Arabic. There is therefore a certain range of pronunciation for many words. Hadith is sometimes pronounced "hadīs," for example, and Qur'an, "Gur'an."

4. All citations are from William Chittick, *The Sufi Path of Love: The Spiritual Teachings of Rumi* (Albany: State University of New York Press, 1984); page numbers are given after each citation.

5. From his last album, *Swan Song.*

6. See Fethullah Gülen, *Love and Tolerance: Toward a Global Civilization* (Somerset, NJ: The Light, 2004).

Chapter 23

1. The key phrase within the verse is translated below by three well-regarded translators. Muhammad Marmaduke Pickthall: "And those of whom ye seek content (by marrying them), give unto them their portions as a duty. And there is no sin for you in what ye do by mutual agreement after the duty (hath been done)." Muhammad Asad: "And unto those with whom you desire to enjoy marriage, you shall give the dowers due to them; but you will incur no sin if, after [having agreed upon] this lawful due, you freely agree with one another upon anything [else]." Thomas Cleary: "For since you derive enjoyment from them thereby, give them their recompense as prescribed. But there is no blame on you if you come to terms of mutual agreement in this regard after the determination of the allocation."

Chapter 24

1. The restriction of women prayer leaders to female groups only is currently being challenged in the United States by some in the progressive Muslim community.

Chapter 25

1. Muslim, *Saḥīḥ*, (Arabic text with commentary by Al-Nawawi, Beirut: Dar al-Thiqafa al-Arabiyya 1324/1929), "Friday prayer," Vol. 6, p. 141, English translation of Abdul Hamid Siddiqi, n.p. Dar al-Manar, n.d., Vol. 2, p. 405).

2. Babylonian Talmud, *Sanhedrin* 38b (the name, Yoḥanan rendered in Arabic is Yaḥyā). In the Rabbinic Jewish calendar there are 12 hours in a day.

3. Muslim, 6:144 (Siddiqi, 2:406). This *hadith* is followed immediately by another that adds another interesting nuance to the natural competition between monotheisms: "God turned away those before us from the Friday (lit: the Day of Congregation = *yawm al-jumu'a*). Saturday (lit: the Sabbath day = *yawm al-sabt*) for the Jews and Sunday (*yawm al-aḥad*) for the Christians. God came to us and guided us to Friday. He made Friday, Saturday and Sunday. Thus they come after us on the Day of Resurrection. We are the last [religious community] among the people of this world and the first on the Day of Resurrection to be judge before [all] creations."

Chapter 26

1. Presumably the common fast during daylight hours.

2. Bukhari, *Ṣaḥīḥ, al-nikāḥ* 1 (Kazi 7:2).

3. Bukhari, *Ṣaḥīḥ, al-nikāḥ* 4 (Kazi 7:4).

4. Al-Qaradawi, 148–149.

5. A number of excellent and responsible works have been produced in the past few decades that reopen public discussions on important gender issues. These include Leila Ahmad, *Women and Gender in Islam* (New Haven, CT: Yale University Press, 1992); *Feminism and Islam: Legal and Literary Perspectives*, ed. May Yamani (New York: New York University Press, 1996); *Islam, Gender, and Social Change*, ed. Yvonne Yazbeck Haddad and John Esposito (New York: Oxford University Press, 1998); Khaled Abou El Fadl, *Speaking in God's Name: Islamic Law, Authority and Women* (Oxford: One World, 2001).

6. Bride and groom do not sign their wedding contract in the traditional Jewish system either, but rather than a male guardian as in Islam, unrelated male witnesses sign the contract in traditional Judaism.

7. Bukhari, *Ṣaḥīḥ, Nikāḥ* 67 (Kazi 7:51–52), *Nikāḥ* 69 (Kazi 7:52). The intervening *hadith* explains that silence is considered consent because a young girl feels shy and may not speak up to express her agreement.

8. Commentators tend to associate this with legal captives taken in war (compare Deut. 21:10–17).

9. Harald Motzki, "Marriage and Divorce," *Encyclopedia of the Qur'an* (Leiden: Brill, 2003), 3:278.

10. Bukhari, *Buyū`* #432 (Kazi 3:237–238. My translation is contrary to that of Khan). This same *hadith* is given several other times. See also Bukhari, *fīl-`itq* #718 (Kazi 3:432); *Maghāzī* #459 (Kazi 5:317); *Nikāḥ* #135, 136, 137 (Kazi 7:102), etc.

11. Ibn Ḥanbal *Musnad*, 5:173, 306. For the payment of the bloodwit, see Bukhari, *Farā'iḍ* #732 (Kazi 8:483), *Al-i`tiṣām bil-kitāb wal-sunna* #420 (Kazi 9:313–314).

12. al-Qaradawi, 202.

13. A second tradition is given on the authority of `Ā'isha as well: "Two old women from the Jews of Medina came to me and said: 'The people of the grave are tormented in their graves.' She said: I disagreed with them but I did not consider it fitting to believe them. They left and the Apostle of God came by and I told him: O Apostle of God, two old women from the Jews of Medina came to me and claimed that the people of the grave are tormented in their graves. He said: 'They are correct.' They will be tormented [such a great] torment that the animals will hear them. `Ā'isha said: After that I never saw him in prayer without seeking refuge from the torment of the grave. Muslim *Ṣalāt 76, al-masājid* 24 (Siddīqī 1:290 #1212–1214; Ar. 410–11 #123–125). See also *Al-Bukhari, janā'iz, `ādhāb al-qabr* (Kazi 2:256) *Sunan al-Nasā'ī* 4:103–104 (*janā'iz, ta`ūz min `ādhāb al-qabr*).

Chapter 27

1. And the commentators add, "and you have found it before it died and properly slaughtered it."

2. Compare Leviticus 11, Deuteronomy 14.

3. Http://www.isna.net/downloads/ISNA_Halal_Program_Brochure.doc.

4. Because Islam emerged out of a largely pastoral economy and social system, it reflects those pastoral origins. That is why the word for meat in Arabic is *laḥm*, while the same term (*leḥem*) in the agrarian economy of ancient Israel means "bread" in Hebrew. The reason for this difference is that the Semitic base meaning of that root is actually food or major food item. Some biblical passages use *leḥem* to refer to food in general (Gen. 28:20, Psalm 136:25), and the Qur'an uses *laḥm* to refer to fish (Q.16:14) as well as the meat of land animals (16:115). There is purportedly a Semitic language once spoken by peoples who made their living from fishing in which *leḥem* refers specifically to fish.

5. Khat (Arabic, *qāt*) is a flowering plant native to tropical East Africa and the Arabian Peninsula. It contains an amphetamine-like stimulant called cathinone.

6. Addressing people with "peace" (*salām*) is proven to be a statement of extreme merit elsewhere in the Qur'an (Q.37:79,109,120,130, 27:59, etc.).

7. Shiu-Sian Angel Hsu, "Modesty," in EQ 3:403. The Arabic is probably related to the Hebrew *`erva* with a reversing of the last two letters (Arabic also has another form with the same root as the Hebrew to denote nakedness). See Leviticus 18:6–19.

8. The Gemara on this Mishnah does not explain it either. Rashi (d.1204) explains that the first term describes the custom of Arab women to cover their heads and faces except for

their eyes, but he may be describing Arab customs he may have heard about in his own day, a full millennium after the closing of the Mishnah. His description of the Median custom is similar to another custom among some Arab women as well. Rashi explains that the Median women hold one corner of a shawl-like garment in their mouth and tie the other side with the assistance of a small stone or nut to keep the knot in place (which functions like a button).

Epilogue

1. For guides to dialogue between Jews and Muslims, see Leonard Swidler, Reuven Firestone, and Khalid Duran, *Jews, Christians, Muslims in Dialogue: A Practical Handbook* (New London, CT: Twenty-Third Publications, 2007); *The Children of Abraham: Jews and Muslims in Conversation* (New York and Washington, DC: Union of Reform Judaism and the Islamic Society of North America, 2007).

2. Swidler, Duran and Firestone, 15.

3. Babylonian Talmud, *Ta'anit* 23a.

4. Fazlur Rahman, *Islam* (New York: Holt, Rinehart & Winston), 1966, 241.

APPENDIX

Islam and Judaism: Some Related Religious Terminology

Allāh	الله	*Ha*ʾ*el*	הָאֵל	God
*Qur*ʾ*ān*	القُرْآن	*Miqrā*ʾ	מִקְרָא	scripture
āya(*t*)	آيَة	*ōt*	אות	verse/sign
salām	سَلاَم	*shalōm*	שָׁלוֹם	peace
assalāmu ʿ*alaykum*	السَّلاَمُ عَلَيْكُم	*shalōm* ʿ*aleykhem*	שָׁלוֹם עֲלֵיכֶם	greetings
ḥajj	الحَجّ	*ḥag*	חַג	pilgrimage/holiday
furqān	فُرقَان	*purqān*	פֻּרְקָן	Qur'an/redemption
kitāb	كتَاب	*katav*	כָּתַב	book/write
ṣalāt	الصَّلاَة	*tzlōta* (*ṣ*^{e}*lōta*)	צְלוֹתָא	prayer
ṣawm (*ṣiyām*)	الصِّيَام الصَّوْم	*tzom* (*ṣōm*)	צוֹם	fast
ṭahāra	طَهَارَة	*ṭāh*^{o}*rāh*	טָהֳרָה	purity
zakāt	الزَّكَاة	*z*^{e}*khūt*	זְכוּת	required giving/merit
ṣadaqa	الصَّدَقَة	*tz*^{e}*daqāh* (*ṣ*^{e}*daqāh*)	צְדָקָה	charity/justice
al-janna (*jannāt* ʿ*adn*)	الجَنَّة (جَنَّات عَدْن)	*gan* (*eden*)	גַן (עֵדֶן)	Garden of Eden
jahannum	جَهَنُّم	*geh ben hinnōm*	גֵי בֶן-הִנֹּם	Gehenna
rabb	رَب (meaning Lord)	*rav*	רָב	Lord/rabbi
yawm al-dīn	يَومُ الدِّن	*yom ha-dīn*	יוֹם הַדִּין	Day of Judgment
madrasa	مَدْرَسَة	*beyt midrāsh*	בֵּית מִדְרָשׁ	school
*al-samawāt wal-*ʾ*arḍ*	السَّمَاوَاتِ وَالأَرْض	*ha-shamayim veha*ʾ*areṣ*	הַשָּׁמַיִם וְהָאָרֶץ	heaven & earth
al-masīḥ	المَسِيح	*ha-mashīaḥ*	הַמָּשִׁיחַ	messiah
bismillāhirraḥmānirraḥīm	بِسْمِ اللهِ الرَّحْمانِ الرَّحِيمِ		בְּשֵׁם הָאֵל הָרַחֲמָן וְהָרַחוּם	
in the name of God the merciful & compassionate				

Glossary

The definitions and explanations that follow will occasionally include Hebrew linguistic equivalents that convey a similar (but not often identical) meaning, and Jewish religious parallels that are not necessarily equal. Where applicable, verses are indicated where a term may be found in the Qur'an with related, though not always identical, meaning.

Abbasid Refers to a dynasty of caliphal rulers of the Muslim world, whose capital was Baghdad (750–1258 CE).

Adhān The "call to prayer," uttered by the *mu'adhdhin.*

'Adl Social justice (Q.4:58).

Ahl al-Bayt "People of the House," referring to the family of the Prophet, Muhammad (Q.33:33).

Ahl al-Kitāb "People of the Book," referring to members of prior scriptural religions who have legal standing in Islamic religious law but at a secondary status. Jews and Christians and also Zoroastrians have traditionally been in this category (Q.3:65).

Aḥmadiyya A movement following the religious reformer Mirza Ghulam

Ahmad Qadian (d.1908), who are considered apostates by many Muslims because they ascribe to him prophetic status.

Al-Asmā' al-Ḥusnā "The most beautiful names" of God, considered to number 99 (Q.7:180).

***`Ālim***, (pl. *`ulamā'*) One learned in religious knowledge (*`ilm*).

Anṣār "Helpers," namely, the Medinan residents who joined with Muhammad and his Meccan followers in establishing the *umma* (Q.9:100).

`Aqīda A creedal statement of belief.

Asbāb al-nuzūl The "occasions of revelation" of the Qur'an. These are historical events associated with specific sections of qur'anic revelation.

***`Ashūra*** The "tenth" of the month of Muḥarram, most likely corresponding with the 10th of the Jewish month of Tishri and Yom Kippur. Once mandatory, it became a voluntary fast day. The day is especially sacred to the Shi`a because Imām Ḥusayn was martyred on that day at Karbalā'.

Association See *shirk*.

***`Awra*** (Hebrew *`ervah*), literally "genitals." The portions of the body that should be covered (from navel to knees for males, and all but the face, hands, and feet according to the strictest interpreters for females).

Aws (or Banū Aws) A major clan living in Yathrib/Medina when Muhammad emigrated there in 622. The Aws were engaged in a blood feud with a neighboring clan, the Khazraj.

***Āya* (pl. *āyāt*)** "Sign" (Hebrew *ōt*) of God. Also, a verse of the Qur'an (Q.16:101).

Āyat Allāh "Ayatolla." Literally, "sign of God," but in Twelver Shi`ism, the title of a very high position in the religious hierarchy of scholars.

Al-Azhar Located in Cairo, the most prestigious center of *Sunnī* learning in Islam and one of the oldest surviving universities in the world.

Baraka (Heb. *Berachah*) "Blessing" or "spiritual power" (Q.7:96).

Basmala (also pronounced *bismala*) The name of the invocation, *Bismillāhi al-Raḥmān al-Raḥīm* ["In the name of God, the Merciful and Compassionate"].

Badr The location of the first great battle and success of the early Muslims against their Meccan enemy in 624 CE, referenced in the Qur'an in Q.3:123.

Bid`a "Innovation." Deviation from Islamic tradition that is often understood as heresy in Islamic law and doctrine (Q.46:9).

Caliph See *khalīfa.*

Caliphate See *Khilāfa.*

Chador Persian for a long, traditional garment covering most of a woman's skin and figure.

Dār al-Ḥarb See *Dār al-Islām.*

Dār al-Islām "The Abode of Islam," meaning territories under Muslim political control. The rest of the world is known as the *Dār al-Ḥarb,* "the Abode of War."

Da`wa "Call" to Islam, proselytizing of Muslims; prayer [calling out to God] (Q.13:14, 30:25).

Dhikr (also pronounced *zikr*) "Mentioning" or "remembering" God; the distinctive Sufi form of meditative spiritual practice (Q.13:28).

Dhimmī A person whose status is defined by the *dhimma* ("protection," "obligation"), meaning a member of the "People of the Book" (*Ahl al-Kitāb*) who has legal status in Islam protected by the state, but at a lower status from Muslims (Q.9:10).

Dīn "Religion" (Q.109:6).

Du`ā' "Calling" upon God in prayer. Spontaneous or unofficial, to be distinguished from the formal prayer service called *ṣalāt* (Q.3:38).

***Faqīh* (pl. *fuqahā'*)** An expert in *fiqh* (Islamic jurisprudence).

Farḍ "Obligatory" duty, as in the five daily prayers (Q.33:38).

Al-Fātiḥa (Heb. *Petīḥah*) "The Opening," meaning the first chapter of the Qur'an that is also used as a prayer in many contexts.

Fatimid Refers to a great caliphal dynasty that ruled much of the Muslim world from its capital in Fostat (Cairo) (910–1171 CE).

***Fatwā* (pl. *fatāwa*)** A legal opinion (Jewish parallel: *pesak din*) produced by a jurisconsult called a *muftī*.

Fiqh "Understanding" of the law, meaning "jurisprudence."

Furqān "Criterion" or "proof" (related to the Hebrew-Aramaic. *Purqān*); a name for the Qur'an (Q.2:53, 3:4).

Ghusl A full ritual bath that removes major ritual impurity (*ḥadath*) (Q.5:6).

Ḥadath Pollution or ritual impurity, divided into two types: minor (*asghar*) and major (*akbar*), each of which is removed through a different act of purification.

***Ḥadīth* (pl. *aḥādīth*)** "Report," "event." A paragraph of information communicating the *sunna* of the Prophet Muhammad. *Ḥadīth* also refers to the genre of traditional literature containing these reports.

Ḥajj (Heb. *ḥag*) "Pilgrimage" to Mecca during the pilgrimage month (*Dhū al-Ḥijja*). Pilgrimage at other times is called *'Umra*. A male pilgrim is called *ḥajj* or *ḥajjī*. A female pilgrim is called a *ḥajja*. These are terms of honor (Q.22:27).

Ḥalāl "Permissible," "lawful" (Heb. Equiv. *kosher/mutar*) regarding food or actions. Impermissible is *ḥarām* (Heb. Equiv. *assur*) (Q.16:116).

***Ḥanīf* (pl. *ḥunafā'*)** A qur'anic term referring to a pure or "generic" monotheist such as Abraham (Q.3:67).

Ḥamās "Zeal," "fanaticism." An acronym for the "The Islamic Resistance Movement" [*Al-ḥarika al-muqāwama al-islāmīya*].

Ḥaram "Sanctuary" or sacred area such as at Mecca, Medina, or Jerusalem. The term also means "sacred," "forbidden," "holy" (Q.29:67).

Ḥarām See *Ḥalāl.*

Ḥijāb "Partition," "barrier" (Q.17:46). In post-qur'anic literature, often refers to the covering of a woman's hair and sometimes also the cheeks and neck.

Ḥijāz "Barrier," referring to the western Red Sea coastline of the Arabian Peninsula extending into the interior to an uplifted ridge running parallel to the coast; the region in which is found the holy cities of Mecca and Medina.

Hijra "Emigration" (Heb. *Hagīrāh*), usually referring to the emigration of the Prophet and his companions from Mecca to Medina in 622 CE.

Hilāl The crescent moon marking the beginning of months in the Islamic calendar; a symbol of Islam (Q.2:189).

Hizbullah "The Party of God."

***Ḥudūd* (sing. *ḥadd*)** "Limits," traditionally derived penalties or punishments for theft, adultery, fornication, bearing false witness, etc. (Q.2:229).

***`Ibāda*** "Worship" (Heb. *`avodah*) (Q.18:110).

***`Īd*** "Festival" (Heb. *`ēd*) (Q.5:114). The two canonical Islamic festivals are *`īd al-aḍḥā*, "The Feast of Sacrifice" associated with the *Ḥajj*, and *`īd al-fiṭr*, "The Feast of Breaking the Ramadan Fast."

Iḥrām Special state of ritual purity signaled by wearing special clothing (also called *iḥrām*) when engaging in the *Ḥajj.*

I`jāz al-Qur'ān "Miraculous nature of the Qur'an." Refers to the notion of inerrancy of the Qur'an.

Ijtihād Independent legal reasoning, engaged by a person called a *mujtahid.*

***`Ilm* (pl. *`ulūm*)** "Knowledge," "science." See *`Ālim* (Q.7:52).

Imām "Leader," as in one who leads the daily prayers (Q.2:124). The term is used by the Shi`a to refer to the descendants of Muhammad through `Alī, who have been invested with divine guidance. An *imām* may also be a simple religious teacher.

Imāmī Refers to a branch of Shi`ism also called "Twelver" because it recognizes 12 holy *imāms*.

Imān "Faith" (Heb. *emunāh*) (Q.3:193). One who has faith is a *mu`min* (Heb. *ma'amīn*) (Q.16:97).

Irtidād See *ridda*.

Islām "Submission" (Heb. *hashlamah*) (Q.3:19).

***Ismā`īlīs*** A major branch of the Shi`a that takes its name from the 6th *imām*, Ismā`īl.

Isnād The list of people who passed a *ḥadīth* down through the generations. The more reliable the *isnād*, the more authentic the *ḥadīth*.

Isrā' The miraculous night journey of Muhammad in which he is said to have flown from Mecca to Jerusalem on a Pegasus and then ascended to heaven from the rock now covered by the Dome of the Rock on the *Ḥaram* (Temple Mount) (Q.17:1).

Jahannum A qur'anic term for hell (Q.3:12, 4:93), paralleling a common English term, *gehenna*, which derives from the Hebrew, *geh hinōm* (Josh. 15:8, 2 Chron. 28:3).

Jāhiliyya "Ignorance." The period in Arabia before the revelation of the Qur'an (pre-Islamic Arabia) (Q.5:50, 48:26).

Jāmi` "Friday Mosque," main mosque for the Friday congregational prayers.

Janāza "Funeral bier," funeral service.

Al-Janna "The Garden" (Heb. *gan/ginnah*). A qur'anic term for Paradise, the hereafter for the righteous (Q.2:35, 7:42).

Jihād "Striving," especially in terms of engaging in the religious path. Also, divinely authorized war (Q.2:218, 25:45–52, 60:1).

Jinn (sing. *jinnī*) "Genies." A type of creature created by God from fire that is powerful and often, though not always, evil or mischievous (Q.55:14–15).

Ka`ba "Cube." A stone cubic building in Mecca that serves as the main sanctuary in Islam.

Kāfir "Infidel," "ingrate," "unbeliever" (Heb. *kofer*) (Q.50:2).

Kāhin Soothsayer or diviner (Heb. *Kohen*) in pre-Islamic Arabia (Q.52:29).

Kalām "Speech," "discourse." *`Ilm al-kalām* ("The knowledge of Discourse") is dialectical or systematic theology.

Khalīfa Caliph, "Successor" or "deputy," especially of the Prophet, later to become the title of the leader of the dynastic Muslim empires (Q.38:26).

***Khārijī* (pl. *khawārij*)** Kharijites. A strict and radical sect in early Islamic history.

Khātam al-anbiyā' "Seal of the prophets." A qur'anic reference to Muhammad (Q.33:40), who was the last of God's prophets according to Islam.

Khaybar The Jewish town in Arabia that was captured by Muhammad in 628.

Khazraj See Aws.

Khilāfa Caliphate of the great dynastic Muslim empires (Umayyad, Abbasid, Fatimid).

Khitān Circumcision.

Khuṭba The sermon preached in the weekly Friday congregational prayers by the preacher, who is called (*khaṭīb*).

Kiswa The richly brocaded cloth covering over the Ka`ba.

Kitāb "Scripture," "book." The term is often used in the Qur'an for "book of revelation" (Q.2:2 10:1).

Madhhab (pl. *madhāhib*) School of law; usually referring to one of the four surviving schools: the Hanafi, Maliki, Shafi`i, and Hanbali.

***Madrasa* (pl. *madāris*)** Religious school (Heb. *beit midrash*).

Mahdī "Guide." Messianic figure who will appear at the end of days and usher in a new order; particularly important among the Shi`a.

Mahr (Heb. *mohar*) Wealth, usually in the form of gold jewelry, that the groom is required to give to his wife by the time of marriage.

Ma`rifa Mystical knowledge or understanding.

Masjid "Place of prostration," mosque (Q.7:29).

Al-Masjid al-Aqṣā "The Distant Mosque," referring to the third most sacred mosque of Islam in Jerusalem (Q.17:1).

Al-Masjid al-Ḥarām "The Sacred (or holy) Mosque," referring to the primary mosque of Islam in Mecca (Q.2:149–150).

Maṣlaḥa The public interest or welfare of the community.

Matn The actual text or content of a *ḥadīth* that follows the *isnād* (the list of people who passed it down through the generations).

***Mawlā* (pl. *mawāli*)** A term to describe both the adopted and the adopting member of an Arab tribe; a non-Arab convert to Islam in early Islamic history; "patron," "master" (Q.47:121).

Mawlānā Title or term of endearment applied to some religious masters such as Mawlānā Jalāl al-Dīn al-Rūmī.

Mawlid "Birthday," especially of a saintly person, with special festivities.

Mawlid al-Nabī "Birthday Festival of the Prophet."

Miḥrāb Usually decorated recess in the wall of a mosque indicating the direction of prayer toward Mecca (Q.38:21).

Minbar The raised pulpit in a mosque from which the sermon (*khuṭba*) is given.

Al-Mi`rāj "Ascension." Especially, the ascension on Muhammad's "Night Journey" (*al-isrā'*) from the rock in Jerusalem to heaven.

Misbaḥa *See subḥa.*

Mu'adhdhin ("*muezzin*") The one who calls the community to prayer.

Muftī Jurisconsult who gives a learned opinion called *fatwā*.

***Muhājirūn* (sing. *muhājir*)** "Emigrants." Especially those who followed Muhammad from Mecca to Medina on the Hijra in 622 (Q.9:100).

Muḥrim One who is in the state of ritual purity called *iḥrām*.

Mujtahid One who engages in independent legal reasoning called *ijtihād*.

Mulla Persian form of the Arabic word, *mawlā*, meaning "master" of religious sciences; a religious authority.

Mu'min "Believer" (Heb. *ma`amin*). One who has faith (*imān*) (Q.16:97).

Murtadd "Apostate."

***Muṣḥaf* (pl. *maṣāḥif*)** "Codex," "volume," especially of the Qur'an.

Mushrik See *shirk*.

Muslim "One who has surrendered" to God; an adherent of the religion of Islam (Q.2:127–128).

***Mutakallim* (pl. *mutakallimūn*)** One who practices systematic philosophy (*kalām*).

Mu`tazila The "rationalist" school of Islamic philosophy.

***Muwaḥḥid* (pl. *Muwaḥḥidūn*)** "Unitarian," meaning one who believes in divine unity (*tawḥīd*); a member of the 12th century fundamentalist North African movement called *al-muwaḥḥida* ("Almohad" in Western texts) that conquered Spain from more liberal Muslims and imposed draconian rules on Muslims and non-Muslims alike.

Nabī Prophet (Heb. *navī*).

Najāsa Polluting matter that can rend a person ritually impure (such as wine, urine, blood, and the saliva and other fluids of pigs and dogs).

Najs "Impure," "unclean" (Q.9:28).

Najrān A city near the border of today's Saudi Arabia and Yemen, and home to a well-established Christian community at the time of Muhammad.

Al-Nār (Heb. *nēr*) "The Fire" of hell; a qur'anic term for hell (Q.2:24).

Niqāb Veil that covers the entire face.

Nikāḥ "Marriage" (Q.24:60).

Niyya "Intention," especially as spiritual preparation for a ritual act (Heb. equiv. *kavvanah*). Without proper formal *niyya*, the ritual is considered invalid.

Al-nūr al-Muḥammadī "The light of Muhammad" believed by the Shi`a to be a special essence of prophecy that is passed down to those descendants of Muhammad through the line of `Ali to the Shi`i imāms.

People of the Book See *ahl al-kitāb, dhimmī.*

Pīr A Persian word similar in meaning to the Arabic, *shaykh*, and that refers to a Sufi spiritual guide.

Al-qaḍā' wal-qadar "The divine decree and predestination."

Qāḍī Religious judge appointed by the ruler whose judgments are binding.

Qāri' "Reciter" of Qur'an (Heb. equivalent: *qore'*). One who knows the complex rules of Qur'an recitation and who has memorized the text of the Qur'an. May be male or female (Q.96:1–3).

Qibla The direction of prayer toward Mecca (Q.2:144–145).

Qiyās Legal hermeneutic parallel to that of the Jewish *heqesh* by which legal decisions and arguments are made on the basis of analogy.

Qubba A domed structure, typically over the burial site of a holy person. The Arabic name for the Dome of the Rock in Jerusalem is *qubbat al-ṣakhra.*

Qur'ān "Recitation," especially in reference to the scripture of Islam (Q.12:3).

Quraysh The ruling tribe in Mecca at the time of Muhammad (Q.106:1).

Rak'a The prayer cycle of postures that includes standing, bowing, kneeling, prostrating, and sitting back on the heels.

Rasūl "Messenger." A prophet with a divine message intended for a specific people (Q.14:4), almost synonymous with *nabi* (prophet).

Ra'y "Opinion." The personal opinion or deduction of a legal decider or Qur'an interpreter.

Ribā "Interest" (Heb. *ribīt*). Any gain from lending goods or money (Q.3:130, 30:39).

Ridda "Apostasy," especially in relation to Islam. Also called *irtadd.*

Ṣadaqa "Charity" (Q.9:60) (Heb. *tzedakah*), given freely and at any time. *Ṣadaqa* is not the same as *zakāt*, which as required giving, is more closely associated with the Jewish practice of *tzedakah.*

Ṣaḥīḥ "Sound," especially in reference to *ḥadīth*; the name of certain authoritative collections of *Hadith* such as *ṣaḥīḥ bukārī*, meaning "the sound *hadith*(s) of Al-Bukhārī."

Sajda, sujūd "Prostration." One of the most central acts in the cycle of motions the Muslim worshiper engages in formal prayer (*ṣalāt*) (Q.2:125).

Sakīna (Heb. equivalent *shekhīna*) Special divinely sent tranquility that may descend on God's servants (Q.48:4).

Salaf Pious ancestors; early Muslim community.

Salafiyya Puritanical form of revivalist Islam based on assumptions of how the generation of Muhammad and his followers lived out their religious lives.

Ṣalāt Formal prayer, as in the five formal daily prayers (Q.2:43–45).

Ṣawm, Ṣiyām "Fasting" (Heb. *tzōm*) (Q.2:183–185).

***Sa`y*** A ritual during the H.ajj that is said to commemorate the running of Hagar between two points near Mecca in search for water for her child Ismā`īl.

Shahāda/Shahādatayn A formal statement that bears witness to God's unity and Muhammad's prophethood. Making this statement with true intent before proper witnesses is the formal ritual of conversion to Islam.

Shahīd "Witness." Also, martyr, one killed in battle (Q.4:41,69).

Sharī`a "The way to the water hole." Refers to Islamic law based on Qur'an and tradition (Jewish equiv. *halakhah*) (Q.45:18).

Shaykh "Elder," "tribal leader," "religious scholar," "Sufi master," or a title of respect. Feminine form: *shaykha* (Q.12:78).

Shayṭān "Satan" (Heb. *ṣatān*) (Q.4:60, 5:90).

Shī`a "Party," "faction."

Shī`at `Alī "The party supporting `Ali." Those who believed Muhammad had chosen `Ali to become his successor (*khalīfa*) after his death.

Shirk "Association," especially of anything with God (Q.31:13) (Heb. equiv. *shittūf*); idolatry. One who engages in *shirk* is a *mushrik* (Q.2:221).

Shūra "Consulation" (Q.42:38) or council.

Subḥa, misbaḥa Prayer beads in a loop of 11, 33, or 99 to aid in the recitation of the 99 "most beautiful names of God."

Ṣūfī A Muslim mystic.

Sulṭān "Ruler," including governor of a region or military commander.

Sunna "Custom," "way of behaving," especially of Muhammad. The *Sunna* of the Prophet consists of the sayings and behaviors of Muhammad that are transmitted in the *Ḥadīth* (Q.17:77).

Sunnat A popular term commonly used for circumcision and the genital mutilation of females.

Sunnī Common name for the Muslim majority officially called *Ahl al-Sunna wal-Jamāʿa* (The People of the [Prophetic] Custom and the Community).

Sūra Chapter of the Qur'an (Q.24:1).

Tafsīr "Explanation," "commentary" of the Qur'an.

Ṭahāra "Purification" (Heb. *ṭaharah*). Includes a number of ritual purification rituals and is a common synonym for circumcision.

Takbīr A term to describe saying *"Allāhu Akbar:"* "God is most great."

Takfīr Charging or accusing someone of being an unbeliever (*kāfir*).

Tajdīd Revival, renewal.

Tajwīd The act of reciting the Qur'an melodiously according to strict rules to ensure proper pronunciation and meaning.

Ṭalāq Divorce (Q.65:1).

Talbīya The act of uttering the pious formula, *Labbayk allahumma labbayk* . . . : "I am here, O my God, I am here. . . ." It was recited as part of the *Ḥajj* ritual in the pre-Islamic period and is uttered repeatedly during the Pilgrimage to this day.

Taqiyya The practicing of religious dissimulation in the face of danger, such as practicing outwardly one form of Islam but secretly believing and practicing a different form.

Taqlīd "Imitation." Accepting a legal or theological position on blind faith without engaging in independent, critical reasoning.

Ṭarīqa "The way." A Sufi method of spiritual discipline or a formal Sufi school or order.

Tartīl Slow, clear recitation of the Qur'an according to strict rules to ensure proper pronunciation and meaning.

Taṣawwuf The Sufi way, sufism.

Tashahhud "Testimony." The recitation of the *shahāda* at a specific time in the ritual prayer (*ṣalāt*).

Taslīm Uttering *al-salāmu `alaykum* (peace to you); greeting in general; uttering *al-salāmu `alaykum* at the end of formal ritual prayer.

Ṭawāf "Encircling." The ritual circumambulation (walking around) the Ka`ba in Mecca (Q.2:125).

Tawba "Repentance" (Heb. *teshuvah*) (Q.4:17–18).

Tawḥīd Maintaining the unity of God.

Ta`wīl Qur'an interpretation that tends toward allegorical or symbolic readings.

Tayammum Ritual ablution using clean sand or earth rather than water (used only under exceptional circumstances) (Q.4:43).

***Ta`zīya*** "Consolation." The Shi`i passion play commemorating the martyrdom of Imām Ḥusayn at Karbalā'.

Tilāwa Recitation of the Qur'an in general (Q.2:151).

***`Ulamā'*** See *`Ālim.*

Uḥud The name of a famous battle in Medina (625 CE) in which Muhammad was wounded and many of his followers and supporters killed from the Meccan attack.

Umayyad Reference to the clan within the tribe of Quraysh called the *Banū Umayya*; the first caliphal dynasty with its capital in Damascus (661–750 CE).

Umma (Heb. *ummāh*). The international community of Muslims; a community having a common religion (Q.2:128, 3:113).

`Umra The "lesser pilgrimage," which can occur any time during the year and has fewer ritual obligations than the "greater pilgrimage" commonly referred to as *Ḥajj* (Q.2:196).

Wahhābīya The Arabic term for a puritanical Islamist movement founded in 18th-century Arabia by Muhammad ibn `Abd al-Wahhāb (Eng. Wahhabi movement).

Wājib Obligatory (Jewish parallel: *ḥōvāh*).

***Walī* (pl. *awliyā'*)** A friend or protégé, protector; Muslim "saint" (Q.2:107).

***Waqf* (pl. *awqāf*)** Private endowment of property for religious purposes such as the building and maintenance of mosques, schools, hospitals, or other socially beneficial purpose.

Wuḍū' The lesser ablution or washing, which renders ritual purity before engaging in certain ritual activities such as prayer or Qur'an recitation.

Yathrib The oasis town to which Muhammad emigrated in 622 CE, known afterward as *madīnat al-nabī* (Medinah).

Zakāt Required annually alms tax calculated on the basis of one's wealth (Q.2:277).

Zam-zam The sacred well near the Ka`ba in Mecca.

***Ziyāra* (pl. *ziyārāt*)** "Visitation" to a holy shrine or grave of a holy person.

Zuhd Asceticism.

Bibliography

Abū Dāwud al-Sijistani, *Sunan*. Translated from the Arabic by Ahmad Hasan. New Delhi: Kitab Bhavan, 1993.

Abou El Fadl, Khaled. *Speaking in God's Name: Islamic Law, Authority and Women*. Oxford: One World, 2001.

Ahmad, Leila. *Women and Gender in Islam*. New Haven, CT: Yale University Press, 1992.

Ahmed, Salahuddin. *A Dictionary of Muslim Names*. New York: New York University Press, 1999.

Asad, Muhammad, trans. *The Message of the Qur'an*. Gibraltar: Dar al-andalus, 1980.

Baron, Salo. *A Social and Religious History of the Jews*. 18 vols. New York: Columbia University Press, 1957.

Brown, Daniel. *A New Introduction to Islam*. Oxford: Blackwell, 2004.

Bukhārī, *Ṣaḥīḥ*. Translated from the Arabic by Muhammad Muhsin Khan. Lahore, Pakistan: Kazi Publications, 1979.

Char, S. V. Desika. *Hinduism and Islam in India*. Princeton, NJ: Markus Wiener, 1993.

Chittick, William. *The Sufi Path of Love: The Spiritual Teachings of Rumi*. Albany: State University of New York Press, 1984.

Cleary, Thomas, trans. *The Qur'an*. Chicago: Starlatch Press, 2004.

Cohen, Mark. *Under Crescent and Cross: The Jews in the Middle Ages*. Princeton, NJ: Princeton University Press, 1994.

Coulson, N. J. *A History of Islamic Law*. Edinburgh: University of Edinburgh Press, 1964.

Denny, Frederick Mathewson. *An Introduction to Islam*. New York: Macmillan, 1985.

Donner, Fred M. "From Believers to Muslims: Confessional Self-Identity in the Early Islamic Community." *al-Abhath: Journal of the Faculty of Arts and Sciences, American University of Beirut* 50–51 (2002–3): 9–53.

Esack, Farid. *The Qur'an: A Short Introduction*. Oxford: Oneworld, 2002.

Firestone, Reuven. *Journeys in Holy Lands: The Abraham-Ishmael Legends in Islamic Exegesis*. Albany: State University of New York Press, 1990.

——. *Jihad: The Origin of Holy War in Islam*. New York: Oxford, 1999.

——. *Children of Abraham: An Introduction to Judaism for Muslims*. New York: Ktav, 2001.

——. "The Failure of a Jewish Program of Public Satire in the Squares of Medina." *Judaism* (Fall 1997): 438–452.

——. "Holy War in Modern Judaism? 'Mitzvah War' and the Problem of the 'Three Vows.' *Journal of the American Academy of Religion* 74 (December 2006): 954–82.

Goitein, S. D., and Jacob Lassner. *A Mediterranean Society: An Abridgment in One Volume*. Berkeley: University of California Press, 1999.

Guillaume, Alfred. *The Life of Muhammad: A Translation of ibn Ishaq's Sirat Rasul Allah*. Oxford: Oxford University Press, 1955.

Gülen, Fethulla. *Love and Tolerance: Toward a Global Civilization*. Somerset, NJ: The Light, 2004.

Haddad, Yvonne Yazbeck, and John Esposito, eds. *Islam, Gender, and Social Change*. New York: Oxford University Press, 1998.

Halkin, Hillel, and David Hartman. *Epistles of Maimonides: Crisis and Leadership*. Philadelphia: Jewish Publication Society, 1985.

Hoyland, Robert. *Arabia and the Arabs: From the Bronze Age to the Coming of Islam*. London: Routledge, 2001.

Hsu, Shiu-Sian Angel. "Modesty." *Encyclopedia of the Qur'an*, 403. Leiden: Brill, 2003.

Ibn Ḥanbal, Aḥmad. *Musnad*. Beirut: Dar al-Sadr, n.d.

Ibn Hishām, *Al-sīra al-nabawiyya*. 2 vols. Beirut: Dar al-Thiqafa al-Arabiyya, n.d.

Ibrahim, Izzadin, and Denys Johnson-Davies. *Forty Hadith Qudsi*. Beirut: Dar al-Qur'an al-Karim, 1980.

Jullābī, Hujwīrī, `Alī bin `Uthmān al-. *The Kashf al-Mahjūb: The Oldest Persian Treatise on Sufism*. Translated by Y. S. Nicholson. London: Luzac, 1967.

Kalmin, Richard. *Sages Stories, Authors and Editors in Rabbinic Babylonia*. Atlanta, GA: Scholars Press, 1994.

Khadduri, Majid. *The Islamic Law of Nations: Shaybani's Siyar.* Baltimore: Johns Hopkins University Press, 1966.

Lawrence, Bruce, ed. *Messages to the World: Statements of Osama Bin Laden.* London: Verso, 2005.

Le Strange, Guy. *Palestine under the Moslems: A Description of Syria and the Holy Land from* A.D. *650 to 1500.* Beirut: Khayats, 1965.

Martin, Richard C. *Islam.* Englewood Cliffs, NJ: Prentice Hall, 1982.

Massignon, Louis. *Hallaj: Mystic and Martyr.* Translated by Herbert Mason. Princeton, NJ: Princeton University Press, 1994.

Meri, Josef. *The Cult of Saints among Muslims and Jews in Medieval Syria.* New York: Oxford University Press, 2003.

Motzki, Harold. "Marriage and Divorce." *Encyclopedia of the Qur'an*, 276–81. Leiden: Brill, 2003.

Muslim, *Ṣaḥīḥ bisharḥ al-nawawī.* Beirut: Dar al-Thiqafa al-Arabiyya, 1929.

Muslim, *Saḥīḥ.* Translated from the Arabic by Abdul Hamid Siddiqi. N.p. Dar al-Manar, n.d.

Nasā'ī, al-. *Sunan al-nasā'ī bisharḥ al-suyūṭī waḥāshiyat al-imām al-sanadī.* 4 vols. Cairo: Dar al-Masriyya al-Lubnaniyya, n.d.

Nelson, Kristina. *The Art of Reciting the Qur'an.* Cairo: American University of Cairo Press, 2001.

Peters, F. E. *The Hajj.* Princeton, NJ: Princeton University Press, 1994.

Peters, Rudolf. *Jihad in Classical and Modern Islam.* Princeton, NJ: Markus Wiener, 1996.

Pickthal, Marmaduke, trans. *The Glorious Qur'ān.* Istanbul: Enes Matbaasi, 1999.

Qaradawi, Yusuf, al-. *The Lawful and the Prohibited in Islam.* Translated by, Kamal El-Helbawy, M. Moinuddin Siddique, and Syed Shukry. Indianapolis, IN: American Trust Publications, n.d.

Rahman, Fazlur. *Islam.* New York: Holt, Rinehart & Winston, 1966.

Ringgren, Helmer. *Studies in Arabian Fatalism.* Uppsala: A. B. Lundequistska, 1955.

Swidler, Leonard, Reuven Firestone, and Khalid Duran. *Jews, Christians, and Muslims in Dialogue: A Practical Handbook.* New London, CT: Twenty-Third Publications, 2007.

Tennant, F. R. *The Sources of the Doctrines of the Fall and Original Sin.* New York: Schocken, 1968.

Tirmidhī, al-. *Al-Jāmi` al-ṣaḥīḥ.* 2 vols. Beirut: Dar al-kutub al-`ilmiyya, n.d.

Vaglieri, L. "*Ghadīr Khumm.*" *The Encyclopaedia of Islam.* 12 vols, 993–94. New Edition. Leiden: Brill, 1983.

Wagner, Judith Romney. "Halakhah and Sharī`a: Roots of Law and Norms of Conduct in Theocratic Systems." *Central Conference of American Rabbis Journal* (Fall 2000): 81–95.

Wasserstein, David. "Islamisation and the Conversion of the Jews" in *Conversions islamiques. Identités religieuses en Islam méditerranéen Islamic Conversions. Religious identities in Mediterranean Islam.* Edited by Mercedes García-Arenal. European Science Foundation. Paris: Maisonneuve et Larose, 2001.

Watt, W. Montgomery. *Muhammad: Prophet and Statesman.* New York: Oxford University Press, 1961.

Wielandt, Rotraud. "Exegesis of the Qur'an: Early Modern and Contemporary." *Encyclopedia of the Qur'an,* 124–42. Leiden: Brill, 2002.

Yākūt, *Mu`jam al-Buldān.* 7 vols. Beirut: Al-Kutub al-`Ilmiyya, 1990.

Yamani, May, ed. *Feminism and Islam: Legal and Literary Perspectives.* New York: New York University Press, 1996.

Scriptural Index: Verses from the Qur'an and the Bible

Qur'ān

Hebrew Bible

New Testament

Subject Index

Aaron, 87, 110
al-`Abbās, 63
`Abbasid Dynasty, 62–65, 137, 254
`Abdū, Muhammad, 73, 119
abortion *(ijhāḍ)*, 219
Abraham
as an Islamic prophet, 87
and genealogical lines, 6
and idol worship, 151
at Mecca, 171–72
in the Qur'ān, 19–21, 110, 153
as a *ḥanīf*, 12–13, 257
"Abraham" (Sūra 14), 106
Abū Bakr, 42, 44, 45–46, 201
Abū Ḥanīfa, 136
Abū Hurayra, 185
Abū `Imrān Mūsā Ibn Maymūn (Maimonides), 66, 97–98
Abū Karib As`ad, 11–12
Abū Sufyān, 30
Ābū Ṭālib, 22
Abū Zayd, Naṣr Hāmid, 119
activist Islam, 75
acts *see* behavior, five categories of
Adam, 110, 208
adultery, 188–89
ahl al-Bayt (people of the Prophet's house), 131, 199, 254
ahl al-Kitāb see People of the Book
`A'isha, 44, 49, 224, 251n13
Akbar, 71
alcohol, 228–29
Alevi-Bektashi community (Sufi), 198
Allāh *see* God
amir (prince), 67
analogical reasoning *(qiyās)*, 138–40, 264
ancestor, pious *(salafi)*, 75, 264
Andalusia *see* Umayyad Spain
angels, 85–86, 224
animals, 83, 173–74, 210–11, 225–26, 227
annulment *(faskh* or *tafrīq)*, 221
`aqīqa (sacrifice after birth), 210–11
al-Aqsa Mosque, 61